THE
INEVITABLE
AMERICANS

☆

THE
INEVITABLE
AMERICANS

By

John Greenway

NEW YORK : *Alfred A. Knopf*

1964

L. C. catalog card number: 64–10789

THIS IS A BORZOI BOOK,
PUBLISHED BY ALFRED A. KNOPF, INC.

FIRST EDITION

To my Son

Contents

THE
INEVITABLE
AMERICANS

☆

A Word to Begin

There is strange and wonderful news coming out of the Soviet Union these days. Those Russian scientists report a woman—a Russian, of course—who can see, color and all, with her fingertips. Another band of Soviet scientists have revived a triton lizard that had been solidly frozen under twenty-five feet of Siberian ice for five thousand years—not far from the place where another Soviet citizen is about to celebrate his one-hundred-and-forty-sixth birthday. Everybody knows about the Soviet physician who grafted a new head on a dog. And about geneticist Lysenko, who changes a field of barley to wheat by sowing in a few seeds of Michurinism. Everyone in America seems to take these things seriously, for, after all, those amazing Russians can do anything.

The American papers have different news to report. One of the most prosperous and best-loved American newspapermen begins an article by calling the United States "mealy mouthed" for its behavior in the Congo. The same issue of the local newspaper in

Boulder, Colorado, has a Letter to the Editor from a young man who says: "I am beyond despondency. I am so thoroughly disgusted I cannot find words for it." For what? For something else those mealy-mouthed Americans did or failed to do.

Possibly this young letter writer was one of the audience of fifteen hundred well-informed students who crowded into the auditorium at the University of Colorado to give a thunderous standing ovation a little while ago to a handsome officer of the United States Army who compounded a mass of half-truths, false inferences, equivocations, and palpable lies about the behavior of the unfortunate American prisoners of war in Korea into as vicious an attack on our national character as Pravda could concoct. When one lone girl rose after the talk to point out what she thought was an obvious distortion of fact, this American audience led by this American army officer crushed her back into her seat with derisive laughter.

If any single incident made me decide to write this book, this was it. It is about time someone spoke up for America, unpopular though this stand may be. The other side has been heard long enough. The particular calumny heard at the University of Colorado is circulating at this moment in 600,000 copies—500,000 printed and 100,000 tape-recorded—to tell the nation it is rotten to the heart.

Your bookshelves probably are brightened by the jackets of books like *The Organization Man*, *What Ivan Knows That Johnny Doesn't*, *A Nation of Sheep*, *The Ugly American*, and perhaps even Mrs. Trollope's scathing *The Domestic Manners of Americans*, still in print and selling well in this country after 132 years. Surely you have some George Bernard Shaw, who made much of his good living lecturing Americans on their doltishness. Who does not know the American, the officious money-grubber stalking the innocent world

For the sake of the almighty dollar
And whatever else he could gain,

as it was so nicely put by one of our patriotic poets, John Alexander Joyce. There is even a new book entitled *Is Anybody Happy?* telling us that American civilization is so crassly materialistic that Americans do not even enjoy sex any more.

The purpose of *The Inevitable Americans* is to shatter the false mirror on the American wall, not by defending Americans, but by showing, through anthropological observation of their culture, that they are inevitable, the culmination of the civilization begun when the first Mesopotamian farmer pushed a dibble stick into the Iranian foothills. The approach will be analytical, comparative, and historical, as well as anthropological; several basic aspects of American life will be examined against the patterns established by other societies, primitive and sophisticated, to point up the unique disparities that together establish the culture of the United States. We will look at the Old Stone Age natives of Australia, the better to see ourselves; we will go back in our own history at least as far as the Anglo-Saxons, to see ourselves in the pugnacious, proud, prudish, practical, unimaginative, sentimental, democratic, muddling, acquisitive, bibulous, gullible, credulous, and gloomy folk who sloshed mead around Heorot.

All of this will be in the philosophical frame of cultural determinism, which argues that Americans—like everyone else in the world—were driven by their cultural genes to become what they are and what they will be, so that there is no purpose in censuring Americans for not being Russians or Englishmen or angels or even ants, which the Chinese are trying to emulate.

There should be some hope in this for the grieving and reluctant nay-sayer, who may thus learn that what makes Americans bad also makes them good. He may even be brought to appreciate that, while America may not be the best country in the world, it is the best country in the world for Americans.

John Greenway
BOULDER, COLORADO
August 1, 1963

☆ I ☆

The Tyranny of Culture

If we are going to understand this tyrannous thing anthropologists call culture—the thing that makes Americans inevitable—we will have to begin with its simplest and most tangible products, such as what you have in your pockets. Since the cigarettes come out oftenest, let's look at them first.

Ten years ago you and your fellow Americans smoked 400 billion cigarettes annually. Since then, you have learned that scientific tests prove that tobacco is a dirty weed that satisfies no normal need, that

> *It makes you thin, it makes you lean,*
> *It takes the hair right off your bean,*
> *It's the worst darn stuff you've ever seen,*

besides giving you lung cancer, so this year you will smoke 600 billion. Advertising tells you that cigarettes taste good, that filters turn the nicotine every way but loose, that it's what's up front or out back that counts, but it never tells you that you began smoking because your high-school crowd exerted social coercion to get you hooked and that you persist because you are addicted to a real narcotic. Freud offered another reason for the popularity of cigarettes, but I intend to keep this book as free from obscenity as possible and I will not mention it.

Unless they are king- or imperial-sized cigarettes, your smokes come in a package sealed with a blue stamp on the top. Now, without looking, do you know why the stamp is on the package? You should, if you believe that man is in control of his behavior because man is a reasoning creature. Tax, you say? That tax was repealed years ago. You say then that it lets you tear open a convenient third of the top? Possibly; but even if you know nothing about industrial engineering you can contrive at least a half dozen better designs. If you are a Spanish American living in rural New Mexico, you do have a reasonable use for the stamp—you stick it on your forehead to cure headache.

The pack probably features in its design a V-shaped symbol of some sort, frankly as on the Parliament box or covertly as on the Newport package. Why do none of them use an X, which is just as esthetically satisfying? Because the V has unobtrusively become a status symbol in our society. You can follow its evolution by examining the change in the design of automobiles in the last decade or so, beginning with the hood symbol of the Cadillac, our high-status car, and with its imitation in the more plebian automobiles, some of which borrowed the symbol with the lame excuse that it indicated a V-8 engine. Quickly the symbol settled on the back of the trunk and progressively became more elongated and its angle more obtuse, until the utter end was reached in the design of the back of the 1959 Chevrolet.

If you smoke Camels, you should know that the R. J. Reynolds

Tobacco Company tried to reduce the size of the camel to give a bit more room for advertising copy, but you reasonably felt that you were being cheated, and you forced the retention of the old-size dromedary.

If you are a rural American, you chew rather than smoke the nicotine into your system at the rate of 30,000 tons a year. Ten years ago you masticated 43,000 tons, and a century ago you chewed nearly all the tobacco consumed in America, but foreign visitors so shamed you by their mordant criticisms of the nasty habit of spitting tobacco juice over everything that you are giving it up, except in the backward areas of the United States, in accordance with the anthropological principle that obsolescent traits persist longest on the periphery of a culture.

So, instead of a plug, you probably have a package of chewing gum in your pocket, for habits are never lost, the psychologists tell us, since they are a gratification of the organism; they are only substituted for. American floors are no cleaner now than they were a hundred years ago, only stickier. As for nastiness, look under the next lunchroom table you sit at and see scores of gum wads stuck to the underside of the table top.

To light your cigarettes in this atomic age, you have a mechanical lighter that operates on the ancient principle of the flint-and-steel.

You have a watch, because Americans are obsessed with time. If you were a Hopi Indian you would have none; the Hopi have no concept of time. Unless you are a Phi Beta Kappa working in a non-academic profession, your watch is on your wrist; if you are a professor you do not show your key, for that would be pretentious. In industry, however, your Phi Beta Kappa key helps you establish rapport with other intellectuals ashamed of how they are earning their living.

You have other keys in your pocket, because American social organization is weak in its internalized restraints. In less enlightened societies, incest tabus are extended to make people behave;

we put locks on the bedroom doors. You are not aware that the number of keys you carry in ratio to the number of doors open to you is a gauge of your social status. As a janitor, you have a hundred keys to open a hundred doors; as chairman of the board, you need none, for other people open doors for you. You may, as chairman of the board, have a key to a lady's apartment, but this is not so much a key as a trophy.

You have a nuisance of coins in your pocket. They are symbols of value according to the decimal system, which the mathematicians do not find particularly logical. Some of your coins carry the declaration "In God We Trust," for societies make catchwords of ideas they have ceased to believe, and not since the Druids have the faithful regarded this slogan as acceptable collateral. The main function of coins is to activate cigarette machines and parking meters, but you cling to the idea that they have a more mystical value. The silver coins are milled, that is, their edges are crenelated, because once upon a time silver was valuable enough to justify "sweating" the edges off coins; but not within the memory of the oldest inhabitant could a man make a living wage by filing off slivers of silver. However, the tyranny of culture, which makes no pretensions to reasonableness, requires that our mints go on cutting milling into silver coins.

In your wallet (which, according to the etymology of the word, was once a basket carried on your back), you have paper currency. This is inscribed with resounding proclamations of its reliability, though, if you are a Republican, you suspect your dollar bill has suffered a depreciation since 1933 to a real value of 56 cents, whatever that means. Regardless of your politics, you know that, despite Roosevelt, currency still has a mystical value. But if coins as a medium of exchange are obsolete, paper currency is at least obsolescent: it is now being replaced by checks and credit cards, several of which you have in your wallet. These too are transitionary to an even more efficient means of drawing from the national wealth, your thumbprint on a national credit account. There is nothing you can do about the further evolution of coins or currency, for within twenty years after Darwin's *The Origin of Species* it was discovered that money evolved just like biological organisms, without interference or assistance by human beings. In fact, if you knew how little you affect your own behavior, you would now be pulling from your pocket a handkerchief to mop your brow or a pillbox of antacids or aspirins. Earlier in your cultural history, you would have worn the handkerchief around your neck—and indeed you still do, though this has evolved (with what help from your own volition you can assess) to your tie, which has no utilitarian function at all. The headache and stomach medications are also traditional to our civilization; the ailments were noticed as peculiar to Americans a century ago.

Buried down in the lint of your pocket, there is probably a paper clip or two, for, with every other man, woman, and child in the United States, you use 400 pounds of paper every year.

It would not be fair to carry this inventory of unreason into an examination of a woman's handbag, though it would be infinitely more profitable to our purpose of showing the intrusion of culture into human affairs. No man doubts that in his wife's handbag there may still be lurking in a corner a Paleolithic *coup-de-poing*. Nor would it be fair to look into our minds, for they are cluttered with far more junk than our pockets, including vastly greater quantities of lint, as well as a few woolly caterpillars. But let's have a quick look at the rest of you.

You are probably sitting in a chair, a by no means universal repository for the relaxed human body. Since only Freud has given us a persuasive reason for the popularity of chairs among Americans, I will offer none, and will note merely that in the list of the hundred best-designed products of industrial civilization described in the final chapter, thirteen per cent are chairs and another fourteen per cent are automobiles, which provide the same method of repose.

The temperature of your room is about 72 degrees, which most of mankind, including all foreign visitors to the United States, find intolerably hot.

You are wearing a suit of heavy or light fabric, depending on the season of the year, though you spend about 95 per cent of your time in heated interiors, even in winter. If you are a woman, the design of your dress was not created in the mind of Dior or Balenciaga, but by culture. Alfred Kroeber showed that since the time of the first Queen Elizabeth, fashions in Western dress have been swinging like a pendulum between the voluminous skirt and the sheath, with a periodicity of about fifty years.

You may be eating as you read; if so, at the threshold of your consciousness, your conscience is nibbling too. In a less affluent society, you would try to gain rather than to lose weight as a symbol of your economic position. Look at the handle of your coffee cup. If you can get your finger loosely through the hole, you have probably borrowed or stolen this book, for the evolution of coffee-cup handles has tended toward a smaller size for at least half a century, and large-handled cups linger on only in deprived households. Flinders Petrie, the great Egyptologist, was able to set up a chronological table for dating Egyptian pots on the basis of this evolution as it occurred during the time of the pharaohs—who knew no more about natural selection in pot handles than you do. If you are very wealthy, the spoon in your saucer keeps in its design the hinge of the pecten shell which set the model for stylish utensils two thousand years ago. And most illogical of all, an ethnological study of the peoples of the world tells us, is your idea that the woman who poured your coffee married you for love.

You need not feel individually harried by all of this. I like to think myself emancipated from the tyranny of culture, yet I obey not only its orders but its etiquette, and would not use the first personal singular pronoun in this book if the publisher, whose power here is stronger than that of culture, did not insist on it. I should feel much more comfortable using the editorial "we," though I do not have a tapeworm. I know, too, that the English language has about two dozen different vowels, but I spell with the five substitutes the Greeks introduced in place of the unused sounds in the Phoenician alphabet they borrowed three thousand years ago. Yes, the preceding sentence is a morass of orthographic anachronisms, but I would not venture the spelling "Foneshun alfabet" even if Mr. Knopf would allow it. I am more than a little dubious about the propriety of using contractions in so serious a work as this, but as an extreme effort of my free will, I will use one in the next sentence.

Why don't we eat dogs? Why do Polynesians consider rice disgusting and raw fish delicious? Why do we bring trees into the house at Christmas and paint eggs at Easter? Why do the natives of Australia call their son's son "grandfather"? Why do we make jokes about our mother-in-law? Anthropologists who have asked questions about the behavior of hundreds of societies, savage and civilized, and who have received answers, from savages and savants alike, that we do what we do "because it is the custom," "because people have always done things like that," or "Just because," have been forced to the conclusion that we have nothing to do with what we do. It is culture that runs the show. Before bringing more evidence to this point, let us define culture and examine its processes.

THE NATURE OF CULTURE

To the anthropologist, culture does not mean the ability to approbate Château d'Yquem and abominate Coca-Cola or to wear "black tie" instead of a "tux." It would be easier for us to understand culture as a concept if its discoverers had given it an entirely new and unambiguous name, as Norbert Wiener did with cybernetics.

Anthropologists are now in much the same position as the followers of Linnaeus when they tried to construct a definition of "species"—and "to define," it should be remembered, means to isolate a concept and surround it with a semantic barrier. The early scientific naturalists found that no definite boundary could be devised, that species were not atomistic, as the Biblical account of creation implied. For a long time they ignored the embarrassing borderline cases by building a buffer corridor between contiguous species. Buffer corridors are as abhorrent to biology as they are to politics, but, as Sir Charles Lyell put it nearly a century ago, "what they wanted was names, not things."

Still, names are important. In order to talk about anything more complex than the simplest emotive states and physical drives, we must have words. Stick us with a pin and we exclaim without need of symbolic utterance (though whether we yell "ouch," "aïe," "ach," "aй," "hpæt," or " 痛ⱱ " is entirely determined by culture), but any talking or thinking that can be called human depends on words, or, more properly, symbols. Whatever cannot be named cannot be conceived. Anyone who reads the earliest writers in English must be impressed by the handicap they had in trying to describe concepts named so simply and unthinkingly by us, but for which they had no words. Chaucer had no more trouble figuring his customs accounts in Roman numerals than he had in trying to write of Renaissance concepts with medieval English. Galileo got himself into hot water with the Church principally because he tried to express astronomical phenomena with theological language. Even as late as the beginning of the nineteenth century, Erasmus Darwin, grandfather of the evolutionist, was, like Chaucer, forced to describe chemical processes with poetry. A modern chemist would show the natural formation of potassium nitrate in this way:

$$N_2 + O_2 \rightarrow 2NO$$
$$2NO + O_2 \rightarrow 2NO_2$$
$$4NO_2 + O_2 \rightarrow 2N_2O_5$$

$$N_2O_5 \begin{bmatrix} \text{water} \\ \text{rain} \end{bmatrix} + KOH = KNO_3$$

$$\Big\downarrow \begin{array}{l} + \\ H_2O \\ \text{crystallization} \end{array}$$

Erasmus Darwin wrote it this way in *The Botanic Garden*:

> *Hence orient nitre owes its sparkling birth*
> *And with prismatic crystals gems the earth;*
> *O'er tottering domes the filmy foliage crawls,*
> *Or frosts with branching plumes the mould'ring walls,*
> *As woos Azotic Gas the virgin Air*
> *And veils in crimson clouds the yielding fair.*

which is almost as bad chemistry as it is poetry.

In defining species, it was not the psychology of naming that was wrong, as Lyell contended, but the thing itself, for the concept of species did not exist except in an arbitrary sense. Textbooks in elementary biology define species as "a homogeneous interbreeding group, below a genus and above a race," which is as empty as the answer "Not far" to the question "How far is it?" Where any definition of species is scientifically meaningful, it is wrong. "A species is a biological population which when interbred produces fertile offspring." But biologists have bred fertile organisms not only across species barriers, but over even higher taxonomic hurdles. The Russians (who else?) crossed a radish with a cabbage, and the only reason you have not heard about it is that the product had the root of a cabbage and the head of a radish—hardly surprising in view of the ideological inhibitions of the Soviets about making anything commercially profitable. This most convenient of all definitions of species breaks down in the other direction as well, for the difference between a Chihuahua and a Saint Bernard is only racial, yet there are practical as well as genetic difficulties in mating these two dogs.

Eventually, the biological taxonomists realized that species could not be defined because species did not exist in the absolute sense—species were changing continuously in all but a few cases—and this realization was the greatest intellectual discovery in the history of the world—for if species change, then species evolve, and what becomes of the divinity of man?

It may be that culture is also indefinable by any criteria that restrict its possession to human beings, but until this has been determined, we can heed Lyell: take the things and let the naming go. No physicist would commit himself to the absolute correctness of the atomic theory, but he can build hydrogen bombs on the basis of it, and right now that is all that is required of it. Even the demolished concept of species is viable; the eminent geneticist Theodosius Dobzhansky says that, in spite of its indefinability, the working classification known as "species" is one of the most useful in biology.

Most social scientists who define culture follow the enumerative approach of Sir Edward Burnett Tylor, who in 1871 called it "that complex whole which includes knowledge, belief, art, law, morals, custom, and any other capabilities and habits acquired by man as a member of society." But enumerations can never make a definition, since they cannot be applied deductively to unincluded material. Other students of man shovel everything into "the whole of social tradition," as Robert Lowie did in his *Introduction to Cultural Anthropology*. Psychologists disregard the content and emphasize the pragmatic aspects; C. Dawson, in *The Age of the Gods*, for example, says that culture was "a particular adjustment of man to his natural surroundings and his economic needs." And some, infected with that chronic disease of social scientists, logorrhea, define culture as does John P. Gillin, who wrote in *The Ways of Man* that it "consists of patterned and functionally interrelated customs common to specifiable human beings composing specifiable social groups or categories."

What all these people have been looking for is some means of separating man from the animals by his works, since he cannot be separated from them by his physiology. A summing up of definitions would hold that culture is what man has and animals do not have, which is wrong where it is meaningful and meaningless where it is right. The ants not only have means of communication, domestication of lower animals, agriculture, war, and a sweet tooth, but they imitate human behavior distressingly well. As militarists, they are hardly distinguishable from the Spartans, to choose a classic example, or the Watusi, to choose a contemporary one; in the peaceful sphere of their activities, they are hardly distinguishable from the Chinese Communists, who look to them as models.

It has been said (allegedly first by Benjamin Franklin) that man is the only tool-making animal, but one of Darwin's famous Galápagos finches makes a wooden prod to dig insects out of trees, and there are many other craftsmen in the animal world, ranging up to Sultan, Köhler's chimpanzee genius, which (or who) fashioned a ball-and-socket joint to elongate a stick to retrieve bananas.

The notion that culture is simply learned behavior and its products, and therefore exclusively human, dies hard, though it has been confounded by a number of professional iconoclasts. Dr. Zing Yang Kuo demonstrated that kittens raised with rats in the absence of a rat-killing mother never killed rats of the species of its companions. Kenneth Oakley, the destroyer of Piltdown Man, showed that birds in one locality of England discovered how to peck the paper caps off milk bottles, and that this trait spread quickly among the species all over Britain.

"Language is our Rubicon," said Max Müller three quarters of a century ago, "and no brute will dare to cross it." But man, more eager for communication, has paddled his way across to the brutes. R. L. Garner claims that he can converse with monkeys wherever in the world he finds them—a feat that should encourage the Esperantists. Furness says he can "almost" speak with orangutans. Father Landois, possibly to find out what really happened in the Garden of Eden, studies the speech of snakes; Karl von Frisch, the speech of bees; Bastian Schmid, the speech of hens; Georg Schwidetsky, the speech of lemurs (from which he derives, with evolutionary consistency, the speech of human beings); Konrad Z. Lorenz, ducks and geese; and M. P. Fish, appropriately, fish.

The most persuasive definition of culture yet constructed, and the last hope of setting man off from the lower beasts, is that of anthropologist Leslie A. White, who says that culture is anything founded on the symbolic process, from mother-in-law jokes to satellites. The symbolic process is the "stands-for" relationship and, so far as we know, is exclusively human. It is fundamentally different from the "equals" relationship, the signal reaction, which seems to be the upper limit of subhuman cerebration. The dinner bell, to Pavlov's dogs, did not *stand for* dinner; it *was* dinner. When the bell rang, the dogs did not speculate whether they were hungry just then, or what was for supper, or whether they felt like a heavy dessert, or whether the food might more charitably be sent that day to starving North Koreans; they did not, it is thought by some, even say grace. They salivated. The difference between the symbolic process and the signal reaction is not simply a matter of stupidity, which is comparative, but a matter of intelligence, which is absolute. Social stability requires man to act most of the time tropismatically according to the signal reaction, but no animal can do otherwise—and that makes all the difference.

Man made culture, as he is now making cybernetic machines. But somewhere in the last twenty millennia it got away from him, though most of us refuse to admit it. "Cultures don't paint their fingernails," says the opponent of cultural determinism, "people do." Of course people paint their fingernails, and culture could not exist without man, but man today is no more responsible for culture than the violin is responsible for Oistrakh. For the moment at least, let us willingly suspend our disbelief in the absolute tyranny of culture and say, with the cultural determinists, that culture is a superorganic entity with a will and mind of its own— omnipotent but not omniscient. As long as man is allowed to muck up the equation, culture cannot be understood.

THE PROCESSES OF CULTURE

No one has ever seen electricity, but we know its nature and its processes. So with culture: we can see it only in its manifestations,

by separate societies—these losses can be irretrievable. When the Maori left Havaiki in their great canoes and migrated to cold New Zealand, where the paper mulberry would not grow, the Polynesian bark cloth was forever lost to them. If a culture is growing, losses are replaced, as the Maori replaced *tapa* with flax cloth, with more complex or efficient substitutes. Most cultural losses come about through displacement, as the bow and arrow was displaced by gunpowder and the horse by the automobile.

One amusing phenomenon associated with cultural losses is what Robert Marett called metataxis—the transvaluation of obsolescent cultural items from implements of subsistence to implements of recreation; or, to state the process more simply, things on the way out become toys. The bow and arrow was obsolescent as a weapon in the Middle Ages and obsolete in the Renaissance, but it still hangs around as a toy, not only among children, but among adults as well, just as the activity with which it is associated—hunting—is itself a metatactic toy, left over from Paleolithic times, like many of its practitioners. The horse also is obsolete as a means of transportation, except in certain professions and societies that themselves survive more for their romanticism than for their utility, but the horse will endure for many years yet, riding ingloriously in horse trailers behind its insolent displacer, the automobile. One is tempted to say that culture has put the cart before the horse. Cultures that are progressing rapidly leave enormous piles of this kind of detritus behind them. One reason Americans are so play-conscious, as the envious world censures us, is that in our culture there are so many metatactic toys to play with.

It may be that functional items come in also as toys, though not enough evidence has been assembled to establish this as a principle of cultural change. Very probably the hunting bow was first invented as a musical instrument; it is hard to imagine how the principle of transferring vertical tension to horizontal propulsion could have been discovered otherwise. In the ancient civilizations of the New World the wheel was known only as a toy. In later

American civilization, the bicycle and the automobile were both established first as adult toys.

Some obsolescent cultural forms are like the gift portrait of the rich, aging, but testate aunt—too ugly to use, but inexpedient to throw out just yet. Sir Edward Burnett Tylor called these things survivals—items that persist beyond their usefulness. The end of this chapter contains illustrations of these in profusion; for the moment, a few examples are the electoral college, states' rights, and cod-liver oil.

Another amusing cultural process is transculturation, a term Melville J. Herskovits coined to describe the reborrowing by one culture of an item previously lent by it to another; again more simply, cultural ping-pong. A "riding coat" once worn by English-women was borrowed by the French, who, having as much difficulty with English pronunciation as Englishmen have with French, called it a "redingote." Long after fashion threw the riding coat out of the British wardrobe, Englishwomen reborrowed the apparel from the French, taking the French term with it, and "redingote" it remains. American Chinese, according to unimpeachable witnesses, have been seen to eat chow mein, an American dish invented in imitation of Chinese food. In the area of non-material culture, the concept and practice of civil disobedi-ence in imitation of Gandhi's supposedly successful precedent was recently employed by American antiracist objectors. Gandhi said he got it from Thoreau; and Thoreau, as a Boston Brahmin, got it from the Indian philosophers. At this writing, an American folk singer and professional protestant is carrying the gospel of the sit-in technique to the peoples of India. Before the coming of the white man, Polynesians doted on fresh fish, but the American business genius taught them to like the canned variety better. Today Japanese are commissioned to catch fish in the Ryukyus by the Americans, who can it in San Francisco and ship it to the Polynesians. In payment in kind, the Polynesians sell *muumuus* to American women; this shapeless garment was hastily designed by early American missionaries in the Pacific to cover the huge and naked bodies of Polynesian maidens.

Like any efficient monolithic organization, culture guards against the varied dangers of too-rapid movement by instilling in the influential members of a society attitudes of conservative opposition. The resulting apparent resistance of a culture to change is called cultural inertia. Its most obvious vehicle is the Haves, and the vehicle for rampant change is the Have Nots. Opposition to progress is always couched in specious phraseology such as: "George Washington warned us against entangling alliances" and "We must recapture the self-reliant spirit of '76." However, the basis of the conflict between the Republicans and the Democrats of the world is simple: the existing culture gave the Haves a major share at the feast and they are fat and content; the existing culture gave the Have Nots rather small potatoes, and they are hungry for a change, any change. Inequitable distribution of wealth means that the Haves are vastly outnumbered, but since their share of power is as disproportionately great as their share of wealth, a tactless Have such as Jay Gould could declare publicly: "I can hire one half of the working class to kill the other half," and prove his point. The only danger to the power and position of the Haves was expressed well by Lord Acton, but better by those who misquoted him: "Power corrupts, and absolute power corrupts absolutely." The vested interests will often thwart their best interests just for the sake of avoiding change. One of hundreds of ready examples is the Southern slaveholders, who could not be persuaded by their Northern friends that free labor was cheaper, more efficient, and crueler than slave labor.

Not all opposition to cultural change is as sensible or as simple as that of Barry Goldwater. Often there seems to be no reason for it other than sheer human perversity, and it is therefore nearly unpredictable. Anacleto Apodaca found a good example of unreasoning cultural inertia among Spanish-American farmers in the Rio Grande Valley in New Mexico. Since pre-Columbian days, the Indians of this region and their mestizo descendants have been growing as their staple crop a species of corn miserably poor in color, taste, yield, and nutrition. The United States government in its officious kindness sent an agriculture agent into the valley in 1946 to introduce one of the greatly superior American hybrids. The agent was no fool; he did not rush in with the new corn, but first laid a groundwork of education, so that at the end of the second year sixty of the eighty-four farmers were growing the hybrid corn, and enjoying all the advantages (including a double yield) that the agent had promised. Yet in the next year all but three of the eighty-four farmers had gone back to the Indian corn. Why? After exhaustive analysis of the situation, Apodaca could find no better reason than this, given by all the farmers: "My wife don't like that hybrid, that's all."

Lest the resistance to progress on the part of these farmers be attributed to the notorious stolidity of foreigners, well known to every American, consider a recent case from the white Protestant United States. About five years ago John P. Repko, a packaging genius at the Dobeckmun Division of Dow Chemical Company, conceived the idea of de-shelling eggs and marketing them (with yolks visible but unbroken) in small individual plastic containers the size and shape of teabags and joined together in rectangular dozens by perforated plastic, like sheets of postage stamps, so that the housewife could tear off one or several eggs, as she needed. This package had every advantage over nature's invention, except that it was not much good for Easter egg rolls. These eggs could be stored in one tenth the space of eggs in shells, thus saving not only refrigerator space but shipping costs. Danger of breakage at home and in the store completely disappeared; moreover, cracked eggs at the dairy no longer had to be disposed of as unusable or made into odious egg powder. In cooking, the plastic-packaged eggs ended all the messiness and bother of boiling, frying, or poaching eggs. A boiled egg did not have to be watched blindly against a clock; when it reached its proper consistency, the housewife could see it, and take it out of the water. An egg to be fried could be opened neatly over the frying pan—no more need to break it open on the edge of the skillet and watch the yolk drip down into the stove. Hard-boiled eggs could be opened quickly and their plastic cover easily and completely disposed of—no more concern for getting shell sherds in the teeth or on the toast. In short, the plastic-packaged egg was one of the most brilliant inventions in the history of American marketing. Have you ever seen one?

Other institutions besides the Haves tend to hold up cultural progress—even some alleged Have Nots do. Some trade unions give themselves the impudent luxury of impeding change; the inventor of the shovel was probably run out of the cave by hand-scrabbling men who complained that he was throwing them out of work. American housing would be far cheaper and more plentiful if the carpenters' union did not encourage the retention of local building codes. In California today there are twenty-three different legal heights for handrails, depending on geographical location, and 4,688 separate laws and regulations covering the building industry. These make mass production impossible. In Australia, butcher shops have the carcasses of beef hanging free to all the flies that come in by the unscreened doors, and housewives get their meat wrapped—if it is wrapped at all—in old newspaper. Yet the butchers' union successfully resisted the introduction of American cellophane meat packaging on the grounds that it was unsanitary.

What Galbraith in *The Liberal Hour* called social nostalgia— the romantic yearning for the past—manifesting itself in "charm," as in San Francisco beyond the freeways, is a more general brake to progress. This is not very harmful so long as it is limited to collecting antiques, but it aggravates cultural lag when it is intruded into the serious things of life, such as government. Fortunately for the future of the United States, Americans have been bound by the irrationality of the past much less than other people;

or, as the British put it, Americans "have no respect for tradition." Respect for tradition means that the traditionalist's civilization is over the hill, for his attention is always drawn back to the time of his country's greatest glory. Thus Queen Elizabeth rode to her coronation in 1953 in an eighteenth-century coach, not a Rolls-Royce.

The phrase "cultural lag" used in the last paragraph was introduced by William Fielding Ogburn forty years ago to describe the friction that results when parts of a culture move at different speeds, producing disruptions and maladjustments in society. The most sweeping instance of cultural lag in our civilization is the conflict between a stagnant society and a runaway technology; this conflict produces hundreds of traumata, such as technological unemployment and the breakdown of the family. Indeed, everything that looms as a problem of society is the result of one cultural lag or another.

Here again, institutions that inhibit change often accomplish quite the opposite of their intention. One purpose of religion is to make man's hostile environment bearable to him, but religion always and everywhere preserves a dead past, especially if it is a vital religion. The vestments of Catholic priests are only superficially different from the clothing used in the Roman Empire at the time of Christ; the nun's habit is only superficially different from ordinary women's wear at the time of the founding of these orders in the Middle Ages. This extreme conservatism of religion is not limited to modern institutions. St. Patrick's Cathedral in New York, surrounded by disrespectful skyscrapers, has a pre-Columbian counterpart in the kivas the tourist sees in Mesa Verde National Park. These underground churches of the Pueblo Indians, modeled on the ancient pithouses of the Basketmaker ancestors of the Pueblos, were similarly five hundred years behind the secular architecture that rises all around them. Liberal critics of American social history unfairly accuse the churches of supporting the forces of oppression for ulterior purposes, when actually the situation is one of different conservatisms unintentionally allied.

Strangely enough, the military, on whom the existence of modern society absolutely depends, is almost as conservative as the Church. Hitler's Wehrmacht contained one million horses, besides its better publicized panzer tanks. The Queen's Guards in London were so far in the past that they had to be guarded from American tourists by policemen until a barred promenade could be built for them. In the eighteenth century Benjamin Franklin tried to tell General Braddock that marching soldiers stiffly through the woods was not the best way to fight Indians. Braddock ignored this civilian advice and his army was destroyed, but neither he nor his military posterity learned anything from this and similar debacles. Today at the Air Force Academy in Colorado Springs one may see the choice of America's youth marching in stiff array like Braddock's men, bellies in, chins down, in the close-order formation that was suicidal two hundred years ago, and carrying swords— though, if Ben Franklin were around today, he might officiously suggest that in modern jet warfare a pilot could not get more than one effective swipe at an enemy pilot in combat. But no real harm is done, since jet fighter planes are just as obsolete as swords or soldiers, no matter how they are marched.

Ironically, in view of the conservative nature of the military mind, no social movement is more productive of rapid technological change than war. The most powerful force in man's existence is competition—it is more fundamental than culture, as Darwin proved—and war is the essence of competition. Almost every great invention was suggested or developed by war—the first stone tools a million years ago were weapons; the first bronze artifacts were weapons; the first iron implements were weapons; and the first real use of the wheel and the horse was in warfare; so also with the first atomic implements. Those who deplore military exploitation of atomic energy may be right, but they ignore history. They are as naive as the Trojans who stood on the battlements remarking, as the great horse was dragged in: "It just goes to show what wonderful things the mind of man is capable of when he turns his thoughts to peace."

World War II and its continuance in the present cold war have been the greatest stimulus in history. They produced the jet engine and the guided missile; they led to the development of previous medical discoveries such as penicillin, DDT, and sulfa; they are responsible for the controlled release of atomic energy, the fall of the British Empire, the extinction of France as a world power, the focusing of the two most powerful ideologies in history, the first steps toward the conquest of space, and the end of the two-pants suit. Even greater things may be produced by the cold war, so long as it is fought in the manner of modern master chess— with all the action in the notes, in the What-Might-Be-Done-If-My-Opponent-Makes-a-Mistake. But this is something else we have nothing to do with.

Whatever people have comes to them through independent invention — "polygenesis" — or through borrowing — "diffusion." Among the great intellectual accomplishments, the zero is a classic example of the polygenetic invention—at least three different iso-lated cultures produced it. The alphabet, on the other hand, is a classic example of diffusion—wherever true writing and the alpha-bet are found, they can be traced to their original inventors, a Semitic people who lived on the western fringes of the Near East around 2000 B.C.

Much of the making of America is due to unabashed borrowing of the inventions of others. Ralph Linton dramatized this Ameri-can characteristic in his stimulating introduction to anthropology, *The Study of Man*:

Our solid American citizen awakens in a bed built on a pattern which originated in the Near East but which was modified in Northern Europe before it was transmitted to America. He throws back covers made from cotton, domesti-cated in India, or linen, domesticated in the Near East, or wool from sheep, also domesticated in the Near East, or silk, the use of which was discovered in China. All of these materials have been spun and woven by processes invented in the Near East. He slips into his moccasins, invented by the Indians of the Eastern woodlands, and goes to the bathroom, whose fixtures are a mixture of European and American inventions, both of recent date. He takes off his pajamas, a garment invented in India, and washes with soap invented by the ancient Gauls. He then shaves, a masochistic rite which seems to have been derived from either Sumer or ancient Egypt.

Returning to the bedroom, he removes his clothes from a chair of southern European type and proceeds to dress. He puts on garments whose form originally derived from the skin clothing of the nomads of the Asiatic steppes, puts on shoes made from skins tanned by a process invented in ancient Egypt and cut to a pattern derived from the classical civilizations of the Mediterranean, and ties around his neck a strip of bright-colored cloth which is a vestigial survival of the shoulder shawls worn by the seventeenth-century Croatians. Before going out for breakfast he glances through the window, made of glass invented in Egypt, and if it is raining puts on overshoes made of rubber discovered by the Central American Indians and takes an umbrella, invented in southeastern Asia. Upon his head he puts a hat made of felt, a material invented in the Asiatic steppes.

On his way to breakfast he stops to buy a paper, paying for it with coins, an ancient Lydian invention. At the restaurant a whole new series of borrowed elements confronts him. His plate is made of a form of pottery invented in China. His knife is of steel, an alloy first made in southern India, his fork a medieval Italian invention, and his spoon a derivative of a Roman original. He begins breakfast with an orange, from the eastern Mediterranean, a cantaloupe from Persia, or perhaps a piece of African watermelon. With this he has coffee, an Abyssinian plant, with cream and sugar. Both the domestication of cows and the idea of milking them originated in the

Near East, while sugar was first made in India. After his fruit and first coffee he goes on to waffles, cakes made by a Scandinavian technique from wheat domesticated in Asia Minor. Over these he pours maple syrup, invented by the Indians of the Eastern woodlands. As a side dish he may have the egg of a species of bird domesticated in Indo China, or thin strips of the flesh of an animal domesticated in Eastern Asia which have been salted and smoked by a process developed in northern Europe.

When our friend has finished eating he settles back to smoke, an American Indian habit, consuming a plant domesticated in Brazil in either a pipe, derived from the Indians of Virginia, or a cigarette, derived from Mexico. If he is hardy enough he may even attempt a cigar, transmitted to us from the Antilles by way of Spain. While smoking he reads the news of the day, imprinted in characters invented by the ancient Semites upon a material invented in China by a process invented in Germany. As he absorbs the accounts of foreign troubles he will, if he is a good conservative citizen, thank a Hebrew deity in an Indo-European language that he is 100 per cent American.

Linton did not lose the emphasis of his argument by pushing it as far as he might have done. In the last phrase, for instance, he could have shown that the decimal system is another ancient importation and that the word "American" itself was borrowed from the first name of a Florentine explorer, Amerigo Vespucci. He notes only one modern American contribution to the average citizen's morning—certain bathroom devices; but nothing in the bathroom is originally American or modern. Linton possibly had in mind H. L. Mencken's notorious bathtub hoax.

Diffusion, however, does not account for the origin of things any more than natural selection accounts for the origin of species. The human propensity to simplify concepts too hard for the mind to comprehend gives credit for inventions to man, for man is obviously the creator of the products of culture, as he is the creator of culture itself. Nothing is more logical. In an article entitled "What Makes a Genius?" in the November 12, 1955, issue of *Saturday Review*, Delbert Clark gives this list of the greatest geniuses of civilization: Alexander, Archimedes, Aristotle, Beethoven, Brunelleschi, Buddha, Caesar, Cézanne, Copernicus, Marie Curie, Dante, Darwin, Einstein, Erasmus, Fleming, Franklin, Freud, Giotto, Goethe, Gutenberg, Hannibal, Hertz, Leonardo da Vinci, Machiavelli, Michelangelo, Napoleon, Newton, Pasteur, Praxiteles, Saint Paul, Shakespeare, Socrates, and Van Gogh. We will not quibble over objections such as that the incidence of genius, being a biological constant, must appear with equal frequency throughout the species of *Homo sapiens,* and therefore one or two Oriental geniuses besides Buddha (who came from Benares anyhow, hardly in the farthest East) might in generosity have been included. But even a slight knowledge of any of the persons on Clark's list will blow them away. Almost at random, let us look at Fleming.

In 1928 Alexander Fleming was working with a batch of pathogenic organisms he had set out in a line of Petri dishes. He noticed one morning that the *Staphylococcus aureus* was dying around a green mold—*Penicillium notatum*—in its dish. Fleming reported the phenomenon in the *British Journal of Experimental Pathology,* but nobody paid much attention to it, not even Fleming, who confessed later: "I had not the slightest suspicion that I was at the beginning of something extraordinary." In fact, Fleming had too little knowledge of chemistry to do much with his discovery. Going back into bacteriological history, we might give some credit to John Tyndall, who made the same discovery in 1876, and took no more notice of it than Fleming. After Tyndall, many scientists independently discovered penicillin, including Pasteur. Even further back, the effect, if not the process, was known in the Middle Ages, but it was disguised in herbal compounds to evade prosecution by the Church. Fleming was arbitrarily selected for genius when the exigencies of World War II led to the isolation of the antibiotic substance of *Penicillium notatum* in 1941—a three-year research effort under the direction of Sir Howard W. Florey and Ernst B. Chain. As always, Americans improved the invention: modern penicillin is not the Englishmen's *Penicillium notatum*, but *Penicillium chrysogenum*, discovered by Kenneth Raper of the U. S. Department of Agriculture on a rotten cantaloupe he picked up at a Peoria market in 1943. And like many of the other wonder drugs, penicillin is independently rediscovered at the great pharmaceutical houses every few days.

William Fielding Ogburn in 1922 compiled an impressive list of polygenetic inventions to show that inventions invent themselves when culture is ready for them. An up-to-date list of this sort would occupy several volumes the size of this book, though each invention is attributed to a Great Man, whose greatness actually lay in his good fortune of being in the right place at the right time. Sometimes, however, not even this opportunism is enough to assure recognition as a genius. The name of Charles Wheatstone is not known to many Americans, yet he is given credit by some historians of science for the invention of the concertina, the electric telegraph, the stereoscope, the self-exciting dynamo, the electric clock, the printing telegraph, and the typewriter, among other things. One wonders at this moment who will get the Nobel Prize for discovering the anti-XI-minus particle, found independently in 1962 by scientists at the Brookhaven National Laboratory at Upton, New York; CERN, the Swiss nuclear research center at Geneva; the French nuclear research laboratories at Saclay; and the École Polytechnique at Paris. Like the first knot, these things invent themselves.

THE FALLACY OF "WE"

All of us are aware of the forces of "custom," as one aspect of culture is called, in table manners and social behavior, for example, but when we find that culture can even make us see things that are not there and hear sounds that have not vibrated, the control culture exerts on us becomes so frightening that we easily understand why man is reluctant to give up his fancy that he has freedom of will. But the evidence that man lacks such freedom is overwhelming. The Japanese artists who painted Admiral Perry's sailors with slant eyes did so because they simply could not see the absence of the epicanthic fold in Caucasians. The German immigrant who says "I go to bet" when he means he intends to retire, rather than attend the races, speaks as he does because he cannot hear the difference between a dental surd and a dental sonant. Likewise the Polynesian who takes the Lord's name vainly as "Keristi" and the Spaniard who has trouble with his "bowels" demonstrate the effect of culture upon physiology. In the matter of vowels, incidentally, a fairly convincing example of the tyranny of culture is available to any American who has not studied the history of his language in the phenomenon known as the Great Vowel Shift.

For reasons not entirely agreed upon by linguists, in the fifteenth century in England the long vowels began to shift up the "vowel triangle" (the imaginary triangle in the oral cavity representing the position of the tongue in the formation of vowels). The vowels already at the top of the triangle became diphthongs. This change is so regular that one can without much difficulty translate the language of Chaucer's poetry into modern English by raising the long vowels one or two steps (the short vowels have not changed in more than a thousand years) and dropping off the inflectional endings that even in Chaucer's time were already crumbling as a result of another linguistic process.

The pertinent thing about the Great Vowel Shift is that it is still going on, though only linguists are aware of it, and its progress is in perfect accordance with all the relevant anthropological principles. We have already seen several examples of the rule that cultural movement takes place fastest at the center of a culture and slowest in the marginal areas. Today, in cultural backwaters

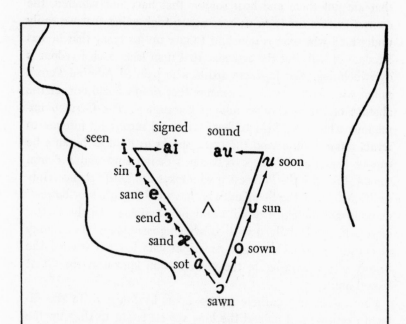

THE VOWEL TRIANGLE

The lowest long-vowel sound that can be made with the tongue at the point of lowest depression is the ɔ (symbols are from the International Phonetic Alphabet), as in "sawn." As the back of the tongue is raised, successive vowel sounds are made until the highest, 𝘶 as in "soon," is reached. As the front of the tongue is raised, another series of vowels is formed until the highest possible in this position, i as in "seen," is reached. Arrows indicate the direction of the Great Vowel Shift.

such as rural Ireland, one can hear the vowels of the eighteenth
century. When Alexander Pope in *The Rape of the Lock* described Windsor Castle:

> *Here, thou, great Anna! whom three realms obey,*
> *Dost sometimes counsel take and sometimes tea,*

he was not writing "eye rhymes." Because of the Great Vowel
Shift we have lost the rhyme of the first couplet in Jonathan
Swift's slap at the hierarchy of parasitism:

> *Naturalists doth observe a flea*
> *Hath smaller fleas that on him prey;*
> *And these have smaller still to bite 'em,*
> *And so proceed* ad infinitum.

whose last rhyme identifies the Dean, if this were not already
common knowledge, as a Protestant, for, in their root-and-branch
Reformation, Protestants revived an earlier Latin than that used
by the Catholic Church.

In the United States today there are similar cultural hinterlands
as in Ireland, where they still sing:

> *You work all day*
> *For the sugar in your tea.*

In Colorado one hears "hawrible" for "horrible," "ruff" for "roof,"
"crik" for "creek," and "rut" for "root," all pronunciations one
step down on the vowel triangle. Even the "cultured" American
shows some backwardness in relation to mother country, as the
story about the Englishman, the Irishman, and the American
shows. It seems that an Englishman insisted that the word
"neither" should properly be pronounced "nigh-ther," whereas an
American championed "nee-ther." To settle the argument, they
appealed to an Irishman (which makes this a most unlikely tale)
to judge which of them was right. "Nayther of ye," he ruled.

The most recent example of a clear shift upward is the change in the pronunciation of "falcon," which all but the most modern dictionaries give as "fawlcon" or "fawcon." But the Ford Motor Company, wiser in such matters, shot the word up the vowel triangle to "faalcon." Despite the great power of business, this does not prove that it can run against the current: the manufacturers of Pall Mall cigarettes have not been able to impose upon smokers the "proper" low-position pronunciation of this trade name.

In the sciences, too, the tyrannical direction of culture works against what man thinks is fact. For more than a century physicists believed that, to achieve polychromatic effects with light, filters from the three primary colors were necessary, but recently Edwin H. Land, inventor of the Polaroid camera, demonstrated that full-color photographs can be made by using only a small fraction of the yellow spectrum. However, it will be some time still before photographers and teachers of art abandon their pigments of the imagination. And Lord Hailsham, Britain's first Minister for Science in charge of outer-space experiments, sits at a desk lit by three candlestick lamps.

It is not for want of edification that our world is going wrong— if it is going wrong, which is doubtful. Our publishing houses seem to be filled with surrogate parents who cannot put pen to paper without writing "We must. . . ." Billy Graham says: "We must recapture the American challenge" and "We must recapture the courage of our fathers"; Adlai Stevenson says: "We must return to the reality principle"; Clinton Rossiter says: "We must show the way to enduring peace"; C. P. Snow says "we" must halt the bifurcation of culture into science and the humanities; Leo Szilard says "we" must stop making hydrogen bombs; William H. Whyte, Jr., says "we" must become nonconformists; Ashley Montagu says "we" must put an immediate end to war and race prejudice, to start with, and to this end he has pledged the efforts of all anthropologists in an official proclamation to the United

Nations. From all sides we are exhorted to do something about the ways of the world, and only rarely does a wise man with a more sensibly directed supplication come along—such as the otherwise unidentified "M. H." who wrote to the editor of *The Denver Post* asking him: "Will you please do something about inflation?"

Even if it were possible for any individual or group to do any of these things, it would be necessary first to have general agreement that they should be done, but "we" cannot even agree that the Bomb should be done away with. To see the power of human society when it is in full agreement about what should be done, let us look at the record of achievement in an activity that since the first person died in an automobile accident in the city of New York on Christmas Day in the year 1900, has maimed, crippled, and killed 66 million Americans—more than all the casualties in all our wars. "We" ought to do something about this because "we" are responsible for killing more than 38,000 of ourselves with automobiles each year, and because this is probably the only field of human endeavor in which there is unanimity of intention to improve or change things. Each year since 1931 the Travelers Insurance Companies have published statistics of death on American highways. It is instructive to look into these books from year to year and see the progress of our efforts to stay alive. Here are a few figures comparing the record of 1961 and 1962:

TYPE OF ACCIDENT, CIRCUMSTANCES, ETC.	DEATHS, 1961	DEATHS, 1962
Collisions with pedestrians	7,100	7,100
Motorist cutting in	60	60
Accidents in rainy weather	3,600	3,650
Accidents in icy weather	1,400	1,400
Accidents on Tuesdays	4,410	4,140
Accidents between 10 and 11 p.m.	1,980	1,990
Persons over 75 years of age	2,300	2,300
Car ran away, no driver	30	30

Every year these statistics run on relentlessly through all aspects of the symbiotic relationship between automobiles and Americans. Looking back a couple of years, we find these parallel figures:

TYPE OF ACCIDENT, CIRCUMSTANCES, ETC.	DEATHS, 1958	DEATHS, 1959
Pedestrian killed while walking on rural highway	660	660
Pedestrian killed while standing on safety island	10	10
Vehicle defective; one or two lights out	180	180
Car ran away, no driver	30	30

As long as J. D. DeWitt has been editor of this series of booklets, he has beseeched that "we" join him in the "great work" of doing something about this slaughter. We can avoid being killed while standing on safety islands or walking along rural roads by not standing or walking there, but what on earth are "we" going to do about those thirty driverless automobiles that since 1958 at least have been running about killing us? No one doubts Mr. DeWitt's sincerity in his holy and wholesome crusade, but unless he becomes one of his own statistics, the president of the Travelers Insurance Companies will go on making a very nice living on the assurance that no one is going to do anything about the situation.

The editor of *The Denver Post* might imaginably do something about inflation, but "we" are not going to do anything about the American challenge, or our fathers' courage, or the reality principle, or enduring peace, or the dichotomizing of culture, or hydrogen bombs, or conformity, or war, or race prejudice, or automobile accidents, or anything else, because "we" do not exist—or, to put it more grammatically, "we" does not exist. "We" is a non-referential pronoun, of which the language has one other (the authoritative "they" that is always working mischief on taxpayers); it is the epitome of anthropocentrism, a fallacy that creates gods and Great

Men, a fallacy born of the pitiable human illusion that man is the captain of his fate and the master of his soul.

For thousands of years man thought that the forces that controlled his life were supernatural, and he eventually made them into gods in his own image and likeness, beings full of weaknesses and failings which he could understand and magically coerce. The religious philosophers whom we have personalized under the name of John Calvin carried the idea to its logical conclusion: God was an omnipotent but unreasoning entity whose will man could not influence and who dealt with man without kindness or malice or even recognition, like Caliban's Setebos. This was an unbearable philosophy in a time when there was not even science to turn to for solace, and man reacted violently against it, in the process destroying Christianity as a vital force. The first serious reaction to Calvinism was Antinomianism, which reasonably argued that if God has predetermined our destiny without possibility of alteration, why should we do good, when doing bad is just as meaningless and a lot more fun? By the time the Calvinists had rationalized their way out of this impasse, the situation was lost. In America, where Calvinism was strongest, people accepted with less protest the inevitable cultural evolution toward materialism— so it can be argued that the religion of our forefathers drove us into the materialism that above all else characterizes American civilization. But, like everything else that came to us from Puritanism, this religion prevented us from appreciating our good fortune.

The antinomian objection is made quickly to anthropological Calvinism also, immediately after remarks about cultures and fingernail-painting, but the cultural determinist has a better answer than Calvin or Cotton Mather: we do what we do because we must do it. Whether you are smoking at this moment, or chewing tobacco, or resolving to put this book down and read instead a murder mystery because it offers a happier philosophy (in Joseph Wood Krutch's words, the murder mystery is popular because it "tells over and over again, with what wit and ingenuity it can manage, two flagrant lies: that justice is always done and that man's reason orders his affairs")—whatever you are doing at this or any other moment you do because a cultural pattern of behavior has been fed into you like a taped order into a computer.

This book is part of the order. It tells you that, like the Puritan of old, you can do nothing to be saved—you can only submit as graciously as possible to the inevitable. Submission to most of the shocks of culture is hard, but submission to being an American is the easiest thing in the world. In any event, we are inevitable, and there is nothing we can do about it except appreciate it and enjoy ourselves.

☆ II ☆

To See Ourselves

"I don't like Americans," sneered the Englishman Michael Scott in 1829. "I never did and never shall like them. I have no wish to eat with them, drink with them, deal with them, or consort with them in any way." His snappish countrywoman, Mrs. Frances Trollope, concurred. "I do not like them. I do not like their principles, I do not like their manners, I do not like their opinions." Foreign visitors had been warned by earlier comers such as Henry Bradshaw Fearon:

> In going to America, I would say generally, the emigrant must expect to find, not an economical or cleanly people; not a people of enlarged ideas; not a people of liberal opinions; or toward whom you can express your thoughts free as air; not a people friendly to the advocates of liberty in Europe; not a people who understand liberty from investigation and principle; not a people who comprehend the meaning of the words "honor" and "generosity."

But they came anyhow, not only from England, but from every other part of the world, to see for themselves whether the savages in the American sideshow were really as bad as they had been portrayed. They were indeed, each foreign observer learned (unless he himself were a little queer), and if he came from a nation that had achieved writing, he wrote about the ugly Americans. Some of them, unable to convince themselves that what they had seen was true, came again and again. John Graham Brooks tells us that in 1889 he met a German correspondent who had been to the United States four times and who still insisted that "the Yankee is a tall, gaunt, yellow-faced, hungry-looking dyspeptic . . . generally engaged in selling some very old article, such as a button hook and a cigarette-holder combined, or a pair of socks which change into an umbrella when you touch a hidden spring." Even those who had never been to these dismal shores knew what we were. Like the Russian visitor to London last year who asked to have an American tourist pointed out to him, and, when this was done, was surprised and pleased to find the fellow behaving so well. Like Dr. Samuel Johnson, who filled his poor home with such unfortunate people as a Negro valet (though Johnson had only one suit of clothes, which had to be cut off him when he died), a quack doctor, a blind poetess, and a reformed prostitute, for whom he went out and begged "because nobody else will have them." But of all mankind he excluded from his love the Americans. Like Jonathan Swift, who maligned us as cannibals:

I have been assured by a very knowing American of my acquaintance in London, that a young healthy child well nursed is at a year old a most delicious, nourishing, and wholesome food, whether stewed, roasted, baked, or boiled, and I make no doubt that it will equally serve in a fricassee or a ragout.

The admitted aim of Swift was not to divert mankind but to vex it, but the intentions of the myriad other alien critics of the

Americans were not so clear, even to themselves. Most, like Scott and Trollope, were reacting blindly to the maddening stimulus of the newest barbarians, like a dog with a stick in its ear. But the Americans themselves have always known precisely why they are no good. Here is George F. Kennan, a former distinguished ambassador to Soviet Russia:

> With no highly developed sense of national purpose, with the overwhelming accent of life on personal comfort and amusement, with a dearth of public services and a surfeit of privately sold gadgetry, with a chaotic transportation system, with its great urban areas being gradually disintegrated by the headlong switch to motor transportation, with an educational system where quality has been extensively sacrificed to quantity, and with insufficient social discipline even to keep its major industries functioning without grievous interruptions— if you ask me whether such a country has, over the long run, good chances of competing with a purposeful, serious, and disciplined society such as that of the Soviet Union, I must say that the answer is "No."

Compare this with the bleatings of Mrs. Trollope and you can appreciate that in self-criticism, as in everything else imported from abroad, Americans excel all other people in the world. If Cornelius Tacitus could return in the twentieth century to describe American national character as discerningly as he analyzed the Germanic ethos 1,865 years ago, he would have to put at the head of the list of our peculiarities a unique gift for enthusiastic self-condemnation. We shudder at the Russians who torture other Russians into public confessions of error and guilt, but all that has to be done to an American to make him acknowledge the most heinous faults is to give him the opportunity. Our most significant writers and thinkers have been nay-sayers to their culture; few of them admit or even recognize that their culture gave them not only the cause to censure it, but the permission to do so. The few notable yea-sayers, from Ralph Waldo Emerson to

Norman Vincent Peale, have commended American civilization so foolishly that the cynical reader suspects they were really writing satire. Even Benjamin Franklin, the noblest patriot of them all, expressed his concern that others might find the eagle rather too apt a representative of the Americans to be a proper national symbol:

> He is a bird of bad moral character; he does not get his living honestly. . . . With all this injustice he is never in good case, but like those among men who live by sharping and robbing, he is generally poor and often lousy. Besides, he is a rank coward—the little kingbird, not bigger than a sparrow, attacks him boldly and drives him out of the district.

Franklin went on to suggest as a better choice the "vain and silly" turkey. David Mackay, with his mind on the national American sport of the nineteenth century, proposed the spittoon as the national symbol.

But this is part of being an American. We would be less if we were different.

ANTHROPOLOGISTS AND THE CONCEPT OF NATIONAL CHARACTER

It is fashionable in anthropology today to say that Americans are in fact different—as individuals, never as groups. Margaret Mead, chastened by the criticism directed at her wartime patriotic analysis of America, *And Keep Your Powder Dry*, publicly atoned for her sin by admitting that "a twenty-one-year-old boy born of Chinese-American parents in a small upstate New York town who has just graduated *summa cum laude* from Harvard and a tenth-generation Boston-born deaf mute of United Kingdom stock are equally perfect examples of American national character. . . ." One does not criticize or even characterize people—or anything else—in multiples. Say your foot hurts and you get sympathy; say your feet hurt and you get contempt. One must be careful, too, that the criticized individual does not obviously belong to a militant minority. It is not rhetorical accident that Professor Mead's Harvard graduate was the Chinese and her genetic defective was the Englishman; the positions are by no means interchangeable in this area of rampant egalitarianism. The only national type it is perfectly safe to censure is the majority American, and upon his head is heaped all the censure that used to be distributed more equitably.

That this idea is an aspect of national self-denigration is no more apparent to the people that hold it than is the fact that anthropology, for all its scientific pretensions, is subject to unreasoning fashion. During the first half century of the existence of anthropology, the professional study of man, the Darwin-Spencer evolutionary ordering of humanity was uncritically assumed and just as uncritically attributed to hereditary differences. Then came the Great Depression and the delivery of American opinion into the hands of the Democrats, who are as instinctively environmentalists as the Republicans are instinctively hereditists. Whatever chance there was for the pendulum of anthropological opinion to swing back again ended with Adolf Hitler, whose insane ideas about the natural superiority of the Indo-Germans contaminated for our time any objective consideration of relative cultural capacities on a racial basis. The fact that anthropologists discovered the tyranny of culture did not exempt them from it, and many a linguist who recoils from the word "Aryan" drives to his university in a Volkswagen. Such is the mind of man.

A second fear settling upon the anthropological sheepfold comes from the intrusion of scientism into the humanities. When even students of English literature are applying for computer time, one can understand the reluctance of anthropologists to admit the existence of anything that cannot be measured in the field or replicated in the laboratory. Once upon a time the historian served a tangential function in understanding man, but, as David M. Potter complains in his *People of Plenty*, "to a behavioral scientist who, seeking the determinants of personality, scanned no horizon more remote than the infant's toilet chair, history, of course, could offer nothing relevant." And within the discipline itself, ethnography—the unsystematic description of ethnic groups—has become a dirty word, and ethnology—the analysis of such descriptions—has become, in Ambrose Bierce's definition, "the science that treats of the various tribes of Man, as robbers, thieves, swindlers, dunces, lunatics, idiots, and ethnologists."

But, as Dr. Johnson said about spiritualism, all theory is against the validity of national character; all experience for it. If the Germans of Caesar's time sang weeping into their beer, upheld the chastity of womankind, and butchered their neighbors, and the Germans of the Third Reich sang weeping into their beer, upheld the chastity of womankind, and butchered their neighbors, it is reasonable to assume that Germans in the future will sing weeping into their beer, uphold the chastity of womankind, and butcher their neighbors. If the Americans a century and a half ago stuck tobacco quids under their dinner tables and Americans today stick wads of gum under their dinner tables, it would be advisable in the interests of sanitation to make sure Americans are not chewing when they enter your restaurant. The mere scientific circumstance that weeping in one's beer and chewing one's cud cannot be measured with calipers has nothing to do with the reality. It does not take much to identify a people statistically; the proprietor of Charlie's Place in San Marino recognizes the nationality of foreign tourists infallibly, he says, because Englishmen wear no belts on their trousers, Germans have no shine on their shoes, and Americans look tired and thirsty—for water.

Nor does the diversity of advanced civilizations seriously impugn the validity of national character. Obviously, the Ku Klux Klansman planting a cross on the lawn of a synagogue and the Amish father battling to keep his children out of school are Americans, too, as each would be quick to claim, but these are not the people who make the character of a country. The typical American is the man at the top of the bell-shaped curve, the man who can be questioned in hundreds in Gallup polls and Nielsen ratings and provide an almost absolutely accurate prediction of what a hundred million of his fellows will think and do.

The conclusions of psychologists who have been able to construct tests to measure group behavior tend to corroborate the more casual observations of ethnographers. French contentiousness and Norwegian conformity have often been noticed by foreign visitors, but such judgments had no substance until Stanley Milgram established the fact statistically in 1961. At the universities of Oslo and Paris, Professor Milgram put a large number of subjects (drawn from a wide geographical distribution within each country) one at a time into a closed booth surrounded by similar cubicles. The subject was led to believe that the other booths were occupied, though, as a typical American improvement, Milgram piped into the one occupied booth a multiple tape recording, to save money. On the tape were the voices of five assistants, who gave the uninstructed subject erroneous estimates of which of two musical tones was longer in duration. The Norwegian students conformed, against what their senses told them was the proper answer, sixty-two per cent of the time; French students conformed fifty per cent of the time. Milgram tested these basic reactions by introducing variations. When the subject was told that his answers would be used in airplane-safety design, the degree of conformity dropped to fifty-six per cent among the Norwegians and forty-eight per cent among the French. When the subjects were required to put their answers in writing, the Norwegians conformed to the group opinion at a rate of fifty per cent, the French at a rate of thirty-four per cent. When, to increase conformity, derogatory and critical remarks were made in answer to honest estimates, the Norwegians stepped up their conformity to seventy-five per cent and the French to fifty-nine per cent. On the basis of these figures, Milgram suggested that the greater willingness to conform lent the Norwegians a deep feeling of group identification and

of responsibility to others which manifests itself in stable government and social responsibility, in institutions for welfare, and in
a willingness to pay heavy taxes. The French, on the other hand,
expressed their lack of conformity by being politically unstable,
dissentious, critical, and socially irresponsible.

A similar test was given American subjects in 1955 by Solomon
E. Asch; it will surprise those who enjoy lamenting that America
is a nation of sheep to know that our conformity rate was only
thirty-two per cent. Circumstances, however, can greatly affect the
degree of conformity. Recognizing this, Allen Funt set up a testing
situation among army draftees for his television program "Candid
Camera," which looks for humor in the seemingly unobserved
behavior of ordinary people. Funt marched one uninstructed
draftee into an office with five instructed actors pretending to be
draftees also, to hear another actor dressed as an officer give an
indoctrination talk. After a few moments, the fraudulent draftees
began doing ridiculous things, such as cakewalking around the
officer's desk; the uninstructed genuine recruit followed docilely
at the end of the line. If Funt's motion pictures are to be believed,
conformity of behavior in this situation was a hundred per cent.

In time of crisis, even the military can overlook the objections
against the unscientific nature of ethnology and make some use
of anthropological opinion about national character. Those who
remember newspaper commentary during World War II recall
that American opinion demanded that victory be followed by the
execution of three arch criminals—Hitler, Mussolini, and Hirohito.
Of the three, Hirohito was beyond any possibility of mercy; after
all, he did not belong to a wholly human race. But at this writing
Hirohito is still Emperor of Japan. How this came to be is still
not generally known, though Ruth Benedict has told the story
in a classic analysis of a nation's character, *The Chrysanthemum
and the Sword*. Partly because of her work on the Dionysian-
Apollonian poles of behavior in her *Patterns of Culture*, Professor
Benedict was given an unexpected assignment during World

War II, an assignment that had an effect at least as important for that conflict as the development of the atomic bomb.

Soon after the beginning of the war in the Pacific, it became evident to American military authorities that American victory was inevitable but would be gained only after nearly complete extermination, in hard fighting, of the Japanese army—a process that would result in enormously heavy American casualties. Professor Benedict and a team of anthropologists were asked to probe the Japanese mind to determine what would most likely induce this fanatical enemy to submit to the humiliation of surrender. She had never been to Japan, and her informants were only a few captured Japanese soldiers, yet her analysis of the Japanese ethos— its forced politeness, its internalized aggressiveness, its almost intolerable system of personal obligations, its filial piety, its scorn of self, its concern with spiritual strength, its fear of rejection, its psychic economy, its superhuman requirements both in training for pleasure and in training for pain—led to the most successful military occupation in history, despite an inadequate ambassadorial administration by General MacArthur. Never before had a civilized nation defeated in war given up so quickly and so eagerly so much of its culture to its conquerors. In the matter of the Emperor, Professor Benedict decided that he must be retained: almost none of the Japanese prisoners of war who were her informants could be persuaded to criticize him, though they frequently and bitterly criticized his military and civil officers. Owen Lattimore, too, on the basis of his work in the Orient, had argued for the retention of Hirohito. Yet by 1959 a Japanese sociologist who polled Japanese students found that forty-six per cent of them favored abolition of the emperor system.

Professor Benedict's book drew from Japanese anthropologists astonishment that she was able to probe so deeply into their ethos, though of course she made some mistakes, having so little direct evidence to work with—we knew less about Japan, its culture, and language, than about any enemy we ever fought. Later, criticisms were made of her book; one such rebuttal was *Without the Chrysanthemum and the Sword*, which objected that Professor Benedict had analyzed only the Samurai code, which applied to a minority of Japanese. This objection only strengthened the thesis that in the process of cultural development a country's proletariat simply receives directions from above. In an article in the *Yale Review* in 1953, Douglas G. Haring contrasted Professor Benedict's Japanese with an enclave of Japanese on the isolated island of Amami Oshima, whose history was free of the totalitarian oppression of the dictatorships of the main islands. He found these people to be very different in group character from their cousins.

The anti-American riots of the Japanese in the last few years, which ended in a protest that kept President Eisenhower from visiting Japan, are a predictable reaction to what anthropologists call *malinchismo*—the voluntary abandonment of one's native culture for that of foreigners. By turning internalized aggression against those whose civilization they have borrowed, the Japanese expiate their own guilt.[1]

The term *malinchismo* preserves in dishonor the name of Malinche, the Mexican girl who betrayed her countrymen to become the mistress of Cortés. Her guilt has been shared by all Mexicans since the time of the Conquistadores, as a long succession of commentators, both native and foreign, have attested. From Bernal Díaz del Castillo, himself a Conquistador, and writers such as Father Bernardino de Sahagún and Fernando de Alva Ixtlilzochitl (who described the first cultural shock of the

[1] Harold Strauss calls my attention to the protest of many Japanese that these riots were directed against the Kishi government rather than against the Americans, and cites further the broadcast on February 26, 1963, on radio station TBS (Tokyo Hoso), which revealed that the Zengakuren, whom Americans regard as mad-dog, American-hating Communists, were financed by the notorious rightist, Kiyoharu Tanaka. Being little impressed by people's protestations and less impressed by alleged differences between the Right and Left, and needing anti-American feeling in Japan for my immediate thesis, I am retaining my explanation of these demonstrations, which, in any case, are a fact.

Conquest), to modern writers such as Samuel Ramos (whose *El perfil del hombre y la cultura en Mexico* is the major work on the Mexican national character), José Gómez Robleda, and Leopoldo Zea, there is general agreement that Mexicans look at life through their sense of inferiority. Professor Gordon W. Hewes has summarized these analyses in an article entitled "Mexicans in Search of the 'Mexican.'" Accepting "insufficiency" as the dominant characteristic of the Mexicans, Hewes finds a train of corollary traits: autodenigration, "hothouse Europeanism," hypermasculinity, violence (mainly of the verbal kind), phallic obsession, individualism, morbidity, micromania, sentimentality, introversion, indecision, fatalism, imagination, and alcoholism.

These traits are personified in the *pelado*, the "plucked one," the national nobody, the Uncle Sam of Mexico. The *pelado* reacts to a surrounding hostility and contempt with resentment and violence. He is the mob that shouts "to the wall" in Castro's Cuba. When he can afford it, he goes to the movies to empathize with Jorge Negrete, the excessively masculine actor who has given the name *jorgenegretismo* to the sexual obsession of Mexicans, or to see himself as Cantinflas, the lovable *pelado*. If he competes in sports, he does so as an individual, for he distrusts others too much to play with them. He is a gallinaceous boaster, hiding his inferiority in cruelty to those beneath him on the social scale, though they may only be domestic animals. Since death is the final way to recover personal prestige, the *pelado* is half in love with easeful death. His necrolatry is demonstrated by the bloody iconography of his religious images, the "morbid eagerness" of medical students, the unwholesome attention in the newspapers to the gory details of automobile accidents, the celebration of the Day of the Dead (November 2, on which day candies and pastries are sold in the form of coffins or ornamented sugar skulls, each with a space on its forehead for the name of the intended recipient), the love of automobile racing, and of course bullfighting.

The one-word distillation of national character is admittedly a simplification of the indescribable variety of behavior exhibited by every individual, but it is not indefensible, and it is not applicable only to the Mexicans. Nietzsche gave Ruth Benedict two words for the world: Apollonian and Dionysian—the one signifying people whose approach to life is governed by moderation, non-aggression, non-competitiveness, non-individualism, sociality, gregariousness, conservatism, tradition, and co-operativeness; the other signifying people whose verities of existence are individualism, distrust, combativeness, emotion, treachery, aggression, and frenzy. The only trouble with this classification is that, by the very definition, Apollonians do not exist, for they would long ago have been eaten up by the Dionysians. Another historical philosopher, Oswald Spengler, saw the Greeks as perfect examples of Nietzsche's Apollonian man whose culture was dominated by a single trait—*containment*. In politics, Greek containment was exemplified by the autonomous city state, symbolically enclosed by walls. Greek wealth was in the form of coined money, symbolically circular. Classical architecture was simple, its buildings small in size and aspiration. Art made most use of the single nude figure. Music was bound by the melodic line, its instruments simple and independent rather than harmonious. History was concerned with the present or immediate past. Greek science was as limited as science can possibly be—geometry rather than algebra, static rather than dynamic physics, an earth-bound astronomy. And the "unities" of Greek drama still continue to limit the aspirations of the theater.

Despite the insistent admiration paid to Greek culture through the centuries, it is no model for Western civilization, to which it is antipodal. In the West, political endeavor burst through the protective city walls almost as soon as they were built, and spread into empires, unconfined by time or space. And Western wealth was not comfortable within the traditional bounds of coined money; it is, with us, the manifest destiny of coins to work slot machines while the real business of business is carried on in credit.

From the Gothic cathedral to the skyscraper, Western architecture has been an exercise in structural aspiration, striving always upward and forward. In the arts, sculpture never took hold in Europe or America; it was displaced from the beginning by the more transitory forms of artistic expression, painting and music, and even within these forms the *Gestalt* of the Western world is revealed in its reaching for effects the Greeks would have disdained had it been possible for the Greeks to imagine them. And in science no example is needed of the aspirations of our culture. Again in a word, Western civilization is, in its ultimate American expression, *expansionist*.

Some daring observers of national personalities have tried to trace the origin of what Alfred L. Kroeber called the styles of civilization. Kroeber himself suggested that much of the basic pattern of Chinese culture can be threaded back to the Chinese kitchen, where the basic food is soft—rice husked and boiled—as opposed to the basic hard foods of the West, meat and bread. Meat and bread require tables on which to cut them, and tables require chairs, and knives, and platters, and so on to Emily Post. The Chinese, however, let other foods follow the pattern set by rice; meat and vegetables are cut to morsels in the kitchen and served to diners who need no tables or chairs or knives. The difference in furniture leads to differences in posture, motor habits, and etiquette. As the Chinese sweeps his food into his mouth with chopsticks, he wafts in great quantities of air as well. Since the resultant belch cannot be avoided, the cunning Chinese makes a social grace out of it. Kroeber's explanation of Chinese culture may seem somewhat attenuated, but it is more plausible than that given by Hippocrates 2,400 years ago. Hippocrates argued that the phlegmatic nature of the Chinese was caused by the phlegmatic Chinese weather. And Hippocrates in turn is rather more convincing that Geoffrey Gorer, who insists, in his book *The Great Russians*, that these difficult people were made so by the fact that their mothers swaddled them tightly as infants. Another anthropologist, Ralph Linton, blamed—if that is the proper word—the personality of the Jews on the Jewish father:

The Hebrew Iaveh was a portrait of the Semitic father with his patriarchal authoritarian qualities abstracted and exaggerated. The combination of patriarchal suppression and sexual deprivation has left its mark on the Semitic basic personality. From Moses to Freud, Semites have been preoccupied with sin and sex.

As for the unfortunate Mexicans, Leopoldo Zea attributes their inferiority complex to the superiority complex of the Spanish conquerors; José E. Iturriaga looks for a dietary origin in the traditionally substandard nutrition of Mexico and its consequences—short life expectancy, and high rates of crime and mortality; Samuel Ramos takes the Mexican sense of insufficiency back to the Aztecs and their oppression of the common people.

No such glamorous origins have been proposed for the national character of the Americans, though Frederick Jackson Turner is still occasionally quoted by defenders of TV Westerns:

. . . the frontier is productive of individualism. Complex society is precipitated by the wilderness into a kind of primitive organization based on the family. The tendency is antisocial. It produces antipathy to control, and particularly to any direct control.

. . . to the frontier the American intellect owes its striking characteristics. That coarseness and strength combined with acuteness and inquisitiveness, that practical, inventive turn of mind quick to find expedients; that masterful grasp of material things, lacking in the artistic but powerful to effect great ends; that restless, nervous energy; that dominant individualism, working for good and evil, and withal that buoyancy and exuberance which comes with freedom. . . .

But the land was ours before we were the land's. We were Americans long before we came to America.

THE HERITAGE: ANGLO-SAXONS AND PURITANS

There is much in common between the Americans who drink beer and eat tranquilizers around the garden barbecue and the Saxons who drank honey beer in the ancient *meduselda* and saw life as the brief flight of a sparrow through the warmth of a hall—as the Venerable Bede said—from "winter to winter." They came from a gloomy land, these inconsequential Germans driven west by fiercer barbarians to the east; a country of dark forests running up to misty coasts through which Grendels stalked. Their tempers were not improved by the fogs of Londinium when they came there at Vortigern's foolish invitation. They went on eating pork, cheese, and salt fish, drinking honey beer, killing each other at the slightest provocation, and disputing at no provocation at all. There are some good things to be said for the Angles and Saxons and Jutes: they were courageous, prudent, loyal, and moral. Chastity was not with them "the rarest of the sexual aberrations," as Housman defined it. Most important, they were fiercely democratic; though they had more than enough kings (every hamlet had two or three of them), their hereditary rulers got the minimum of respect and obedience in time of peace. For all their savagery and uncouthness, they loom more nobly in our ancestry than the Puritans, to whom we sadly owe so much more as the progenitors of our way of life.

The Puritans did not invent themselves in the middle of the sixteenth century, as some think. There were budding Puritans all along the corridors of English history, such as the merchant saint, Godric of Finchale, who journeyed in the twelfth century

to Denmark and Flanders and Scotland; in all which lands he found certain rare, and therefore more precious, wares, which he carried to other parts wherein he knew them to be least familiar, and coveted by the inhabitants beyond the price of gold itself; wherefore he exchanged these wares for others coveted by men of other lands; and thus he chaffered most freely and assiduously. Hence he made great profit in all his bargains, and gathered much wealth in the sweat of his brow; for he sold dear in one place the wares which he had bought elsewhere at a small price.

It is a fact that in the early seventeenth century fourteen of fifteen American settlers were not Puritans; indeed, in colonial America the Puritans were outnumbered by the Negroes. America, except for its slaves and its Puritans, was just as English as the Mother Country—but those Puritans made the difference.

It is an anthropological truism that the first dominant settlers establish the cultural pattern to which all later comers must conform. Just as all Americans speak the language of the Puritans, so also do they think with the minds of the Puritans. The Melting-Pot Theory that gives equal credit to the multitudes of non-English immigrants for the making of America is a fairy tale concocted for the solace of immigrants who cannot trace their ancestry to the *Mayflower* and the *Amelia*. Those who persist in the delusion that more recent settlers have contributed substantially even to American food should test their belief Down Under in Australia now that it has opened its gates to southern Europeans, and have a go at Italian-Australian spaghetti. But at the present time there are some forty million Americans who were born abroad or who are the children of foreign-born parents, and they must be allowed their satisfying delusions until they too have absorbed Puritanism, its ethic, and its mythology.

As his contribution to the observance of the 300th anniversary of the landing of the Pilgrims, Charles A. Beard assembled for the *New Republic* this list of characteristics drawn from his reading of commentators on the Puritans:

Godliness	philistinism
thrift	harsh restraint
liberty	beauty hating
democracy	sour faced fanaticism
culture	supreme hypocrisy

industry	canting
frugality	demonology
temperance	enmity to true art
resistance to tyranny	intellectual tyranny
pluck	brutal intolerance
principle	grape juice
a free church	grisly sermons
a free state	religious persecution
equal rights	sullenness
a Holy Sabbath	ill temper
liberty under law	stinginess
individual freedom	bigotry
self government	conceit
a gracious spirit of Christianity	bombast

Beard did not dote on the Puritans or their identifiable descendants, and his list is intended to confute those who acknowledge the Puritans as the makers of American culture. It is easy to sympathize with him and his numerous followers in this generation, for it is within the realm of human imagination to conceive of more lovable forebears than the Puritans. But his list is quite valid, so far as it goes, and the characteristics he has set in opposite columns are complementary traits, often found in the same individual in seventeenth-century Massachusetts. Samuel Sewall was a conceited, canting, bigoted, philistinistic demonologist, but he was at the same time a thrifty, frugal, industrious, temperate, plucky man of principle with as gracious a spirit as Christianity will allow. It was natural for a Puritan governor to write:

> If we should change from a mixt aristocracy to a mere Democratie, first we should have no warrant in scripture for it; there was no such government in Israel. . . . A Democratie is, amongst most civilizations, accounted the meanest and worst of all forms of Government.

But they had a democracy, in spite of what they thought to the contrary.

One does not have to go to the Puritans alone to find an abundance of evidence that a people are the worst judges of their own actions. Doubtless, Governor Winthrop was unaware that he was epitomizing the Puritan ethos when he enumerated his reasons for not shooting birds out of season, as paraphrased by Samuel E. Morison in his *Builders of the Bay Colony*:

1. It is illegal
2. It offends the neighbors
3. "It wastes great store of tyme"
4. "It toyles a man's bodye overmuche"
5. It endangers his life
6. It brings no profit
7. The penalty for shooting birds out of season is heavy
8. "It brings a man of worth and godliness into some contempt"
9. After he has gone shooting with "wounds of conscience" he has missed most of the "fowle that came his way, and often returned with an empty bag"

Our legacies from Puritanism are not easily summarized, though they fill the rest of this book. For the remainder of this chapter, let us see ourselves as others have seen us in observations whose profundity is frothed over by supercilious humor. Arthur M. Schlesinger, Sr., summarizes the traits noticed by most visitors, in a useful guide paragraph:

> . . . a belief in the universal obligation to work; the urge to move from place to place; a high standard of average comfort; faith in progress; the eternal pursuit of material gain; an absence of permanent class barriers; the neglect of abstract thinking and of the esthetic side of life; boastfulness; a deference for women; the prevalence of spoiled children; the general restlessness and hurry of life, always illustrated by the practice of fast eating; and certain miscellaneous traits such as overheated houses, the vice of spitting and the passion for rocking chairs and icewater.

THE RIP-TAILED ROARERS

Anglo-Saxon poetry was so full of bragging that the god of poetry himself was named Bragi. Here is Beowulf (in J. Duncan Spaeth's translation), telling King Hrothgar why the other heroes urged him to come take care of the monster Grendel:

> *For well they approved my prowess in battle,*
> *They saw me themselves come safe from the conflict*
> *When five of my foes I defeated and bound,*
> *Beating in battle the brood of the monsters.*
> *At night on the sea with nicors I wrestled,*
> *Avenging the Weders, survived the sea-peril,*
> *And crushed in my grip the grim sea-monsters*
> *That harried my neighbors.*

By the time Beowulf got to the Kentucky frontier, he was considerable fiercer. It is told of Davy Crockett that he addressed Congress with this sort of legislative dignity:

Congress allows *lemonade* to the members and has it charged under the head of stationery—I move also that *whiskey* be allowed under the item of *fuel*. For *bitters* I can suck away at a noggin of aquafortis, sweetened with brimstone, stirred with a lightning rod, and skimmed with a hurricane. I've soaked my head and shoulders in Salt River, so much that I'm always corned. I can walk like an ox, run like a fox, swim like an eel, yell like an Indian, fight like a devil, spout like an earthquake, make love like a mad bull, and swallow a nigger whole without choking if you butter his head and pin his ears back.

Farther west there was the cowboy roarer who described himself thus:

Raised in the backwoods, suckled by a polar bear, nine rows of jaw teeth and holes punched for more, a double coat of hair, steel ribs, wire intestines, and a barbed wire tail, and I don't give a damn where I drag it.

Some of the British visitors to the frontier, seeing the epic braggarts on their best behavior, allowed that there was some exaggeration in these boasts. Crockett and Fink and most of the other backwoods roarers were mainly imaginative, but Bully Bill Sedley was a fact. Bully Bill, a Mississippi flatboatman who wore the red turkey feather in his cap as champion of his barge, got drunk one night in New Orleans, took up a club, broke into a circus menagerie, and beat a tiger to death.

American boasting came over with the Pilgrims. In 1668 the Reverend William Stoughton expressed the feeling of all Massachusetts when he said that God "hath sifted a whole nation that he might send choice grain over into this wilderness." The Puritans were not being allegorical when they called themselves the Saints.

Coming to a big country, the early immigrants drew out quality to quantity, and the phrase "biggest in the world" became the merest intensive adjectival precedent to any American noun. John Graham Brooks said in *As Others See Us* that:

> There just comes to hand an official document of the Jamestown Exposition from which, among many, I take these sentences: "greatest military spectacle the world has ever seen," "grandest naval rendezvous in history," "greatest gathering of warships in the history of the world," "the largest military parade ground in the world," "the greatest military and naval parade ever witnessed," "the greatest display of gorgeous military uniform," and "the greatest military and naval celebration ever attempted in any age by any nation."

A few experienced visitors tried to protect themselves from this chronic disease of "congenital eminence," but at the slightest flagging of caution it was on them again. Brooks tells of the English bishop who could not resist expressing his delight upon visiting an obviously unpretentious Eastern college. He confessed to its president that it was so very restful to find a school that was not, in endowment, in rapid growth, in distinction of alumni, or in some other way, the biggest in the country. The president looked at him in dismay; "But we do cover more *space* than any college in the United States." Said the bishop later: "From this time I avoided all occasions of bringing this extraordinary endowment into play."

Brooks goes on to quote a visitor who swore he took this paragraph from an Ohio paper:

> This is a glorious country! It has longer rivers and more of them, and they are muddier and deeper, and run faster and rise higher, and make more noise, and fall lower, and do more damage than anybody else's rivers. It has more lakes, and they are bigger and deeper, and clearer and wetter than those of any other country. Our rail-cars are bigger, and run faster, and pitch off the track oftener, and kill more people than all other rail-cars in this and every other country. Our steam boats carry bigger loads, are longer and broader, burst their boilers oftener, and send up their passengers higher, and the captains swear harder than steamboat captains in any other country. Our men are bigger and longer and thicker; can fight harder and faster, drink more mean whiskey, chew more bad tobacco, and spit more, and spit further than in any other country. Our ladies are prettier, dress finer, spend more money, break more hearts, wear bigger hoops, shorter dresses, and kick up the devil generally to a greater extent than all other ladies in all other countries. Our children squall louder, grow faster, get too expansive for their pantaloons, and become twenty years old sooner by some months than any other children of any other country on earth.

The habit is hard ground into the national character. Only the United States compiles lists of the hundred best books and the ten greatest sports stars and the twenty best-dressed women and the forty top tunes and the one most beautiful woman in the universe. Only in America would a professor get a freshman English composition asking: "Where else in the world can you ride from one end of Manhattan to the other for a dime?" It is an accepted fact that Colorado (which is not especially known to the rest of the nation in superlatives) has 90 per cent of the land in the United States over 10,000 feet and would be, if flattened out to sea level, larger than Texas. But not many flatland tourists know that there is a garage near Telluride that claims to be the biggest in the world, that nearby is the finest scenery in the United States, that just a few miles away there is a bridge whose owners claim is the highest in the world, that in Lyons, Colorado, a quarry advertises itself as the "world's largest producer of Colorado sandstone," and that along one of the Colorado highways there is a hamburger stand that offers the "largest hamburgers in the world" (next door a lunchroom sells "the biggest hamburgers on the block").

This sort of thing annoys foreign travelers so much that they cannot see the insecurity that prompts it. Only Lord Bryce, in the most perceptive of travel books, *The American Commonwealth*, appreciated that American boasting was the other side of the coin of autodenigration, and he greatly preferred bragging to the habit of some Americans of pleasurably censuring themselves and their country to strangers, a habit whose incidence has grown much stronger of late.

The early Americans tried to see things as they should be, not as they were, and to this natural custom in a new country was added the Puritan heritage of Calvinistic self-examination for indications of heavenly election; but one dare not look deep into oneself without finding many more indications of damnation. This is why James Truslow Adams said that all the virtues of Puritanism were negations.

THE JOINERS

Misery loves company, we are assured, and Americans delight in it. The first New England settlers came to this country as Congre-

gationalists and found Indians (those whom Providence had not
graciously removed by smallpox) who were more congregational
than any other primitives on earth. De Tocqueville sums up the
result:

> The political associations that exist in the United States are
> only a single gesture in the midst of the immense assemblage
> of associations in that country. Americans of all ages, all
> conditions and all dispositions, constantly form associations.
> They have not only commercial and manufacturing com-
> panies, in which all take part, but associations of a thousand
> other kinds—religious, moral, serious, futile, extensive, or
> restricted, enormous or diminutive. The Americans make
> associations to give entertainments, to found establishments,
> for education, to build inns, to construct churches, to diffuse
> books, to send missionaries to the antipodes. . . .
>
> The first time I heard in the United States that a hundred
> thousand men had bound themselves publicly to abstain from
> spirituous liquors, it appeared to me more like a joke than a
> serious engagement; and I did not once perceive why these
> temperate citizens could not content themselves with drink-
> ing water by their own fireside.

De Tocqueville is held above all other foreign commentators on
American culture (except perhaps Lord Bryce), not because he
refrained from criticizing his hosts, but because he tried to understand the reason for their failings—and he was humorless enough
to keep from couching his observations more sharply than his
English colleagues. Here is Charles Dickens on the subject of
temperance, for instance, after he fell foul of a temperance hotel:

> . . . I never discovered that the scruples of such wincing land-
> lords induced them to preserve any unusually nice balance
> between the quality of their fare and their scale of charges;
> on the contrary, I rather suspected them of diminishing the
> one and exalting the other, by way of recompense for the loss
> of their profit on the sale of spirituous liquors. After all, per-

haps, the plainest course for persons of such tender con-
sciences would be a total abstinence from tavern keeping.

No comment is needed on the most numerous and most enthusiastic of American associations, religion—or more exactly,
churches. As Frederick Marryat remarked:

> The fact is, that there is little or no healthy religion in their
> most numerous and influential churches; it is all excite-
> ment. . . . I believe it to be the case in *all* religions in
> America, for the Americans are a people who are prone to
> excitement, not only from their climate, but constitutionally,
> and it is the *caviare* of their existence.

The Yearbook of American Churches for 1963 reported 116,-
109,929 members in 258 religious bodies, but these figures are
limited only to the respectable—that is, the least heretical—of
American denominations. There are no recent figures for the sect
in Los Angeles that began when a housewife brought home an
apparently quite dead and decapitated rooster and threw it into
her sink, from which it leapt to the floor and began running about.
This was a Sign, and since it happened in Southern California,
the lady founded a church that was soon full of members. The
last that was heard from this temple was that its officers were
contemplating the establishment of an associated mortuary.

MRS. BLOOMER'S PROGENY

The frenzied enthusiasm of the churchgoers on the American
frontier had a result noticed after the normal period of human
gestation. Preacher Casy in *The Grapes of Wrath* worried about
this paradox:

> Here's me preachin' grace. An' here's them people gettin'
> grace so hard they're jumpin' an' shoutin'. Now they say
> layin' up with a girl comes from the devil. But the more
> grace a girl got in her, the quicker she wants to go out in the

grass. An' I got to thinkin' how in hell, s'cuse me, how can the devil get in when a girl is so full of the Holy Sperit that it's spoutin' out of her nose an' ears. You' think that'd be one time when the devil didn't stand a snowball's chance in hell. But there it was.

The Americans, since they were good Puritans, tried to channel their emotion into more spiritual endeavors by improving on the prudery of their forebears, which did not last long in the old country. From the time that the martyred head of Charles the First bounced away from the bloody axe until Cromwell's own dour cranium bobbed on a pole in a traveling circus, England was a mirthless place where Puritans hanged cats on Monday for killing rats on Sunday. But when Charles the Second restored the kingly head to the kingly crown, England went on a debauch of merriment and misbehavior that Kathleen Winsor described in *Forever Amber*. For most of the century that followed, blatant immorality was a patriotic virtue, and those who provided the amenities of vice—the vintners and the songsters—prospered as they would not prosper again, purveying to the hedonists who hung about the court and the clubs. But that was in England. In America it was different. If immorality was a patriotic act in England, then morality was a patriotic act in America, quite apart from any abstract value in morality. American Puritanism made sure that Charles's Cavaliers stayed down in the Southern boondocks with their dallying slaves so that it could eventually produce Amelia Bloomer, who put the voluminous Turkish trousers on herself and other American ladies, rendering them practically impregnable.

It is a slander on the English to call latter-day prudery "Victorian," for it was the Americans, not the British, who were its most assiduous proponents. Even Mrs. Trollope, whose name belied her morality, thought the American ladies a bit silly on this point. She tells of visiting a public park in Cincinnati in 1827 where an ice-cream concessionaire advertised his stand with a signpost cut in the form of a Swiss peasant girl. Unfortunately, her petticoat was so short that her ankles were exposed, and a delegation of ladies protested.

> The affrighted purveyor of ices sent off an express for the artist and his paint pot. He came, but unluckily not provided with any colour that would match the petticoat; the necessity, however, was too urgent for delay, and a flounce of blue was added to the petticoat of red, giving bright and shining evidence before all men of the immaculate delicacy of the Cincinnati ladies.

Nothing in this amusing country amused the indefatigable Captain Marryat more than American prudery:

> I was requested by a lady to escort her to a seminary for young ladies and on being ushered into the reception room, conceive my astonishment at beholding a square pianoforte with four *limbs*. However, that the ladies who visited their daughters might feel in its full force the extreme delicacy of the mistress of the establishment, and her care to preserve in their utmost purity the ideas of the young ladies under her charge, she had dressed all these four limbs in modest little trousers, with frills at the bottom of them.

Many an Englishman besides Marryat committed an unforgivable breach of etiquette in asking for breast of chicken at American tables. Sexually pertinent regions of even chicken anatomy were not mentioned in mixed company in America. One had to refer then, as one does now, to white meat and dark meat, not so much because of the color of the substance as because of its strategic location. The only real change over the years is that today we are conscious of our prudery. The Puritans unwittingly awarded Hester Prynne the first athletic letter in indoor sports to wear on her sweater; modern Puritans in Hollywood make special scenes in orgiastic period motion pictures for the overseas trade and give the native moviegoer Roman gracious living with courtesans garbed in unassailable bloomers.

THE SEMPITERNAL HOT STOVE

American heat was chastely surficial—another indication, said the visitors, of American infantilism. As Freud might have remarked:

If you find your lonely bed at night as chilly as a tomb
And you curl up 'neath the blankets like a worm in a cocoon,
It's not temperature that moves you, but a longing for the womb.

James Fullarton Muirhead at the end of the nineteenth century tied the two characteristics together in his book *The Land of Contrasts* when he recalled that he "summoned a blush to the cheek of conscious sixty-six by an incautious though innocent reference to the temperature of my morning tub."

The earliest item on the list compiled by *Fortune* of the hundred best-designed consumer products of the age of industry (see Chapter 10) is Franklin's stove, an invention that took the heat out of the chimney and put it into the room, to the extreme discomfort of English travelers, who since the time of the Norman invasion had been used to cold behinds from August to July. British visitors were driven nearly out of their senses by indoor temperatures in America. Dickens, during his 1842 visit, steeled himself to the general decrepitude of American interiors, but he could not abide "the presence of the eternal, accursed, suffocating, red-hot demon of a stove, whose breath would blight the purest air under heaven." And reliable Mrs. Trollope was sure the poor complexions of Americans were attributable to their stoves, just as their warped physiognomies were attributable to their habit of chewing tobacco. T. C. Grattan, the Anglo-Irish diplomat who in 1859 published his observations on the United States in the ironically titled *Civilized America*, objected that the Americans took the stove out of the parlor and put it into the cellar, gigantically enlarged and empowered:

The method of heating many of the best houses is a terrible grievance to persons not accustomed to it, and a fatal misfortune to those who are. Casual visitors are nearly suffocated, and constant occupiers killed. An enormous furnace in the cellar sends up, day and night, streams of hot air, through apertures and pipes, to every room in the house. No spot is free from it, from the dining-parlour to the dressing-closet. It meets you the moment the street door is opened to let you in, and rushes after you when you emerge again, half-stewed and parboiled, into the wholesome air.

American visitors to England need not be told of the two great hardships they will have to bear in that country—frigid rooms and indestructible toilet paper—but they should be warned that the same conditions obtain in the colonies. Every American traveler in Australia, without exception, huddles the entire winter under "rugs" before the "electric fires" that are obtainable in some metropolitan centers, just as every Australian traveler in America, without exception, throws open the windows upon his arrival in a hotel. In point of fact, you will be told, the coldest temperature ever recorded in Sydney was 37 degrees above zero—but it should be made clear that this is outside temperature; indoors it gets much colder.

THE SICK AMERICANS

The early English visitors blamed the superheated interiors of the United States for the national hypochondria that most of them noticed. This is not much of a reason (though it is still to be heard in Australia, where Americans are assured that exposure to artificial heat causes chilblains), but anthropology cannot offer a better one. It is easy enough to say that this or that general characteristic is an ancient import, but so is everything else, and that which explains everything explains nothing. Anthropology has only recently discovered the concept of culture; it has not yet had time to explain it. Every people somewhere in their history have a choice of selecting from several apparently satisfactory courses, and in so doing enter an irreversible path. So far as we can tell, the Navahos came into the Four Corners region of the Southwest with very little except ferocity and envy; they drove out the peaceable Anasazi folk, but they kept the looted culture of the Pueblos. But for some unknown cause they reoriented it away from agricultural fertility toward curing of illness. In historical times, hypochondria is so thoroughly woven into the Navaho ethos that an epidemic of good health could wipe them out. For some unknown cause also, this is the path chosen by the Americans.

Probably the path toward hypochondria was taken in Anglo-Saxon times, for the oldest English literature is well spattered with curing charms. Felix Grendon, who has written the best general discussion of Anglo-Saxon leechdom and wortcunning, shows that the earliest Englishmen had refined the techniques of magical curing found among all primitive peoples. Pope Gregory the Great, who advised his missionaries to create Christian feasts out of the displaced Germanic pagan rites, expediently retained heathen practices under a veneer of Christianity. He permitted the Germanic shamans to continue applying herbal remedies together with supplications to superior spirits, but he insisted that the superior spirits be changed to Christian deities—angels, saints, and martyrs in place of demons, gods, and magicians. The early substitutions are still efficacious, according to modern spiritual physicians, and can be used in do-it-yourself therapy. Here are a few of the common and uncommon illnesses and the proper saints to whom one should apply for intercession:

AGUE: Sts. Pernel and Petronella
BAD DREAMS: St. Christopher
BLEAR EYES: Sts. Otilic and Clare
BLINDNESS: St. Thomas à Becket
BOILS AND BLAINS: Sts. Roque and Cosme
CHASTITY: St. Susan [It is not clear whether this is for retention or cure of chastity.]
CHILDREN'S DISEASES: St. Blaise

COLIC: St. Erasmus
DANCING MANIA: St. Vitus
EPILEPSY: Sts. Valentine and Cornelius
GOUT: St. Wolfgang
GRIPES: St. Erasmus
IDIOCY: St. Gildas
INFECTION: St. Roque
LEPROSY: St. Lazarus
MADNESS: Sts. Dympha and Fillan
PALSY: St. Cornelius
PLAGUE: St. Roque
QUINSY: St. Blaise
SMALLPOX: St. Martin of Tours
SORE THROAT: St. Blaise
TOOTHACHE: St. Appolonia

In Anglo-Saxon times, the syncretism of pagan and Christian curing and of the holy sign (early, the hammer of Thor; later, the crucifix) are illustrated by this charm for "elf-shot"—an imaginary cattle disease caused by eating elves:

If a horse is elf-struck, take a knife of which the handle is horn from a tawny ox and on which are three brass nails. Then inscribe a cross on the animal's back and on each of the limbs that you can hold on to. Then grasp the left ear, pierce it in silence. This you must do: take a stick, strike the horse on its back, then it will be well. And on the horn of the knife inscribe these words:—
Benedicite omnia opera domini dominum.
Be the elf who he may, this will suffice as a cure for him.

We have come a little way from this, but not very far. The ℞ on your wonder-drug prescription is a derivative of the sign ♃ which was written in ancient times at the head of a curing charm to propitiate Jupiter into letting the formula work properly. And Dr. Mundy's Soothing Syrup is the end point of an evolution which began in our culture with heathen magical liquids and

proceeded through baptism, holy water, and the oil of Extreme
Unction to the fantastic remedies written by the great Puritan
intellectual, Cotton Mather. New Englanders will object to this
slight on Mather and note that he championed smallpox inoculation. This is true, but certainly the appeal of this specific in
Mather's mind was its resemblance to homeopathic magic.

The publication history of leechbooks is unbroken to the
present time. One sample among uncounted many is *Divine
Remedies: a Textbook on Christian Healing*, published by the
Unity School of Christianity of Kansas City, Missouri, in 1945,
which gives magical charms to cure any ailment, from ingrown
toenails to falling hair. It advises as a prefatory caution that:

> It is well for anyone, when beginning healing prayers, first to
> deny the medical name of the seeming inharmony. It is good
> not to call inharmonies by any of the terms applied to them;
> because they are in reality nothing, and should not be given
> any kind of name to explain their error meaning. To name a
> disease tends to give it a place and power in consciousness;
> therefore deny the name.

Anyone who doubts that Americans are obsessed by illness evidently has not seen many late late movies on television, along
with the interspersed advertisements for aspirins and antacids
demonstrated by some quite remarkable anatomical schemas.
When next you see the pounding hammers and oscillating springs,
remember that at least one nineteenth-century visitor remarked
that we were a "headachy and dyspeptic people." We would
probably spend a good deal more than the current annual one
billion dollars for blatantly quack cures (exactly that spent on
ethical medicines) if two other Puritan qualities—officious prayer
and miserliness—did not work to help our pockets if not our
bodies. The most niggardly Puritan of them all, Samuel Sewall,
records that on the tenth day of February, 1708, he issued these
directives to God:

Perfect what is lacking in my Faith, and in the faith of my
dear Yokefellow. Convert my children, especially Samuel and
Hannah; Provide rest and settlement for Hannah; Recover
Mary, save Judith, Elisabeth, and Joseph; Requite the labour
of love of my kinswoman Jane Tappin, Give her health, and
find out Rest for her. Make David a man after thy own heart.
Let Susan live and be baptised with the Holy Ghost and with
fire. Relations. Steer the Government in this difficult time,
when the Gouvernour and many others are at so much
Variance; Direct, incline, overrule on the Council Day fifth-
day Feb. 12 as to the Special Work of it in filling the Super.
Court with Justices; or any other thing of like nature, as the
Inferior Court of Plymouth. Bless the Company for the
propagation of the Gospel, Especiall Govr. Ashurst, etc.
Revive the Business of Religion at Natick, and accept and
bless John Neesnumin who went thither last week for that
end. Mr. Rawson at Nantucket. Bless the South Church in
preserving and Spiriting our Pastor; in directing into suitable
Supply, and making the Church unanimous: Save the Town,
College. Province from invasion of Enemies, open, Secret,
and from false Brethren. Defend the Purity of Worship. Save
Connecticut, bless their new Governour; Save the Reformation under N. York Government. Reform all the European
Plantations in America: Spanish, Portuguese, English, French,
Dutch; Save this New World, that where Sin hath abounded,
Grace may superabound; that CHRIST who is stronger,
would bind the Strong man and spoil his house; and order
the Word to be given, Babylon is fallen. Save our Queen,
lengthen her Life and Reign. Save France, make the Proud
helper stoop (Job ix, 13). Save all Europe; Save Asia, Africa,
Europe, and America. These were genl. heads of my Meditation and Prayer; and through the bounteous Grace of GOD,
I had a very comfortable day of it.

Which is surely more than God could say.

☆ III ☆

Bringing Up Americans

In the lunar desolation of central Australia a boy is about to become a man.

In the last few weeks he has suffered through the preliminary rites, learning some of the esoteric lore about his totemic ancestors who made this land in the distant *alchera*—the Dreaming; his penis has healed somewhat from the circumcision ceremony, and his clansmen decide he is ready for the *arilta* operation. They construct the *apulla* ground, scrabbling away the sparse gray saltbush from the brown sand and red bedrock; other relatives have painted his body with the ancient designs carved into the totemic stones; the eagle down has been glued to his chest with coagulated human blood; the women have been driven away in terror before the *churinga* was whirled into the voice of the spirits. He is given a fascis of bundled spears to hug, deadening his senses against the exquisite pain to come, and his clansmen on hands and knees begin to form the human operating table, each taking the proper place assigned to him according to the rules of their bewildering social organization. The initiate is led to this *tapunga* and is laid across it on his back as the ritual surgeon flicks his stone knife into a fine edge with his thumbnail. Other assistants, also relatives of the boy, hold him down as the *peininya* seizes the boy's penis, inserts a long emu bone into the urethra, and makes the first incision. The flesh breaks open suddenly like a slit sheet of stretched rubber, as living flesh does when it is deeply cut, but the surgeon cuts on in nicking strokes through the layers of flesh to the emu bone. And still he cuts, cuts, cuts along the exposed emu bone until at last the boy's penis is slit wide along its entire length from the glans to the scrotum. It is a good job, this one, and the *peininya* steps back proudly as the quivering boy is helped to his feet and led to a small fire, over which he squats, his blood sizzling as it drips upon the embers. The boy is proud, too, for he has gone through the ordeal without crying out, and he is congratulated by his clansmen. He is no longer a boy, but a man.

Some social anthropologists, especially the Freudians, are misled by the somatic locus of the operation into thinking subincision has something to do with sex. One of them, a writer who has propounded such other arrant nonsense as the "natural superiority of women," argues that the rite is performed because the men want to imitate the women's menstruation, a sort of perverted Penis Envy. Why they should want to do such a weird thing he does not explain, probably feeling that such people are not accountable for their actions.

But subincision is simply a mnemonic, not different in kind from the act of the odious soap tycoon in *The Hucksters* when he spat upon the polished mahogany table at a conference of his advertising executives, to make them remember something he was saying. What is associated with unforgettable acts is similarly unforgettable. The Aranda initiate will never forget what happened to him at the *arilta*, nor will he forget what he learned in association with it, just as any male reader of the foregoing paragraphs with any sense of empathy will remember some of the things said in this chapter. Association of trauma with events im-

mediately surrounding it has been recognized, at least since the
time of Simonides, as the most effective educational device known
to man—or, for that matter, to any animal organism.

In the case of the Aranda boy, what he must never forget is
that to be a man in aboriginal Australia means a great deal more
than being able to reproduce himself. It means he must be able to
preserve himself and his people, which is far more difficult. Life
in this most hostile of all inhabited environments is almost impos-
sibly hard. A man can roam for days in the red desert of the
island continent and see no other living thing except insects, ants,
and Americans testing their missiles. If a horde of two or three
dozen natives cannot find food every few days, they die; and
where the whole of life is survival, reproduction is only a recreation. There is no "reproductive urge" among the higher animals;
if there were, nature would not have made its preliminary act
so pleasurable.

The fallacy of calling initiation rites such as the *arilta* "puberty
ceremonies" is exposed by the fact that where survival is precarious these rites are usually severe physical experiences; where life is
easier, the initiation rites begin to lose both their pain and their
meaning. In the more favored coastal areas of Australia, subincision was replaced by tooth evulsion (in which the upper central incisor was pounded out), cicatrization, or depilation. In even
richer places and periods of human culture, the act becomes
increasingly less meaningful and less memorable—the Catholic
Confirmation, the Jewish Bar Mitzvah, voting privileges at the
age of twenty-one, fraternity hazings, and the like. But in central
Australia subincision hurts, and life hurts, too; this is what the
young people must learn. It is a process of learning, then; it is the
end of a youth's formal education. He will learn more as he goes
through life, but the rest will be postgraduate experience.

PRIMITIVE EDUCATION

The anthropologist prefers to speak of "enculturation" rather than
education, because he sees it as a process of making an individual

fit well into his culture. And unless the anthropologist as a teacher overestimates the importance of formal instruction as a means of learning Truths, he recognizes further that it is a process of making young, unculturated, naturally rebellious individuals conform to the behavior patterns of their society. It is fashionable for teachers and other commentators on our civilization to condemn conformity, but conformity is the ideal of the educational process. The purpose of education in ancient Rome was to make the *vir bonus*, the good man; in contemporary Russia, the New Soviet Man; in contemporary America, the Good Citizen. Social goodness is nothing more than social conformity. Fortunately for those of us who exercise nonconformity in small and surreptitious areas of behavior, a secure culture like our own can tolerate a reasonable amount of misbehavior. It is otherwise in the primitive world. Norman Tindale, the Australian anthropologist, is the possessor of rare motion-picture films made some thirty-five years ago among the Pitjandjara people of the Australian desert, which on occasion he can be persuaded to show to qualified persons. In one of these a boy is offered for initiation by his father—a boy who was obviously a genetic homosexual, far too effeminate for Pitjandjara manhood but far too old to remain a child. The other boys on the *tapunga* that day showed their courage by stifling cries of pain when the knife tore them, but this unfortunate not only cried— he screamed and wept and groveled. His father pitiably tried to pass off his son's disgraceful conduct as a joke, but he was clearly mortified with shame. In our society, safe in its great numbers and complex culture from any harm that might result from the weakness of an individual, this boy could have found something useful to do to justify his existence; but he was a Pitjandjara and he had to be a manly hunter. The reaction of his clan was that he had blasphemed the ceremony, that it had been defiled by him. About three months later, Tindale says, his people speared him to death.

This is not to say that enculturation is a simple affair in modern society. The Pitjandjara boy, sharing in his horde's continuous

search for food, is well out of the Devil's hands. The problem of
our youth is ennui. In Curtis Bok's profoundly disturbing book
Star Wormwood, he records the conclusion that his life on the
bench led him to:

> Man turns a corner at twenty-five; that is, he matures at
> twenty-five and not before. Until then he can and should be
> considered a potential killer, raper, and thief, if he has as
> little as five minutes in which to grow bored and make the
> wrong choice. After twenty-five, society can take a chance
> on him. Before twenty-five, society can trust him all the way,
> provided it keeps him constantly busy. Every minute of a
> juvenile's time should be filled.

Adults everywhere, like Judge Bok, have had a lot of experience
with little boys and have concluded that they are a bad lot; and,
like Judge Bok, they have decided that it is best to keep after
them. In Samoa, infants were given into the charge of girls as
young as six years of age. The juvenile surrogate mother then had
to guide her charge into life, teaching it toilet habits, discouraging
its walking upright in the house (the proper method of indoor
locomotion in Samoa was crawling), inculcating an oppressive
series of prohibitions—not to speak to adults while standing, not
to get in the way of grownups, not to do this, not to do that.
These, Margaret Mead says, "were enforced by occasional cuffings
and a deal of exasperated shouting and ineffectual conversation."
Actual punishment came secondhand from the next oldest child,
who was held responsible for the good conduct of any younger
child present. Dr. Mead says that these admonitions became almost perpetual; in *Coming of Age in Samoa*, she describes con-
versations among adults interrupted constantly by "Keep still,"
"Stop that noise," and "Behave yourself," when the child in question had been as still as a mouse. "Just as a child is getting old
enough so that its wilfulness is becoming unbearable," she continues, "a younger one is saddled upon it, and the whole process

is repeated again, each child being disciplined and socialized through responsibility for a still younger one." The young mentors are bullied by their charges, for they will do anything to keep the child from crying; this naturally results in a permissive attitude toward children. "Even Samoan dogs have learned to estimate the proportion of gesture that there is in a Samoan 'Get out of the house.' They simply stalk out between one set of posts and with equal dignity and all casualness stalk in again at the next opening."

Raymond Firth describes the same sort of situation in Tikopian education in his classic study *We the Tikopia*. Some subordination to elders is occasionally required of a child, but most of the time the child does as it likes. There is no segregated instruction, as in our society; education consists of letting the child do whatever it has a mind to try, with advice offered but not enforced. Firth says that children are addressed solemnly by their elders from infancy:

> If the infant does not do as he is told the chief sometimes says to him calmly without the least spark of annoyance, "May your father eat filth!"

Children are continually ordered about by their elders, but since nothing is done if they disobey, they do just as they please.

> If an adult is in a callous frame of mind he tells another, "Fakanimo ko a mata o tau soa"—"Make the eyes of our friend swim," a command to bang the unfortunate intruder on the head without further ceremony.

Education in the higher Polynesian culture of New Zealand was more formal. The earliest education was carried out in the home, but the child was shortly apprenticed to a priest of the profession chosen for it at birth. Sons of priests and the chiefs attended a formal school later—an actual schoolhouse (*whare wananga*) where regular courses of study were conducted and where graduation conferred as much prestige as an advanced university degree does among us. Like the English who overcame them, the Maori required absolutely correct speech, even of small children. No baby talk was permitted, and correct elocution was followed by training in the difficult oratory of the Pacific islands.

Boys in Samoa were required to tend babies also, but were relieved of this responsibility at the age of eight or nine, when they became apprentices to their profession. Co-operation in tasks was encouraged for boys, but not for girls, so, as Margaret Mead says, girls did not learn so well as their brothers. "This is particularly apparent in the activities of young people; the boys organize quickly, the girls waste hours in bickering, innocent of any technique for quick and efficient cooperation."

As the Polynesian boy grew into young manhood, his responsibilities increased. Competition and emulation drew the best efforts from him, but, in a disturbing parallel to our own society, where amiable mediocrity is valued above disagreeable excellence, the good youth is one who does just a bit better than is expected of him. Pushing ambition is deplored just as much as laziness.

Dr. Johnson once said that there was nothing new under the sun in education, and this remark is borne out by reference to methods used by primitive peoples all over the world in bringing up their children. The 163-page monograph by George Pettitt, *Primitive Education in North America*, contains scarcely a principle of education not used by our teachers; and we do not have a single important principle that is not found somewhere in a rudimentary form in Indian education. The first great English anthropologist, Sir Edward Burnett Tylor, said of primitive children: "Their games are in fact their lessons." How excellently this principle is employed in our culture will be described later in this chapter.

But similar principles do not mean that systems are interchangeable. It is one of the most injurious fallacies of our intercultural educators that our system of education, our curricula, is beneficial to the primitive peoples whom we in our sobering position of leader of the world must introduce to Western culture. William Grayden, in his depressing investigation of white contact with the Pitjandjara, *Adam and Atoms* (the title refers to the fact that Pitjandjara territory is now being used as a missile range), shows the harm of educating a child for a culture it cannot join. The Australian government, Grayden accuses, has been forcibly separating native children from their parents to satisfy the desire of the missions to educate them to their own marginal culture, despite Australia's subscription to the United Nations' Universal Declaration of Human Rights. One of these children, a girl reared from infancy at the Warburton Mission in Western Australia, who received the same training as a white child, learned the same domestic habits, ate the same food, wore the same clothing, was, after reaching young adulthood, turned out to marry a bush native and live in the manner of her tribe—with no clothes, no house, and probably very little appetite for snakes, goannas, and witchetty grubs. Grayden concludes: "The training she received for 17 years or more at the Mission has only served to leave her hopelessly ill-equipped for the task of playing her part in fending in the native manner for her family."

So far as the science of physical anthropology has been able to determine, there is no difference in cultural capacity among the several races of mankind, but the difference in cultures is almost infinite. Since education is the process by which an individual is trained to take his place in his culture, to recommend that the educational system of one culture be changed to imitate that of another culture does not make good sense. Indeed, as Congressman Davy Crockett once said of a speech delivered by Andrew Jackson, "it doesn't even make good nonsense."

THE INVIDIOUS COMPARISON:
BRITISH VERSUS AMERICAN EDUCATION

Of the endless criticisms borne by American civilization from within and from without since the first settlers waded to these shores, none has been more monotonously strident than the criticism of our education. Some want us to go back to the Greeks, though they do not specify which Greeks in particular they mean —the Spartans, whose education systematically eradicated all the humane virtues and insinuated the baser vices, and which was adopted by Italy, Japan, and Germany before World War II; or the Athenians, whose education gave us the term "sophistry," and which was consciously directed to aristocratic uselessness, to say nothing of its deplorable practice of poisoning its teachers. Others look to the more recent past, to the Middle Ages, when Europe wallowed in spirituality, which these critics declare they prefer to materialism. These neo-medievalists are still deceived by the most flagrant lie in educational history—that the monks kept knowledge alive in the Middle Ages. If they were to ask themselves who or what was killing knowledge in continental Europe during the Age of Faith, they might realize that the monks and the myriad other Church functionaries did everything they could to destroy knowledge, and were in a fair way of succeeding, until, as one historian expressed it, "civilization was thrust into the brain of Europe on the point of a Moorish lance." But most of our critics look across to the Mother Country, to England, as the cynosure of all that is admirable in modern education.

Naturally the British agree with them. Very few of the hundreds of English tourists who visited the young nation throughout the nineteenth century with pen in hand were able to restrain themselves from monotonous invidious comparisons of American and English education. American colleges and universities were a constant source of amusement to the visiting British until late in the nineteenth century, when the perspicacious Lord Bryce informed his countrymen that the United States had passed England in scientific education. These visitors even went out of their way to ridicule such innocent sources of public edification as the young museums. Captain Marryat notes in his *Diary in America* that he spent a few minutes in the St. Louis museum one day in 1837.

There were once five large alligators to be seen alive in this museum, but they are now all dead. One demands our sympathy, as there was something Roman in his fate. Unable to support such a life of confinement, and preferring death to the loss of liberty, he committed suicide by throwing himself out of a three-story-high window. He was taken up from the pavement the next morning; the vital spark had fled, as the papers say, and, I believe, his remains were decently interred. The other four, never having been taught in their youth the hymn, "Birds in their little nests agree," fought so desperately, that one by one they all died of their wounds. They were very large, being from seventeen to twenty-one feet long. One, as a memorial, remains preserved in the museum, and to make him look more poetical, he has a stuffed Negro in his mouth.

Isaac Weld saw pretty much the same thing (without the stuffed Negro, however) at Princeton:

A large college, held in much repute by the neighboring states. The number of students amounts to upwards of 70; from their appearance, however, and the course of studies they seem to be engaged in, like all the other American colleges I ever saw, it better deserves the title of a grammar school than of a college. The library which we were shown is most wretched, consisting for the most part of old theological books not even arranged with any regularity. An orrery contrived by Mr. Rittenhouse stands at one end of the apartment, but it is quite out of repair, as well as a few detached parts of a philosophical apparatus enclosed in the same glass case. At the opposite end of the room are two small cupboards which are shown as the museum. These contain a couple of small stuffed alligators and a few singular fishes in a miserable state of preservation, from their being repeatedly tossed about.

The English educational system we are advised to emulate has some admirable features, but they are not suited to a democratic culture. Since the interpretation of British history for Americans has traditionally consisted of tracing the evolution of democracy in the island kingdom, it cannot be insisted too much that England, until forced to change its ways by the success of the United States, was not a democracy, except in the Athenian sense of democracy—that is, a democracy for the upper classes. To give the system a more honest name, it was a broad oligarchy. Real democracy in England ended with the conquest of the Anglo-Saxons at Hastings; since then it has been an oligarchy trapped out as a democracy. The great events of British political history, from the Magna Carta to the Reform Act of 1884, have been oligarchic acts. The last Reform Bill, for instance, is taught in American surveys of English history as the successful conclusion of a century-long struggle for universal franchise, but in actual fact it gave the vote to only five million out of Britain's population of 31.4 million. And since education is the means whereby a culture perpetuates itself, English education is good only for an oligarchic culture. Through much of the history of Britain the only way for a poor child to figure in the educational process was as the subject of an experiment—for example, the infant boy who was locked up in a cellar by King James I, who wanted to find out whether, when he let the child out at the age of ten, the child would naturally be speaking Hebrew. James had other interesting intellectual ideas, some with an unhappy influence upon the American colonies. His occult obsession with witches prompted the obsequious scholarly translators of the King James Bible to include as many references to witches as they could, and this document became the mainstay in the detection and prosecution of the Salem victims in 1692. The looseness of educational standards in England during the time of James and immediately afterward is illustrated by the case of Richard Lovelace, who was to become a rather good minor poet. At Oxford he was famous for his good looks; when the Queen visited the university, her ladies persuaded the officials to grant Lovelace his M.A. without further study.

Beginning with the establishment of Winchester College in 1382, there were indeed schools for *pauperes et indigentes*, but very few paupers and indigents got into them, except to wait at table. Winchester and its followers, the great English "public schools" (Westminster, Eton, Harrow, Merchant Taylor's, Rugby, St. Paul's, Shrewsbury, and Charterhouse), were and continue to this day to be for the rich, except for token integration of less well endowed scholars. They perpetuate, as others have observed, a tribal society by methods not essentially different from those of true tribal societies anywhere in the primitive world. The system has been defended well by a series of resounding slogans such as Wellington's "The battle of Waterloo was won on the playing fields of Eton." But neither Eton nor Wellington had much to do with the victory—it was a little uneducated Flemish boy herding cows who won the Battle of Waterloo for England by advising Blücher's lieutenant, Bülow, to lead his artillery out of the woods above Frischemont instead of below Planchenoit.

The upper classes in England understandably were never very keen on educating the lower classes to become dissatisfied with their station in life, and so it was not until the end of the eighteenth century that the rich finally began to let a little money trickle down into educational charity—and this was only because of the growing agitation of the "nasty, canting, dirty, lousy Methodists," as Cobbett called them. Such schools as existed for the lower classes were liable to closure at any time. As Tawney remarks in *Religion and the Rise of Capitalism*: "King Edward VI's Grammar Schools were the schools which King Edward did not destroy." In the nineteenth century Alfred Lord Tennyson—then a member of the *petit bourgeoisie*—recalls that the rectory school he attended at Benniworth as a child was summarily closed by the local squire because the children were disturbing the game. Tennyson's childhood education illustrates another traditional aspect of British elementary schooling—corporal punishment. After the Benniworth incident, Tennyson went to the Grammar

School at Louth, where the master was so skillful at flogging that he put one boy to bed for six weeks. The great Dr. Samuel Johnson deplored any change in this area of education: "There is now less flogging in our great schools that formerly, but then less is learned there; so that what the boys get at one end they lose at the other." England finally got a system of state-supported schools going in 1870 under the Foster Education Act, but these were established only where the voluntary church system had not erected any denominational schools. The idea that education should be in the hands of the churchmen persisted even in the minds of liberal intellectuals. Ruskin, in *Unto This Last*, does not list teaching among the five great intellectual professions, giving the job over to the "Pastor."

Meanwhile at the universities the monks were still hard at work keeping knowledge alive. Knowledge was so well preserved when the first universities were established that an educated man had to know Latin, for there were no scholarly books in English. After the Fall of Constantinople in 1453, Greek became available for the same purpose (Greek was totally unknown in Western Europe during the Middle Ages). This began one of those revered traditions in English education which last to the present day with accumulated inertial sanctity. In 1959 the question was raised at Oxford University about the wisdom and practicality of retaining a knowledge of Latin as an entrance requirement. The argument that most impressed the assembled dons was an emotional appeal by a fellow of St. Hilda's College for her colleagues to look at the Horrible Example of the American universities, which had abandoned this useful language in their classes. The dons looked and were horrified, and voted 301 to 262 to require incoming freshmen to know Latin. Today less than two per cent of the children who attend elementary schools in Britain go on to matriculate at a university. England has only 1,815 university students per million of population—about the same per capita number as Turkey (1,780)—and four fifths of these are in provincial universities, where they are made, according to Anthony Sampson in his *Anatomy of Britain*, to "feel inferior for life."

This is fine for an oligarchic culture, but not for a democracy. To see what happens when the British system is imitated by another culture, let us look at higher education in Australia, a country completely free and independent of England, but whose official chief of state is the Queen. This, by the way, is a Mystery, like the doctrine of the Trinity, and is past understanding by human minds.

ENGLISH IN THE AUSTRALIAN UNIVERSITIES

Australian professors of English have no exalted opinion of their American colleagues. Since most of them have either been trained in English universities or are intending to take up positions there as soon as their rustication in the colonies is completed, they are masters of the gentle craft of subtle disdain that makes an American Ph.D. feel as if he had taken his degree in Mortuary Science. Although they do recognize—but do not pretend to understand— the presence in American universities of a very few men approaching their own caliber, they are convinced that most American college classrooms begin, like Mr. Dadier's in *The Blackboard Jungle*, with literary discussions of animated cartoons of Jack and the Beanstalk. Their own standards are much higher; the conversational gambit they offer their classes is hardly likely to be less casual than a literary and linguistic analysis of *Ok enn preifar hann um fleskit*, and even the chars who scrub the hall know the difference between an *ibid.* and an *op. cit.*

To an American who remembers one Ph.D. candidate who identified Wyrd as an Anglo-Saxon poet and another who wanted to prepare, for his doctoral dissertation, a concordance to Edgar A. Guest, this studied haughtiness is bound to be disquieting, even though we all know it is founded on nothing more tangible than the empty intellectual arrogance that has kept impressionable foreigners standing in awe of the British for centuries. As Americans, we are not very much concerned, for Americans cannot be made to appreciate the profundity of their own lack of culture. Any British critic will tell you that. But it is the Australians who need our concern—they are without question the most lovable people in the world, but their academic leaders are hard bent on turning them all into proles by such things as the Eleven-Plus examinations that weed out all late-maturing students.

This is, in effect if not in conscious intention, the common goal of Australia's leaders in every field, from the Prime Ministers whose every decision of international importance is guided by the influence it will have toward getting them a peerage, to the idolized jockeys for whom the Queen's accolade is not beyond possibility. But the university teachers of English are most culpable, since, more than anything else, it is the distinction of language usage and accent that preserves the debilitating stratification of Australian society. They could do much to free the class-bound brains of the bulk of the Australian people, and so dredge their country out of the cultural backwater in which it is stagnating, but they are content to let the average Australian go on thinking a bison is something to warsh his fice in.

To American college teachers who see the number and quality of their English majors going down semester by semester, the power of English professors in Australia may seem unreal, but no university student, regardless of his brilliance in the more practical fields of academic endeavor, can get out of his freshman year without being able to discuss to the satisfaction of an implacable grader the linguistic significance of the *Statute of Pleading*.

Let us see how this works.

There are in Australia eleven tertiary institutions of learning: the universities of Sydney, Melbourne, Adelaide, Queensland, Western Australia, New England, and Tasmania, the New South Wales University of Technology, Monash University, Canberra College, and the National University, the latter the only purely graduate school in the country. According to the 1961 *Common-wealth Universities Yearbook*, total enrollment is just under 30,000 students (about one third the size of the City University of New York), of whom some 8,000 each attend Sydney and Melbourne. All these students must pass a year of English study.

Despite the subservience of the Australian universities to English models, they are structured on the Scottish system: the ordinary student reads for a pass degree during three years of study, and Honours students are nominated to take extra work in addition to the pass curriculum, and to go on for a fourth year of study. There are inconsequential variations in procedure and curricula among the several universities, but in general the University of Sydney may be taken as the archetype.

The University of Sydney is housed in the most uncomfortable group of buildings in the Southern Hemisphere. Scholars recognize as one of the chief themes in Australian folklore the illusion that this is a warm country; therefore, though the university roofs are studded with chimney pots (because the English universities have them), they lead nowhere. There are admittedly some fireplaces, and these make excellent repositories for the old examination books, possibly on the homeopathic principle that in burning they emit both heat and light. Some progressive classrooms have gas fireplaces, but they make so much noise that they are not turned on during the school year. The nearby University of New South Wales, in the outer darkness of academic circles (part of its campus is appropriately located in the suburb of Ultimo), broke away from the English medieval tradition and housed itself in a building that, like the Australian hot dog, looks like the real thing. But, shortly after its construction, the roof blew off—doubtless, a divine visitation for its effrontery.

Along the dismal corridors of the University of Sydney moves an English staff of two professors and about a dozen lecturers—but not all at once, for in any year three or four will be on leave, reporting back to England for brainwashing. Normally a staff of about eight will determine what will be the life work of some 1,500 students who annually take courses in English.

The academic year begins in March and ends in September. There are three teaching terms, separated by two three-week breaks (the trimester plan which has been adopted by some American universities). Unlike in American universities, there is no cornucopia of electives; all students must take a total of nine one-year courses to qualify for a degree. A typical arts subject requires compulsory attendance at from two to four hour-long lectures a week; in English courses this means, for the pass student, eighty lectures in an invariable curriculum that offers no free choice of specialization. All students take the same courses and sit for the same examination. Except for two ten-page exercises in the freshman year, the only basis for grading is a three-hour examination at the end of the year. Of the 700 students who take English One, perhaps 60 will be awarded sufficient "credits" to permit them to attempt Honours. Of this number, only a dozen will accept—of the 48 or so who do not so elect, a few will have been offered "credits" in other faculties, which they prefer to English, but most decline because they cannot afford the expense of the additional year.

If the selected Honours student has done exceptionally well among his exceptional fellows, he may go on for an advanced degree, though in Australia there is not the necessity for the M.A. or Ph.D. that obtains in the United States. Should he, however, have taken First Class Honours in his A.B., he will discuss with a supervisor a plan of study. He will not take further course work, for advanced degrees are, with rare exceptions, "external"—that is, the student works on his own, outside of school. After two years of such supervised independent investigation and the writing of a dissertation on the level of a good American doctoral thesis, he will be awarded—perhaps after a year of study in England— his M.A. The enormous prestige that appends to a First Class Honours M.A. will probably dissuade him from studying for the redundant Ph.D, but the degree is available for anyone sufficiently eccentric or sufficiently influenced by American reverence for the honorific "Doctor" to want it. The candidate must, however, bear in mind that his Ph.D. dissertation "shall not be of lower quality than the M.A. thesis."

Our sample Honours student will have, along the way, ever smaller and more select company. As a "fresher," he will sit with about 1,500 other students in classes of from 250 to 450, depending on whether he attends the night or the day lectures, and in this intimacy he will hear one member of the staff hold forth, without benefit of a public-address system, on the criticism, analysis, interpretation, and philosophy of the English works under consideration, with perhaps a little biographical and social background thrown in. In the second year, many of his fellows will have fallen by the way and the classes will have become somewhat smaller, perhaps 150 and 230, respectively. In the third year, 140 or fewer English students will be left, and in the fourth year, he may finally get to speak to his instructor in his class of 12 students.

Personal instruction may be missing, but a university after all is only a collection of books, and a student at the University of Sydney has at his disposal the best university library in Australia (and the third largest library of any kind in the nation), a repository of 570,000 volumes. Should this be insufficient for his needs, he can pay a shilling bus fare and browse among the 900,000 books in Australia's second library, the Public Library of New South Wales, but he cannot take any books out, nor can he take any books in. If he wants to draw books for home reading, he can get off the bus at the 9d zone and enter the public library of the City of Sydney, possibly the worst large-city library in the English-speaking world, where he can find an additional 200,000 books, mostly Bulwer-Lytton.

His bibliographic resources may not greatly impress a student of Harvard, let us say, who has about six million books in his library to refer to, but he is far better off than a student at any other

Australian university, whose libraries comprise from 100,000 to 250,000 volumes, and which are (except for the Eastern universities) isolated from any other sources of information. A student at the outlying universities who is studying American literature is badly off. At any he could carry out, under one arm, all the books on American literature. At Sydney things are better; he would at least need a small wheelbarrow to do the job there.

The truly amazing thing about the English program at the Australian universities is that students are able to answer the questions in the formidable final examinations. Ruth Benedict thought that the most inhuman competition in the world is that thrust upon the Apollonian Japanese student, but she did not look into the case of the Australian fresher. The competition is unmerciful —as fierce as that among American football coaches—and the competitors are even less prepared for it than a Zuñi Indian would be. Reared in an atmosphere of easy beer and "the best sunshine on earth," the young Aussie at the end of his first college year is suddenly jolted in the hardest three hours he will ever face. If you are a teacher of college English, try these questions, taken from a typical Australian examination, on your beanie-pated freshmen, remembering that in the general first-year survey course the Australian fresher does not know where, from Beowulf to Virginia Woolf, the next question is coming from:

The Nonnes Preestes Tale is the first notable example of the English mock heroic. Discuss.

Discuss King Alfred's contribution to the development of a flourishing prose tradition in the Old English period, and the importance of this continuing tradition in the Middle English period.

The influence of Latin upon the English language rose and fell with the fortunes of the church and the state of learning so intimately connected with it. Amplify and illustrate this statement.

What do you know of the history of any *ten* of the following words: them, person, camouflage, cliché, martyr, paraffin, hustings, warrant, scissors, leal, check-mate, cupola, extra, thole, Faraday, Viking, knave?

The unhappy point is that students are *not* able to answer the questions—at least, not to the satisfaction of the examiners. In 1956, sixty-seven per cent of the students in first-year English—including some holders of Commonwealth scholarships—failed out of school, a percentage so high that the newspapers took notice of it and lit fires under the Department of English. The acting chairman of the Department, under whose supervision the red pencils were wielded, left for England before the results were announced and "could not be reached for comment." The return of the official chairman from *his* English recharging afforded the convenient opportunity to "reassess" the papers, and a few flunked students were recalled from Limbo—just enough to return the rate of failure to a healthy and normal fifty per cent. While the vacuum of responsibility existed, the Vice-Chancellor of the University of Sydney allowed as how perhaps "some teachers expect too much from students." He admitted that "of all students who begin a university course, something like 50 per cent graduate," a statement whose mathematics is worth comparing with the fact that the normal fifty per cent failures in English in the first year are augmented by a further third between the second and third years, and a still further drop in the fourth year. But the Vice-Chancellor did not take his degree in math.

The university system is such that it is hard for a student to succeed unless he has been reared in a household of Van Dorens. If his parents have been unable to prepare him for matriculation at a private school, he might just as well reconcile himself to getting a dead-end job with the Postmaster General's Office at fifteen, for the equivalent of the American public schools will qualify him for nothing else, especially if he is a country boy. At Cessnock, in the mining country, the students are studying economic geography out of a text printed in 1927, which describes all of California south of San Francisco as desert. Estimate the chances of success of this student at the universities!

If the student is an aboriginal, he will not be able to get a job with the P.M.G. The best he can hope for is slavery on a sheep station, if he has had the benefit of mission-school training—and the word "slavery" is not used loosely. It hardly seems necessary to add that at the present writing no aboriginal has ever attended an Australian university.

Ill-prepared as the Australian student is for the competition of university life, he needs personal and sympathetic attention from his teachers that he will not get. Not only is the instruction not personal; it is not even adequate. The first-year syllabus cleans up James Joyce in one lecture. One professor, asked how students could answer questions about Burton's *Anatomy of Melancholy* (which consists of almost equal parts of English, Latin, and Greek) after only two lectures, retorted: "They've bloody well got to read it."

So the students fail and pass out of the university community to sell alleged hot dogs in King's Cross. Those who remain learn a lot about English culture, but acquire very little of their own. Until last year, there was not a single chair (professorship) of Australian literature or Australian history in any Australian university, but there are many professors of Greek, this being considered more important in contemporary Australian civilization. Sydney now at last has a Chair of Australian Literature, the funds for which were raised in the following manner: One quarter of the £A80,000 needed was raised by public subscription (this took five years); this sum was used as a lever to pry a further quarter from the Commonwealth government, and this total was matched by a grant from an *American* fund. How important this Chair was in the minds of the professors of English can be seen from a private statement made by one of the men who were responsible for choosing the new Professor of Australian Literature, to the effect that he would not think of putting his best young man into such a narrow and unrewarding post.

The prejudice of the classical curriculum is not restricted to the professors of English; it pervades the entire university, extending even to the students. An editorial in *Honi Soit*, the student paper at the University of Sydney, said, in part:

> A businessman, returning from U.S.A., suggested that all our universities should have a Faculty for the training of Junior Executives in the principles and methods of business and advertising. This, he urged, would best be modelled on the Commercial Faculties of American universities. Well, maybe our University is but a glorified technical school. However, we can be thankful that our concept of education has not yet stooped so low.

This, God bless us all!, in Australia, which needs nothing so much as schools of business administration, except perhaps a revolution against England. You dare not present a check to an Australian shopkeeper—he would recoil from the sight of it faster than he would from the presentation of a pistol; you must take your checkbook into a bank if you want cash. If you go into the King's Cross branch of the Bank of New South Wales, you will see the head teller perched upon his high stool, drawing lines into his great leather-bound ledger with pen and ruler, and in the back room high-collared gentlemen under green eyeshades poking about in roll-top desks. You will find yourself looking to see if Bob Cratchit is back there stealing coals for the fire—but no, Australians do not heat their rooms at all.

On the whole, though, the graduate of the University of Sydney is an excellent product and would not arouse any special criticism in England, where Australians are at least one caste below Americans. But what becomes of the student who passes through the formidable course of study at Sydney?

One of the most brilliant editors of that most brilliant student newspaper, *Honi Soit*, now edits *Weekend*, which pays contributors 10/6 for statements such as: "I'd like to murder Mum." Some of the readers of *Weekend* do murder Mum. Not many pay any attention to *Weekend's* most famous headline: SEX MUST STOP.

Those Honours graduates in English who do not thus distinguish themselves in journalism normally take posts in universities; the pass graduates in English go into high-school teaching, which has the social status of fare collecting on the buses. Brains come cheap in Australia. Even scientists are grossly underpaid. A recent issue of the *Sydney Morning Herald* carried the following advertisements for science and professional graduates:

Electrical engineer, junior, several years' experience: £A1250 ($2,775)

Scientific assistant for Industrial Hygiene, Dept. of Public Health, graduate in science: £A1040 ($2,308)

Geologist, post-graduate study, some field experience: £A1500 ($3,330)

Chemical engineer: £A1400 ($3,108)

Dentist: £A1359 ($3,017); if female, £A1155 ($2,564)

Brains come cheap in Australia because Australian universities, by aping English education, have lost touch with their cultural environment. Like modern poetry, they no longer communicate with the whole community, but only with an ever-decreasing circle of persons who are well and highly educated but who have less and less influence on their civilization. Australia has a population of ten and a half million, but the intellectual community is not much larger than that of London in Alexander Pope's day, and has about the same effect on the general populace as Pope did in his time. About half of this year's twelve or so Honours graduates in English will go on to take their places in the caste, each to train perhaps another five English Honours graduates, who will go on to perpetuate the cycle. The common people are accordingly being turned into a *Lumpenproletariat* at a rate even Minitrue could not achieve, for in Orwell's world of *1984* only eighty-five per cent of the people were uneducated inferiors. In Australia in 1952 the nine universities had only one in 310 of the population, whereas the 1,832 American colleges and universities accommodated one out of every 66. In the same year American tertiary institutions awarded a degree to one out of every 218 in the population; Australian universities conferred degrees upon one out of 2,300. This is what conscious adoption of a foreign educational system has done to a young country bursting with repressed vigor; yet most educational commentators in the United States urge us to give up the most successful educational system in the history of civilization because the one over the fence looks a bit more attractive.

THE LATEST INVIDIOUS COMPARISON: SOVIET VERSUS AMERICAN EDUCATION

Since the first Sputnik, those who entreat us to go chasing after strange gods have turned their eyes away from Greece and England and toward the U.S.S.R. They have been impressed both by Soviet achievements in space and by the statistics of educational growth in Russia. During the first quarter century of Communist control, Soviet literacy increased 600 per cent, an astounding figure—until one looks into it. If a country increases its production of mousetraps from 100,000 to 101,000, there is a growth of only one per cent. If a country raises its mousetrap production from 100 to 200, the growth rate is 100 per cent—but there are 100,900 fewer mousetraps.

The mental attitude of these invidious comparers is well demonstrated in Arthur S. Trace's book *What Ivan Knows that Johnny Doesn't*. Dr. Trace says almost nothing about the difference in

scientific education in Russian and American schools, since everybody knows that in this area Soviet superiority is unapproachable.
(Well, maybe not everybody; a *Saturday Evening Post* survey reported in the December 30, 1961, issue showed that only forty
per cent of Americans think Soviet education is superior to American education.) But Dr. Trace tells us that in the humanities as
well the Russians have pulled far in front. In history, for example.
"Needless to say," says Dr. Trace, "the Communist view of history
shows up in its worst and ugliest outlines in this book [an elementary Soviet textbook], but what needs to be stressed here is
not the interpretation of history but the wealth of detail and the
systematic presentation of it." Or, in other words, it does not
matter that mischievous nonsense is being taught, so long as a
great deal of it is taught, and taught well. Professor Trace also
points out, to our shame, that ninth-grade Soviet students read
the whole of *War and Peace* in one semester; he does not consider whether it might not be better to wait for maturity, when
the novel can be read in a day or two, or to wait for wisdom, so
the tedious thing can be avoided altogether.

If one disregards the evaluations, Professor Trace's book is a
good and up-to-date survey of the Soviet system of education. He
tells us that Soviet students enter school at the age of seven and
attend six days a week during the thirty-five-week term. The first
textbook they use is the *Bukvar* (Preliminary Alphabet); this is
followed in subsequent years by *Rodnaya Rech* (Native Language)
and a series of four readers, and finally, *Rodnaya Literatura*
(Native Literature), from which writers in disfavor such as
Dostoevsky are excluded as unpersons.

The beginning student is taught to read by phonics, which, like
several other elements in the Soviet system, was discarded in this
country more than a generation ago. After the first-grade student
learns the rudiments of reading, he begins to absorb Soviet culture
in such selections as "Spring on a Collective Farm," "The First
of May," "The Song of the Tractor Driver," and "Mama Is an

Airplane Pilot." In the second grade he reads "The Children of Free China," "The Soviet Army," "The Celebration of the First of May," and "How the Workers Lived Before Communism." In the third grade he gets "The Five-Year Plan" and "The Soviet People Are Producing More Milk." And in the fourth grade, ominously, "Be Prepared for the Struggle in the Cause of the Communist Party."

By the fourth grade the Soviet child has amassed a vocabulary of 10,000 words, compared to the American child's accomplishment, at this stage of education, of only 1,800 words. It may be petty to remark that many of the words the Russian child learns are pure Newspeak, but the fact remains the Soviet dictionaries are regularly revised to conform to official truth. And as for the speed with which the Soviet child is hurried along, it could be said that he is taught to run first and crawl later.

It must be admitted, on the positive side, that the energy and thoroughness with which the leaders of the Soviet system have gone about clearing out the remains of the old Czarist education were called for. In the early days of Communist control, advisers were brought in from other countries to guide the inexperienced molders of the new nation. John Dewey was one of these technicians; he encouraged the institution of his method of progressive education, but this lasted only until Stalin, who was a product of a seminary education, heard about it. Stalin's education was rigidly theological, and he made Soviet education just as inflexibly religious, though the subject matter and the missal were rather different. Today the one unavoidable requirement in Soviet schools is a thorough mastery of the works and philosophy of Marx and Lenin. Some of us are beginning to realize that Marxism-Leninism has no validity or relevance whatsoever in the latter part of the twentieth century, except insofar as it helps us understand the Communist mind. It is a theology, nothing more nor less.

When theology is allowed to dominate education, curious results ensue. In no area of Soviet culture is this better demonstrated than in biology, whose dreadful course in Communist Russia has been so well documented by Conway Zirkle in his *Death of a Science in Russia.*

Just how Trofim D. Lysenko rose to the power he was able to exercise in 1936 is not known. Somehow he managed to convince the party leaders that one of the central theses of Marxism-Leninism—that controlled environment can overcome any influence of heredity—was applicable to biology. To support his contention historically, he dredged out of the Russian past an ignorant plant breeder named I. V. Michurin, who had seized upon some of the more foolish ideas of Darwin—of which there were many—and used them to substantiate his anti-scientific attitudes and beliefs in regard to plant hybridization. As for Lysenko's competence in genetics, the English botanist S. C. Harland described a meeting he had with the Russian in 1933, when Harland was visiting the Soviet Union at the invitation of the great biologist N. I. Vavilov (who was later sent by Lysenko to Siberia, where he quickly died). In his *Nature and Man's Fate,* Garrett Hardin quotes Harland's estimation of Lysenko:

> I interviewed Lysenko for nearly three hours. I found him completely ignorant of the elementary principles of genetics and plant physiology. I myself have worked on genetics and plant-breeding for some thirty-five years, and I can quite honestly say that to talk to Lysenko was like trying to explain the differential calculus to a man who did not know his twelve-times table.

Three years after this meeting, Lysenko had attained such eminence in the Soviet scientific world that, as a result of his efforts, an international genetics meeting in Russia passed a resolution that, in the future, genetics and plant breeding were to conform with dialectical materialism. Naturally, Lysenko was opposed by competent scientists, but as Lysenko soared in power, they disappeared. After Lysenko's address to the Lenin Academy of Agricultural Science in 1948, all opposition ceased. He began by informing the 3,000 assembled members that he had been able to change spring wheat into winter wheat, something akin to changing dogs into cats; then he laid down the party line as examined and approved by the Central Committee of the Communist Party:

> V. I. Lenin and I. V. Stalin discovered I. V. Michurin and made his doctrine the property of the Soviet people. By their great fatherly attention to his work they preserved the wonderful Michurin doctrine for biology. The Party and Government and I. V. Stalin personally are constantly looking after the further development of the Michurinist doctrine. For us Soviet biologists there is not a more honorable task than the creative development of Michurin's doctrine and the introduction of the Michurinist method of investigation of the nature of development of living things into all our activity.
>
> Our Academy must foster the development of Michurinist doctrine as taught by the personal example of solicitous interest in I. V. Michurin's activity on the part of our great teachers V. I. Lenin and I. V. Stalin.

Tremendous applause, said the official report, and Soviet genetics was dead.

After the death of Stalin, Trofim D. Lysenko was stripped of his offices and exiled into the remoter parts of the Soviet Union, where, with uncharacteristic humility, he said that he intended to study genetics. But in 1962 Khrushchev, inspecting the Soviet agricultural regions to determine why the wheat crop had failed again, was photographed in pleasant conversation with Lysenko.

The rape of Soviet genetics is the most tragic example of what can happen in an educational system such as the Russian, but there are others. The highly praised foreign-language program in Soviet schools is, as Atkinson and Maleska have put it in *The Story of Education,* simply code deciphering for the purpose of infiltrating the political life of the non-Communist world—nothing whatever about the culture of the people is taught. In fact, the social sciences in Russia are ludicrous. We have to accept some share of the blame for the destruction of the humanities in the Soviet Union, for we awarded the Nobel Prize for literature to a book that had nothing at all to recommend it except a page or two of quite equivocal criticism of Communism. For the rest of its excruciating length, *Dr. Zhivago* is an absurd parody on bad nineteenth-century Russian novels. Those who have managed to struggle through this artless book can be induced to admit that it is rather below a good standard for Nobel Prize novels—which is not, in any case, very high—but they are equally apt to say that, after all, it is Pasternak's poetry that is important. But his poetry, especially that in which he ruminates upon the philosophies of the West, is childish. One cannot imagine any of it being published anonymously in the United States. Pasternak, for all his good intentions, was a product of Soviet education, which deliberately emasculated literature during the whole of his adult lifetime. As the people of Yoknapatawpha County in the books of another Nobel Prize winner would say: "You don't get nothin' from nits but lice."

Without probing into the matter of Soviet education, we can still find enough in bare statistics to dissuade us from any imitation of it. Though Russians pour much more than Americans into their educational program, they get much less for their money. Consider these figures on school attendance published in Charles W. Thayer's *Russia*, keeping in mind that the population of the United States is some 30 million less than that of the Soviet Union:

	U.S.S.R.	U.S.A.
School Attendance, Children		
Primary level	29,500,000	33,400,000
Secondary level	9,000,000	9,000,000
Higher education institutions	2,500,000	3,700,000

	U.S.S.R.	U.S.A.
School Completion, Adults		
Did not complete primary level	52,000,000	21,600,000
Completed primary level only	34,500,000	33,900,000
Completed secondary level only	19,500,000	34,000,000
Graduated from higher institutions	3,800,000	7,600,000

The most important factor in a comparison of the two systems of education—and a factor which is rarely considered by critics of the American institutions—is that the Soviets have what seems at present to be an insuperable handicap in the generally poor content of their culture. Lack of consumer goods is not just a lack of "materialistic" comforts and luxuries—it is a lack of educational facilities. American children learn more in their preliterate play than do Soviet children wrestling with their immense vocabularies of words relating to the imaginary world created by Marx and Lenin. It is doubtful that GUM carries any of the toys available to American elementary-school children. One company—the Allis-Chalmers Science Materials Center—sells such marvelous playthings as science book-labs, in which textbooks, laboratory manuals, and laboratory equipment come packaged for home recreational experiments in chemistry, magnetism, geometry, botany, general physics, jets and rockets, and the like; solar cells and motors; two-way telegraphs; "radio-telescopes"; electronics laboratories; human biology kits; digital and analog computer sets. A myriad of toys is on hand for the ten-year-old to play with which a college teacher thirty years ago would not have been able to understand. Even the dolts are inundated by this rich culture of ours; teen-agers carry transistor radios in their upswept hairdos and read comic books whose art in some cases is superior to the things that hang on the walls of approved Soviet galleries. All the Russians have to counter this deluge of casual education is Agitprop, Komsomol, and the Summer Pioneer Camps—which compound, rather than ameliorate, the felony of Soviet theological indoctrination.

Mention of the domination by Marxist-Leninist theology of Soviet education will not pass the purview of many readers without reminding them of the theological origin of American education. It is quite true that early colonial education was instituted for the single purpose of instilling religious knowledge into the minds of young people. But the chief characteristic of the Puritans, their refractory attitude toward authority, nurtured the seeds of their theology's destruction. So far as the schools of America are concerned, all that was inherited from the Puritans was their rebelliousness. American educational history records an uninterrupted series of vigilant protests lest control fall into the power of any special-interest group, regardless of the sublimity of the particular brand of virtue it was trying to propagate. And we should not forget that the basis of Puritan reformation was reliance on the Bible as the source of all religious knowledge and authority, a reliance so strong that the Puritans felt it was safe to let each man be his own interpreter. This meant that every man was encouraged to learn to read. Naturally, adjuncts to the scriptures were published—John Cotton's *Spiritual Milk for New England Babes, Drawn Out of the Breasts of Both Testaments for Their Souls Nourishment* is an especially distasteful example. But the Puritan emphasis on education laid the legal basis for a public school system by the year 1647. The system endured, though the theology did not, and within fifteen years of the great Puritan migration of 1629 Roger Williams had published the first effective protest against the identification of church and state in America, his *Bloudy Tenent of Persecution.* The spiritual and political vacuum of the New World which attracted the Puritans attracted likewise other religious dissidents—the Dutch Reformed Church to New York, the Catholics to Maryland, the Quakers to Pennsylvania, the Swedish Lutherans to Delaware, and even, during the Cromwellian dictatorship, the Church of England to Virginia. And these denominations and others realized that the only safeguard against the establishment of an official and persecuting church was the establishment of none—or of all, which was the same thing. The latter course was the one first chosen, and was the only form of establishment at the time of the ratification of the Constitution. Finally, the last hold of official religion on the American public-school system was pried loose when the churchmen came to understand that the chief activity of America, making money, was being incomparably better taught in the practical secular schools.

Not only the famous protestants such as Roger Williams in colonial times expended energy in advocating a modern system of education. Benjamin Franklin's prime activity (other than making money) for much of his public life was establishing sensible education. He could have spoken to the point at the meeting of Oxford dons concerning Latin as an entrance requirement; in the eighteenth century he referred to Greek and Latin as the *chapeaux bras* of learning, comparing them thus to the fantastic hats the French carried, because the hats would not fit on their heads. Reliable democrat Thaddeus Stevens poured his ready supply of vitriol on taxpayers who in 1835 protested that they personally were not deriving any benefit from education; Stevens offered to let them have the benefit of the hangman's services which some of their tax money was going to support.

With such people in the unrelenting fight for responsible education, it is not surprising that the English visitor Alexander Mackay noted in his *Western World* in 1849 that literacy in America was nearly complete, except for immigrants from non-English-speaking countries. Today, in the City of New York alone, more than one million children attend school, enough, as the *Saturday Review* of December 15, 1962, noted, "to populate the sixth largest city in the United States."

Many of the aspects of American education that critics unthinkingly condemn are disguised virtues, including the notorious low standards mentioned by nearly every amateur educator from de Tocqueville to the latest Russian official tourists. Most urge us to begin with the primers; to extract the "Oh, oh, oh's" and sub-stitute some elevated literary selections. Shakespeare is a very popular choice, though possibly his advocates would withdraw his name if they knew that among the 20,000 words in his vocabulary there are hidden some 1,400 different terms for sexual acts—about seven per cent of everything he wrote. It might be possible for someone to construct a first-grade reader out of *Finnegans Wake* to placate these critics, but there is some doubt that it would make a really ideal primer.

Probably every young college teacher entering the profession trailing clouds of glory from his new Ph.D. has deplored the low standards of our universities. But if he were to study education in other countries that set arbitrarily high standards—such as Aus-tralia—he might see the efficacy of making as much education as possible available to as many as possible. Indirectly at least, these "low standards," which long ago resulted in the great proliferation of colleges and universities, enabled the United States to be the nation to achieve the atomic age. In his thoughtful history of the atomic scientists, *Brighter Than a Thousand Suns*, Robert Jungk notes that a majority of the physicists expelled from central Europe because of racial or political impurity sought academic positions in England and the other free countries of Western Europe, but

this proved to be less easy than it had appeared, for the num-ber of vacant chairs in European universities and the space available for work in the laboratories were limited. Hardly any country yet understood that the admission of refugees who brought with them no material possessions would be profita-ble rather than a burden.

Only the United States, with its hundreds of universities and institutes, could provide enough appointments for the intellectual refugees. In the first two years after Hitler's acces-sion to power the United States was still suffering from the consequences of the great economic crisis that had begun in

1929. But when Albert Einstein, in the autumn of 1933, accepted the offer of employment at the newly established Institute for Advanced Study at Princeton and transferred his residence from Berlin to that small American university city, the French physicist Paul Langevin, half in jest and half in earnest, made a true prophecy. "It's as important an event," he said, "as would be the transfer of the Vatican from Rome to the New World. The Pope of Physics has moved and the United States will now become the center of the natural sciences."

Obviously, American education is not perfect; in a democracy there are always elements that oppose the main course of progress. It is not universally known by many who cite the "monkey trial" of Dayton, Tennessee, as the event that ended opposition to the teaching of evolution in America, that there is now in Dayton, Tennessee, a William Jennings Bryan University—and you can guess what it teaches. There are, too, those strongly backward-looking people who seriously suggest our return to the McGuffey Readers—enough of them to warrant the publication in 1963 of a paperback edition of the *Sixth Eclectic Reader*. The McGuffey Readers were even adopted as texts by the school board of Twin Lakes, Wisconsin, until authorities brought the board back to its senses by threatening to withhold state funds—an amusing coercion in view of old William Homes McGuffey's diatribes against anyone who accepted government aid.

Few aspects of American civilization have as many mad dogs snapping at their heels as education, but few areas are moving so rapidly into the future, and those who are concerned about the noise of the pack can take heart in the certainty that coming events in education will soon make these particular critics the most outdistanced of all detractors of our civilization.

☆ IV ☆

Behaving Ourselves

TIME AND MORALITY

When the Hebrew children straggled out of Egypt into the wasteland of Sinai, they were a ragged band of nomads despised for their ignorance, poverty, and general nastiness by their civilized neighbors at the rich horns of the Fertile Crescent, and united only by their greater hatred of outsiders and their reverence for a God stolen from the Babylonians and elevated to supremacy by a concept stolen from the Egyptians. The ideas they nurtured along with their skinny goats must have seemed ludicrously backward to the Egyptians and the Babylonians four thousand years ago, but it is the way of the world that the validity of ideas is nowhere near as important as the energy that drives them. And this the Hebrews had in abundance: confidence in their emotional attitudes (one could hardly call them ideas) so overpowering that today these attitudes direct a civilization so far beyond the visions of their flaming-eyed prophets as to make the Hebrew heaven itself look like a nomadic village of goatherds. Of course

the mores of a nomadic village will not work in an atomic civilization, and that is the trouble with our times.

Moses went up into the mountain and came back with a set of
rules for the government of his fanatic band. According to tradition, his tablet had only numerals—Roman numerals—inscribed
upon it; the laws themselves were loose interpretations growing,
like all laws, out of the culture, in this case hard laws for a hard
country. As nearly as scholars can reconstruct from the 34th
chapter of Exodus, the first set of commandments given to the
chosen people enjoined them thus:

1. Thou shalt worship no other god.
2. Thou shalt make thee no molten gods.
3. All the firstborn are mine.
4. Six days shalt thou work, but on the seventh day thou
   shalt rest.
5. The feast of unleavened bread shalt thou keep in the
   month when the corn is in ear.
6. Thou shalt observe the feast of weeks, even of the first.
7. Thou shalt not offer the blood of my sacrifice with
   leavened bread.
8. The fat of my feast shall not remain all night until the
   morning.
9. The first of the first fruits of thy ground thou shalt bring
   into the house of the Lord thy God.
10. Thou shalt not seethe a kid in its mother's milk.

Rudimentary as these commandments were, they still represented a concession to progress which the Hebrews of an earlier
time would have thought dangerously radical, for it was not mur-
dering his sanctimonious brother that got Cain into his first trouble with the Lord in an early period of Hebrew history, but his
impertinence in offering a sacrifice of vegetables instead of meat;
his sin was in his occupation. Jehovah came out of the Sumerian
hills a pastoral nomad like His people, with only contempt for
sedentary farmers. Even in the time of Moses, the Hebrew idea
of paradise on earth was a land of milk and honey, not of corn

and potatoes. The original Decalogue accepts the inevitable march of progress, but it is a grudging acceptance, as several snide digs at the agricultural Babylonians and Egyptians reveal—the prohibition of leavened bread in the first and seventh Commandments, and the rejection of metallurgy in the second.

As we know, Moses went on to give his people a number of ancillary regulations that have been quietly ignored by the inheritors of the Judaeo-Christian ethos—such things as slavery of one's own people, polygyny, witchcraft, witch-killing, and daughter-selling. Our Calvinistic ancestors were much in sympathy with the people of the Old Testament and their God, but even they found some of the ancient precepts irrelevant. Puritans rarely ate goats, and when they did, they found more delectable recipes than boiling them in their mothers' milk. So, by the time of King James, the Decalogue had become the set of rules that some of us know today. For those who do not know them, here they are, in the Protestant version:

1. I am the Lord thy God . . . thou shalt have no other gods before me.
2. Thou shalt not make unto thee any graven image, or any likeness of any thing that is in heaven above, or that is in the earth beneath, or that is in the water under the earth.
3. Thou shalt not take the name of the Lord thy God in vain.
4. Remember the sabbath day, to keep it holy.
5. Honor thy father and thy mother.
6. Thou shalt not kill.
7. Thou shalt not commit adultery.
8. Thou shalt not steal.
9. Thou shalt not bear false witness against thy neighbor.
10. Thou shalt not covet thy neighbor's house, thou shalt not covet thy neighbor's wife.

Since the time King James's seventy scholars translated the Bible, the population of the English-speaking world has increased nearly sixtyfold. Some other changes have also occurred in our civilization, but these rules remain the basis of our official morality, God help us. We cannot hope even for a political change in the organization of heaven—it must forever remain a kingdom, never a democracy.

Over a century ago, in a level of culture as far removed from ours as that of the nineteenth century was from that of King James, the poet Arthur Hugh Clough pointed out several reinterpretations of the ten rules that Moses carried down from Sinai:

> *Thou shalt have one God only; who*
> *Would be at the expense of two?*
> *No graven image may be*
> *Worshipped, except the currency:*
> *Swear not at all, for, for thy curse,*
> *Thine enemy is none the worse:*
> *At church on Sunday to attend*
> *Will serve to keep the world thy friend:*
> *Honor thy parents, that is, all*
> *From whom advancement may befall:*
> *Thou shalt not kill; but need'st not strive*
> *Officiously to keep alive:*
> *Do not adultery commit;*
> *Advantage rarely comes of it:*
> *Thou shalt not steal; an empty feat,*
> *When it's so lucrative to cheat:*
> *Bear not false witness; let the lie*
> *Have time on its own wings to fly:*
> *Thou shalt not covet, but tradition*
> *Approves all forms of competition.*

Clough's poem has been reprinted in many anthologies of humorous verse, but it points up an observation of deadly seriousness: the practice of morality changes with time and almost as fast, but the rules of morality change with molten sluggishness.

The consequent friction which we know as cultural lag causes thereby the breakdown in systems of outmoded morality—our own is the chief example in the world today—and the old folks' condemnation of the younger generation.

Consider one example: that scion of a family far too brilliant and accomplished for his own meager talents, who, like Esau, traded his career for the slim possibility of gulling his relatives and the rest of America into thinking him a polymath. What Charles van Doren failed to understand was that mischief is a safe occupation only on an individual basis; if there are accomplices, the chances of getting caught increase not arithmetically, but geometrically. In his case, hundreds were privy to the conspiracy and therefore exposure of all was certain. So he was caught and shamed by an outraged society. But behind the sensation was the fact that everyone who had been offered answers on the TV quiz shows (with the dubious exception of a prosperous insurance man who was offered an insulting pittance) was corrupted as van Doren was; so many, in fact, that we must infer that in the same situation most Americans would have taken the answers and the money. Many people recognized this awkward fact; some rationalized that the world was a jungle, where one must eat or be eaten; others, more sensitive to abstract rectitude, called American civilization hypocritical for making a scapegoat of the unhappy van Doren.

Van Doren and the moralists can find cold comfort in the case of the Kurnai, a group of related tribes (now extinct) in southeastern Australia whose moral system at the coming of the white man was crumbling under forces they were unable to offset. As we shall see, the Australian aboriginal marriage system is extremely complex, requiring, among many other things, a good supply of exogamous partners. But the Kurnai in the early nineteenth century were declining so fast that there was a scarcity of legal mates, so a couple who chose to marry "wrong" rather than burn, as St. Paul advised, had to elope, for "wrong" marriage was incestuous and liable to capital punishment. Southeastern Australia is one of the more hospitable parts of the continent, and it was possible for a sinning pair to stay away from their people until the heat was off and then, perhaps at the end of a year, to return. They would be reviled, cursed, and beaten, but the marriage had to be recognized as a real if unfortunate fact and the couple would be accepted once again into the tribe. The ironic thing about all this is that, at the time of the coming of the white man, all marriages among the Kurnai were contracted in this way.

Poor Kurnai! Poor Charles van Doren! But also, the poor culture—forced to uphold an outmoded morality because it had to uphold some morality. Culture in the anthropological sense is like the Hebrews' Jehovah, almighty but often confused and blindly angry, often driven to sacrificing a human scapegoat as the alternative to sacrificing itself. As long as things are going smoothly, culture can afford to ignore infractions of the moral law, but when transgressions are brought publicly to its attention, it must enforce the rules, however impractical and obsolescent, for it has no others. The alternative is anarchy and the destruction of culture. Despite the power of culture, it can exist only so long as man exists; therefore, its fundamental task is to preserve man and his societies. This it does by implanting in this intelligent, volatile, and gregarious cannibal a guard of delusive devices, the most important of which is morality. If we were to examine the patterns of conduct of all the various people of the world and draw from this multiplicity of behavior the common denominators of a universal Decalogue, we would see that it is impossible to be specific about morality; it is impossible even to engrave a tablet of ten numerals. We cannot even go so far as to say that "Thou shalt not kill" is an imperative, innate law—as the Deists of the eighteenth century fondly thought—because some societies, such as the Polynesian (whose overriding problem was an environment too easy for their own good) or our own in time of war, find homicide a moral necessity. There is only one numeral on the tablet, only one law common to all humanity: Morality is whatever conduces to the preservation of the group. Depending on the time and the place and the circumstances, there is morality as much in the common laws of Christianity or Judaism as in those of Nazism or Communism. From race prejudice to our paradoxical conduct in opposing Hitler while supporting Stalin, it is all one, and it is all morality.

THE MORALITY OF SOCIETY

In 1787 certain English gentlemen with financial interests in West Indian plantations were concerned about what to feed the slaves who worked the plantations. Someone thought of the manna of the Pacific islands—breadfruit—and in August, 1787, a tough young naval lieutenant named William Bligh was given 46 men, the 215-ton ship *Bounty,* and a commission to get a shipload of breadfruit trees. Bligh was among the most unlovable men in human history, and his personality and conduct, compounded by the length of the voyage, the character of his men, and the hospitality of the Polynesian women among whom the sailors lived for six months while loading the ship with a thousand breadfruit trees, fomented the most dramatic mutiny in British naval history. A few days after Bligh collected his men and started the hard voyage home, a master's mate named Fletcher Christian (whom Bligh had himself selected for the post) led the disaffected sailors to take Bligh prisoner and subsequently put him and eighteen loyal seamen into a small boat with just enough food and water to make dying difficult. Bligh did not die—his fanatical determination to get back to England and to send an expedition to find and hang Christian and the other mutineers drove him to make the most remarkable voyage in the annals of the sea—but that is another story. Christian took the *Bounty* back to Tahiti, collected wives for himself and the eight recalcitrant mutineers who chose to go with him, and sailed away to the far southeast of the ocean, to the tiny island of Pitcairn, where they burned their ship and prepared to make a new life.

It was twenty-three years before the next ship stopped at Pitcairn, and when that captain landed, he found eight or nine Tahitian women, about two dozen children, and one white man. The stories told to account for the strange attrition of the male population are vague and contradictory, but what is obvious is that the white men killed one another fighting over the women. A breakdown in morality, surely? Yes, but not in the ordinary sense; rather, the inevitable result of the importation of a system of rules designed to serve a large society into a situation where a different set of rules was called for. It was not the sailors who were at fault, but their English social organization.

Sigmund Freud wrestled with the problem half a century ago and solved it to his own satisfaction in an influential book, *Totem and Taboo*. Therein he examined the materials of social organization and morality—the incest tabu or "horror," totemism, mother-in-law avoidances, the Oedipus complex, exogamy, and lesser concomitants—and concluded that all this began in the distant dreamtime of mankind with a regrettable occurrence. In those days, Freud theorized, mankind lived in a "primal horde," in which the strongest male—the father—arrogated to himself all the females. Eventually, sons were born and grew to a celibate manhood. Unhappy with this chaste condition but unable to contend singly against the old man, they ganged up on him and killed him. This was in the time of the Anthropophagi, and, not being wasteful, the parricides ate their father, after which repast they divided up the women as mates, their genealogical relationship notwithstanding. Fortunately for the species, remorse for these acts overcame the parricides and they resolved never again to commit such heinous crimes, assuring good behavior in their own offspring by instituting exogamy and the incest horror to prevent the marriage of a son and his mother, and totemism to prevent a father from going the way of all flesh. The taint they could not expunge, and so the remembrance of the sin was carried into subconscious memory in the Oedipus complex.

Freud's brilliant theory is a testament to the febrile imagination of man, but as an explanation for the origin of social organization it has one flaw: it is wrong. The evidence aside, it violates a fundamental rule of logic, Occam's Razor (named for the medieval scholiast who first propounded it): that when we are confronted by two alternative theories, we must choose the simplest one that accounts for all the facts. Freud's theory explains all the facts—all those that his deficient ethnology knew about—but it is Rube Goldbergian in its intricate and unnecessary complexity. Much more persuasive is the anthropological explanation.

In small societies, which of course means all primitive hunting and gathering societies, there are two basic, almost instinctive competitions that can destroy the group: the competition for food and the competition for women. If culture is to preserve itself by preserving man, it must somehow ameliorate or eliminate these competitions; and this it does through social organization, often reinforced by religion, which, as Durkheim explained, is society sanctified. People on a primitive level of existence cannot exploit the environment efficiently in groups of more than forty or fifty individuals; yet, whereas a band of forty or fifty is ideally suited for hunting, it is ill suited to social survival on this level. Thus such groups are delicately balanced between environmental extinction and social extinction. In small societies the two destructive competitions can easily wipe out everybody. If, however, the incest horror could be extended so that a man would be repelled at the idea of marriage or sexual intercourse with any of the women in his immediate society but one or two, the competition for women could immediately be nullified by the best prohibtion of all— a strongly internalized one. If, at the same time, the group should be made to see itself as so strongly unified as to demand—again by internalized directive—distribution of food, the horde would have the best protection against self-destruction. All the social phenomena that Freud derived from the Original Sin of society converge toward this purpose: totemism insures a rudimentary game preservation; mother-in-law avoidance guards against sexual competition between a mother and daughter for a husband; exogamy performs the double function of implementing the incest tabu and strengthening the horde by causing mates to be drawn from other groups (and also, though the primitives are not within a thousands years of understanding it, exogamy widens the gene pool, a biological desideratum); and even superficially disruptive forces such as the Oedipus complex and blood sacrifice have ulterior benefits.

To understand how this relates to our own society, we must stand back several thousand years and see what it was really like in the beginning, not what Freud imagined it to be. *Pithecanthropus* has left no evidence of his social organization (though we know he was a cannibal), so we are forced to infer from the world's last important Old Stone Age people, the Australian aborigines, what it was like when the human world began.

The natives of Australia are not the ideal house guests, and one suspects that the Neanderthals and Cro-Magnons were hardly models of clean-cut humanity, either. William Dampier was the first to describe these living Paleolithic peoples; in 1688, during a recession in piracy in the southern oceans, he nosed his corsair into a bay on the bleak northwest coast of the unknown continent and fell upon the poor, helpless, naked, fly-blown, rat-eating Bard tribe for an ethnographic survey. "The inhabitants of this Country are the miserablest People in the world," he wrote later; "they all of them have the most unpleasant Looks and the worst Features of any People that I ever saw, though I have seen great Variety of Savages." Jonathan Swift got hold of the report and used the Bard people as the basis for his Yahoos in the fourth book of *Gulliver's Travels*.

It can be said for the Australian natives that they had a disconcerting land to live in—a country where Christmas falls in mid-

summer and Midsummer Night in midwinter, where trees shed
bark instead of leaves, where bees dig burrows and fish climb
trees, where anthills are "magnetic" and even mice are marsupials;
a land that breeds such flora as the *Monstera deliciosa* (which
tastes like bananas one day and strawberries the next) and such
fauna as the eclectic platypus, which lays eggs and suckles its
young, has the body of a muskrat, the tail of a beaver, the webbed
feet and bill of a duck, spurs like a rooster, the sting of a scorpion,
and the poison of a rattlesnake. Most important, it is a land that
has no indigenous plants that can be cultivated or animals that
can be domesticated; thus its human inhabitants were doomed to
live a pre-agricultural, Old Stone Age existence.

If Dampier had been interested in serious ethnography instead
of exploitation, he might have sent a man inland to the Aranda
tribe, whose social organization, unlike that of some of the northern coastal peoples, is not quite incomprehensible. Perhaps we can
imagine this reporter acquiring an informant, taking out his note-
book, and constructing a genealogical chart.

"Who is that old man over there?" he might begin.

"Him my father's father—call him *aranga*."

"Ah," muses the ethnographer, "*aranga*—grandfather. Good.
And that little boy chewing on the snake—what is he to you?"

"Him my son's son—call him *aranga*."

"Stap me vitals!" grumbles Dampier's man, slapping shut his
book. "This old fool doesn't know his grandson from his grandfather!" And this would have been only the first and simplest error
that an observer working out of the English social system would
make with the Australian aborigines.

Of course, an Australian aboriginal anthropologist, if there were
such, might have some difficulty with our system.

"Who is that fellow taking beer out of your refrigerator?"

"My mother's brother—my 'uncle.'"

"Ah, yes. 'Uncle' I know—*kamuna*. And who is that man watching the baseball game on your television set?"

"Oh, he's my father's brother—my 'uncle.' "

Whereupon the Australian would mutter: "This old fool doesn't know his *kamuna* from his *wonna*," and go to find a more reliable informant. He could get into a confusing situation with regard to the organization as well—witness the following domestic chaos reported from hillbilly country, where, according to Dwight Latham and Moe Jaffe, such goings-on are not atypical:

Many, many years ago when I was twenty-three
I was married to a widow who was pretty as could be;
This widow had a grown-up daughter who had hair of red,
My father fell in love with her and soon they too were wed.

This made my dad my son-in-law and changed my very life
For my daughter was my mother 'cause she was my father's
*   wife;*
To complicate the matter even though it brought me joy,
I soon became the father of a bouncing baby boy.

My little baby then became a brother-in-law to dad,
And so became my uncle though it made me very sad;
For if he was my uncle then that also made him brother
Of the widow's grown-up daughter, who of course was my
*   step-mother.*

Father's wife then had a son who kept them on the run
And he became my grandchild, for he was my daughter's son;
My wife is now my mother's mother and it makes me blue
Because although she is my wife, she's my grandmother too.

Now if my wife is my grandmother, then I'm her grandchild,
And every time I think of it, it nearly drives me wild;
For now I have become the strangest case you ever saw—
As husband of my grandmother I am my own grandpaw.

Normally, however, there is no comparison between the complexity of our system and that of the Australians. It is one of the apparently inexplicable paradoxes that bewilder students of anthropology that the earth's most primitive people in both physical and cultural evolution have the most complex of all social (that is, kinship) organizations, whereas the Americans, who pride themselves at least on the highest advancement in material culture, have the simplest of all social organizations. Among ourselves, the only meaningful relations are in the conjugal family—wife-husband-children; all others deteriorate into the general American pattern of acquaintanceship. Only Americans who have come from folk groups, which retain the old structure of the extended family (like Midwest farm families), can be sure of the difference between a second cousin and a first cousin once removed. The Australians find the term "cousin" too general to be used at all.

Accompanying the breakdown of the American family is the growth of a generalized pattern of conduct of varying degrees of social intimacy—few very deep—that one person builds with another through a process of verbal experimentation. If you meet an attractive girl on the plane, you begin by talking about the weather—a nonsemantic linguistic device designed not to elicit or convey meteorological information, but to establish communication—and if each is encouraged to go further with the relationship, the consummation has nothing to do with kinship. Not so in wildest Australia. There, in the old days before the white man put an end to such easy solutions of sociological problems, if a man should stray from his own horde territory into that of another, he would not be accepted by the new group immediately, but would first have to sit outside the camp with the old men and talk about their relatives. If the stranger could trace his relationship to someone within the new horde, he would be accepted into it, for now they would know what social category to place him in and therefore how to behave toward him. Otherwise, he would be like a violent paranoid in our society. No one would know what his behavior might be at any time, so the only thing to do with him would be to kill him—insane asylums not being a feature of Australian native culture. This seems to us barbaric at best, since we do not understand the principles of behavior in a system so highly integrated that nearly everything one did in daily life would be determined by one's membership in a social grouping. We have a few vestiges of our primitive social patterns, but they are wholly unconscious. We do not tell our mothers dirty jokes; but do we tell our fathers dirty jokes? Our brothers? Our sisters? In Australian life the joking relationship is clearly and rigidly defined; there is no variance from family to family.

W. Lloyd Warner had the odd experience of witnessing among the Murngin peoples of northern Australia a situation that arose when a dirty joke was told within hearing of the sister of one of the men in the group. The mores had thus been violated, and some action had to be taken in behalf of the social ideals, so the brother took up his spear and hurled it at his sister. He explained to the anthropologist that he did not feel entirely right about throwing a spear at his own sister, but the man who told the joke was in a relationship to him that barred any spear-throwing; his sister was the only person eligible to receive the spear. The naked Australians, too, are subject to life's little ironies.

Marriage, to pursue one of the specifics, is actually a rather minor aspect of behavior since it is an event that occurs only two or three times in the life of an aboriginal. But the other myriad behavioral relationships, which determine that one throw a spear at one's sister, for example, come up again and again. However, understanding the marriage pattern of the Aranda (whose system is the dominant one among the 570 Australian tribes) takes some little attention. The Aranda recognize eight fundamental social categories—*Pananka, Purula, Knuraia, Ngala, Bangata, Mbitjana, Kamara,* and *Paltara.* Everybody is in one or another of these, his membership determined before birth by the rules underlying the following paradigm, which in a simple fashion shows who marries whom and where the children wind up. In addition to the Aranda terms, let us give symbols to these subsections in order to indicate

how these subsections are permuted with genealogical lines later.
In this system of genealogical shorthand (devised by H. K. Fry
of Australia), the initial numeral represents alternative generations ($1, 2, 1, 2, 1, 2, n$), the letter represents the moiety,[1] and
the terminal number stands for the subsection within the given
generation and moiety; all of these concepts—and many others—
are understood in the terms of kinship. To summarize marriage
and descent, therefore, let the base of the arrow represent the man,
the bend of the arrow the woman he marries, and the point of the
arrow the subsection of his children.

This statement is interesting, if tough, for it disposes nicely of
the two destructive competitions. Toward every other woman in
the horde a man would feel incest horror (even the "orgies"

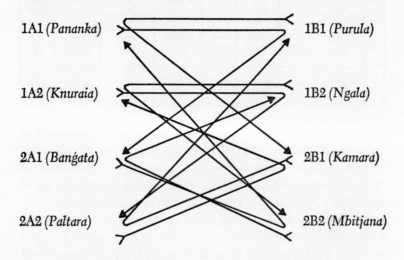

1A1 *(Pananka)*   1B1 *(Purula)*

1A2 *(Knuraia)*   1B2 *(Ngala)*

2A1 *(Bangata)*   2B1 *(Kamara)*

2A2 *(Paltara)*   2B2 *(Mbitjana)*

[1] A moiety is a "half tribe"—a classification into which everything and
everybody is relegated. This is the essence of social dichotomies; the in-group
versus the out-group, Republicans *versus* Democrats, good guys *versus* bad
guys, we *versus* they, hot *versus* cold, up *versus* down. Moieties are always
exogamous—it will be noticed that in the paradigm given here an A never
marries an A, for that would be incestuous.

reported among the aborigines are always engaged in between persons technically eligible to each other as man and wife). Projecting the normal relationship of the forty closest relatives possible in an Australian horde—that is, the ecological group that a person would live with, seeing no others, for perhaps ninety-five per cent of his life—we would have the following pattern:

	A1	a1	B1	b1	A2	a2	B2	b2
1	A1 ARANGA F.F.	a1 aranga f.f.sr.	B1 PALLA F.M.B. W.F.F.	b1 palla f.m.	A2 EBMANNA M.M.B.	a2 ebmanna m.m.	B2 TJIMIA M.F.	b2 tjimia m.f.sr. w.m.m.
2	A1 KATA F.	b1 intoa w.f.sr.	B1 ANTARA W.F. AMBA [H.F.]	a1 wonna f.sr.	A2 MARRA W.M.B.	b2 mala m.	B2 KAMUNA M.B.	a2 marra w.m. nerra [h.m.]
1	A1 KALJA ITIA B EGO MAN SPEAKING	a2 ebmanna f.sr.s.w.	B1 MBANA W.B. NOA [H.]	b2 ankalla f.sr.d. m.b.d.	A2 ILIARRA F.SR.D.H. M.B.D.H.	a1 kwaia itia sr [ego] WOMAN SPEAKING	B2 ANKALLA F.SR.S. M.B.S.	b1 noa W. intanga [h.sr.]
2	A1 ALIRRA S. [B.S.]	b2 namara S.W. [b.s.w.]	B1 AMBA SR.S. [S.]	a2 marra sr.s.w. nerra [s.w.]	A2 MARRA SR.D.H. [D.H.]	b1 amba sr.d. [d.]	B2 KAMUNA D.H. [B.D.H.]	a1 alirra d. [b.d.]
1	A1 ARANGA S.S. [B.S.S.]	a1 aranga s.d. [b.s.d.]	B1 PALLA SR.S.S. [S.S.]	b1 palla sr.s.d. [s.d.]	A2 EBMANNA SR.D.S. [D.S.]	a2 ebmanna s.d.d. [d.d.]	B2 TJIMIA D.S. [B.D.S.]	b2 tjimia d.d. [b.d.d.]

If you study this table closely, you will see that in this group of forty people, roughly the size of an Australian horde, only three women would be eligible to a man as mates, either on a permanent or on a casual basis: his wife, the daughter of his sister's son, and his father's mother. The latter lady would in any case be eliminated, since men are usually able to restrain their passion for women of their grandfather's generation. If he should take a second wife from a generation other than his own, his bride would in fact come from his grandson's generation—this, incidentally, eliminates sexual competition between father and son, and eliminates as well Freud's basis for the Oedipus complex.

In our society the incest tabu is narrower than in any other society, since social safety lies in numbers. Sexual or marriage competition is not very sharp in modern America; if love is unrequited, the unsuccessful suitor simply moves to pastures new. As a rule, we do not kill the competing lover, as the Pitcairn Island mutineers did, for want of a better alternative.

"What about love in all of this?" an American might ask. "Don't the Australian natives recognize Love?" Yes, indeed; all peoples recognize romantic love, but they recognize it for what it is—temporary insanity—and try to pay as little attention to it as possible, for they know it will go away presently of its own volition. Lovers they regard with tolerance and kindness, as we would regard the village idiot. But to establish so important an institution as marriage upon temporary insanity, as we do! That to the ignorant primitives is the ultimate insanity.

We may leave the aborigines for a moment and pursue the bothersome truth in this marriage business. Marriage in Australia and everywhere else in the primitive world is a serious institution. An unmarried adult in Australia is very soon a dead adult. A bachelor would have to live on what he was able to hunt, and in the sterile wilderness of Australia a hunting section produces about as much game as a fair-sized parking lot in Los Angeles. It is the women, we are happy to report, who keep the family going, with snakes and snails and puppy dogs' tails, as well as ants, witchetty grubs, lizards, seeds, and everything else that the human digestive system will absorb. But a spinster is just as helpless as a bachelor: without a husband, she would not only go without game meat; she would be a social outlaw in a land where social outlawry means death. Marriage among the great majority of the people of the earth is a device for economic co-operation, social security, parental tranquillity, and the really meaningful things in life, which do not include Love. Conversely—and unreasonably—our American society and those affected by it are nearly the only ones (a possible primitive exception is the Yurok-Hupa tribes of aboriginal California) that hold these motives to be foolish at best and blasphemous at worst. If we follow our democratic ideals and let truth be established by universal franchise, we must conclude that our system of marriage is unique, and therefore probably wrong.

Having admitted this possibility, we may go on to wonder about other unusual or unique features of our civilization which derive from marriage—the high divorce rate, juvenile delinquency, the status reduction of the aged, rampant infidelity, even household labor-saving devices—and, looming over all, the difficult question: if marriage according to American ideals is the only right marriage, why is it the most unstable marriage in the world?

We must also consider another unique feature of major importance in American and American-influenced societies: the subservient and deferential attitude of men toward women, which underlies the concept of marriage among us. Why do we take off our hats in elevators when women are present, walk on the splattery outside of them on sidewalks, give them our seats on buses, carry their books as schoolboys and their groceries as adults, let them into lifeboats first, and, as the final courtesy, precede them to the grave? No such nonsense among the savages. "Why isn't your wife riding the burro?" asked the indignant white man of the mounted Indian whose wife trudged behind, her head buried beneath a huge bundle of household goods. "Ain't her burro," was the sensible reply. Nothing in our culture seems more imbecilic to the primitives than this gyneolatry of Americans and some Europeans. Women in aboriginal America regularly carried weights of 150 pounds and, far from being a gentling and civilizing influence on their men, were incarnate fiends against wounded enemies. Women in aboriginal Australia were permitted to stay behind the nomadic horde for a few hours when they gave birth to a child, but they had to catch up with the band on their own. As carriers of weights, women are hard to beat, unless their culture has corrupted their minds with the idea that they are clinging vines. Prehistory shows that man's first beast of burden was woman —and, as for the role of women in childbirth, some societies in widely separated parts of the world have instituted the estimable practice of the *couvade,* in which the husband goes to bed for a week or two after the birth of a child and there receives the ministrations of his proud wife and the congratulations of his friends.

Anthropologists are interested in searching out origins or peculiar customs, and since theirs is a legitimately digressive discipline, they can go to literary history as well as to a midden heap for evidence. It is in literary history that the origin of romantic love and *Frauendienst* in marriage is to be found.

Toward the end of the twelfth century, Countess Marie of Champagne imported to Troyes the avant-garde ideas of Provence and set up a Bohemian court of littérateurs, Rabelaisian priests, troubadours, undisciplined artists, political liberals (her husband was nicknamed "The Liberal"), and other beatniks. Her noble pad was already equipped with the greatest writer of the century— Chrétien de Troyes—who simmered, simmered, simmered, until Marie brought him to a boil.

Provence and its environs at this time constituted the most advanced cultural center in Europe, and marriage accordingly was a device for familial alliances, a deadly serious game of connubial Monopoly. Sexual considerations were irrelevant, since one did not throw away ownership of two hotels on Park Place for an empty lot on Connecticut Avenue, regardless of the furtive pleasures to be had thereon. With sex an irrelevancy, there were great disparities in the ages of spouses: the joining of King Richard the Lionhearted and his child wife would have outraged even Vladimir Nabokov. And since love was unconsidered, it had to be found outside marriage; since the nobility had no more pleasurable or profitable activity (the peasants did all the maintenance work of feudalism, and fighting was more rhetorical than actual), adultery became the important recreation of the upper classes. By the time of Marie, rules were necessary, and Marie, as the daughter of one of history's greatest lovers, Eleanor of Aquitaine, was the one to lay them down. Chrétien was getting along in years and had become a bit old-fashioned and stuffy about this (though he invented Sir Launcelot as the perfect model of a Courtly Lover, to replace the uncouth Celtic wencher, Sir Gawain), and did not work at his literary lessons of love as well as Marie wished, so she found a more complaisant amanuensis in her personal priest, Andreas Capellanus, who, as a boastful seducer of nuns, was more amenable to emotion. Under her direction, and perhaps at her dictation, he wrote "one of those capital works," as Robert Bossuat described it, "which explain the secret of a civilization": *De arte honeste amandi,* a 70,000 word codification of the rules of civilized adultery, to which Gaston Paris gave the immortal name of Courtly Love. From his opening definition of love ("a certain inborn suffering derived from the sight of and excessive meditation upon the beauty of the opposite sex") Andreas the Chaplain proceeded to an anatomy of adultery, including such startling dicta as: "Love can have no place between husband and wife," and gave all the necessary directions for the entirety of seduction, from the first casting of calf eyes to a list of gifts to conclude an affair (in our culture, things like bath scales). The book was an immediate best seller among the nobility and remained at the top of the list throughout the late Middle Ages. Its influence was incalculable in its own time and in ours; some maintain that it did more to change the course of Western history than the Renaissance, for every society it touched makes a ritual of seduction and pays unnatural and unjustified deference to women.

Like all the great intellectual concepts, Courtly Love was misunderstood by people to whom it diffused, and its influence in some societies is identified by its perversion. The pushing Englishmen of the fifteenth and sixteenth centuries who came out of the country and elbowed their way up the lower-middle rungs of the social ladder, long after the subtle meaning of *The Romaunt of*

the Rose and *Troilus and Criseyde* (two of the great poems based
upon Andreas's concepts) were lost, got it into their addled heads
that Andreas was not serious about the prohibition of love between married folk, and so their emigrating descendants, we
Americans, say all for love, and the world is very well lost.

Perhaps we give too much credit to the ladies of Champagne.
Lurking outside the walls of Troyes were our old friends, the
nomadic Hebrews. It is they who implanted in our minds the
curious idea that marriage is mostly something to do with sex,
whereas sex is just a pleasant bonus to the acquisition of women
as property. The nomads of the western regions of the Dry World
have always been out of their minds on this subject; when not
poisoning wells and pirating caravans, the men spend their time
seducing women who belong to other clans—the Valentino pictures were not far from the truth—or protecting their own women
from a similar fate. One method of achieving some measure of
safety for their own women without withdrawing from their own
assaultive activities was to sew their women up—but you know
those sheiks. We have already quoted Ralph Linton's remark
about Moses and Freud and sin and sex; remember that the Puritans revived as much as they could the life of the Old Testament.

Since Jews were officially excluded from England before our
Puritan ancestors developed their peculiar brand of Calvinism, the
Semitic conceptions and attitudes came second hand to our founding fathers, through the Old Testament, which in a practical sense
was for them the whole of the Bible. And they knew their Bible—
all of it; they knew about people like Onan and Ooliba and what
went on in the cave at Zoar after Lot's daughters got the old man
soused. The prophets, too, tried to make themselves presentable
for what opportunities came their way; the 133rd Psalm mentions
"the precious ointment that ran down upon the beard, even
Aaron's beard; that went down to the skirts of his garments"—and
that must have been a fetching sight, what with the serpents
and all.

As we have seen, American prudery is notorious, yet nowhere in the world is marriage less durable or conduct—if the Kinsey report is to be accepted—less consonant with stated ideals. But that is what comes of a society's upholding ideals that were obsolete before the society's country was settled.

In every society there is this cultural lag between actual and ideal behavior, but the friction is far less where technological improvements are not hurrying the people out of sight of their mores. For this reason the social organization of the Australian aboriginals is a beautifully efficient machine that compares with our own as an analog computer compares with an Erector set. The Australian aborigines need no chiefs, for the ordinary duties and privileges of a citizen are built into his social organization. If there is a communal hunt of kangaroos, no one orders another to act by shouting: "Hey, mate, stand over there and kill the 'roos when we drive them out of the bushes." If a man kills kangaroos in a general hunt, he does so because it is the mythological function of his clan to kill kangaroos, just as it is the ancient function of another clan to drive them out of the bushes. The Australians need no laws, for in a small society everybody's business is the business of everybody else, and crime literally does not pay. The Australians need no welfare or relief, since food, like wives, is distributed according to the social pattern. If a man kills an emu, he gets to eat that part of the emu reserved for a man in his social position. Perhaps the best part will go to his mother's mother's brother's daughter's husband. Not much trickles down to him from his own kill, but some comes from every line of relatives. The Australians need no government Medicare or federal aid to education, for the clan *inkata*—the wise man and healer—is available to all; that is his duty and their right.

The trouble with the Australian system is that it works only in a small group. As a people acquire cereal agriculture and its concomitant blessings, such as theft and war, the element of the social is driven out by the element of the political. Beyond the horde is the clan—the extended family founded on the precept of one for all and all for one, which calls its members "brother," traces its descent to some fictional ancestor (usually an animal, Freud's totemistic father figure, which one does not eat), and is absolutely inimical to a politically centralized government. We have vestiges of clans, just as we have other social dysteleologies; there are the Elks, who totemistically call one another Elks and brothers and do not eat their fathers; and, more important, labor unions and similar kinship groups whose members on no account will cross another's picket line. Beyond the clan is the tribe, the largest of the purely kinship organizations, whose names, whether Diné, Amazulu, or Inuit, from the polar world to Africa, simply mean "we the human beings," and to whom outsiders are not really human, but an advanced infrahuman primate. In cannibalistic societies, these outsiders are seen as ambulant hamburgers; in more genteel societies such as our own, one may lynch them, but one does not eat them. Or marry them.

Beyond kinship there is the state, a politically organized aggregate of human beings from whom the strong staff of kinship has been taken. This is the system under which we live. Not for us the built-in directives and protections of the horde, the clan, and the tribe; we operate upon a contract, and retain at our own risk vestiges of the purely social phases of our evolution such as the family.

THE MORALITY OF POLITICAL ORGANIZATION

As long as America was an agricultural economy, the obsolescence of the family went unnoticed. Within the memory of man, the family was once a useful institution; on the farm there was a real necessity for a wife, and even for a grandma. Children, too, were productive; if the toddler could not churn butter, he could stand out in the field and be a scarecrow. The family worked as a unit, and in fact was the economic unit, just as the extended family,

the horde, was the economic unit among the aboriginal Australians. But since the Industrial Revolution the family has become
moribund, and steadily the economic unit has become the individual, answerable to none but the state.

If one can become emotionally detached from the situation,
it is beautiful to observe how all aspects of our culture are unobtrusively working toward this end. Take women. Women have
liberated themselves by wonderful and much sought-after labor-
saving devices such as automatic washing machines, TV dinners,
service apartments, baby sitters, and electric can openers; they
have liberated themselves from their function as wives without
providing for acceptance as anything else. It is as true today as
when Dr. Johnson said it: "When a man says he had pleasure
with a woman he does not mean conversation." One sociological
study of college women revealed that only five per cent of them
expected to become housewives. Sit in any laundromat these days,
see the young marriageable men come in with their bundle of
laundry; what do they need a wife for? In the old days a man had
to get married to get his shirts done up, if for no other reason.
Now there is nothing left between a man and a woman except
Love, which, some will agree with Andreas Capellanus, is best
sought outside marriage.

The beauty of the process cannot overcome our involvement in
the shocks and frictions that accompany any moving process. The
breakdown of the American family is no pleasure to those involved
in it. Considering the alternative, the best all of us have to hope
for is old age—but the collapse of the family is hard on senior
citizens, too. Among the primitive Australians one acquires status
mainly by growing old; among the advanced Americans one acquires status mainly by staying young—marrying quickly and temporarily, beating it out to California in a car, and leaving the old
folks to fend for themselves. Or, if you have money to burn and
a remnant of a conscience, buy them a one-bedroom cottage in a
Florida necropolis. It was not long ago—less than a generation—

that the parents of a married couple could still be put to use in watching the babies on movie night; now they are displaced by the baby sitter, who doesn't clutter up the house after you come home. And why cry on Mother's shoulder when you can have a psychiatrist all your own?—someone who not only will listen to your troubles and assure you happy irresponsibility without making a nuisance of himself otherwise, but will prescribe tranquilizers and validate your parking ticket—things Mother never could do.

But, instinctively, man is still a gregarious cannibal. He must cultivate the company of those he intends to devour. So he forms parodies of the older social groupings—unions, manufacturers' associations, and secret sodalities in place of the clan; car pools in place of the hunting pack; bowling leagues in place of phratries; street gangs in place of the horde—all desperate expedients to try to reconcile economic individualism with social conformity. The balance is very hard to achieve, and there are no resources in American education to help a man cope with the difficulties of life in the modern world. On one hand our competitive society drives him to make Phi Beta Kappa, and on the other our conformist society forbids him to wear its key. His religion tells him that in heaven he can ascend, with good conduct and application, through the ranks of the blessed from saint to archangel, but on earth he had better not exercise any individualism, religious or secular, unless somehow he can disguise it as some other quality. If he goes to the movies, he sees anti-cat cartoons such as Mighty Mouse and Tom & Jerry, which reinforce the dislike of his society for the nongregarious, nonconformist, non-leader-following feline and its approbation of the servile, obedient, sycophantic, friendly, organizational canine. If he fails to get the point, watching such things away from the directive group—that is, on television instead of in the crowded theater—electronically augmented reactions guide him to the proper response. Gradually, by hard knocks and subliminal propaganda, he eventually comes to understand what he should have been taught at his baby-sitter's knee: that his society punishes conspicuous nonconformity, even though the nonconformity is in accomplishment of officially admired goals.

As in the case of the Kurnai, as in the case of Charles van Doren, this is not simple social hypocrisy. In Paleolithic times, achieved status was important to the welfare of the group—so a man was trained to his profession and rewarded with food and prestige for being a skilled hunter. In modern times the only important status, so far as the society is concerned, is ascribed status. Advanced socio-economic systems work on the basis of predictable achievement, the actuarially reliable. There is not only safety in numbers, but certainty of profit as well. We are unwilling to accept this fact of life consciously, for all we can do about it is write Letters to the Editor; meanwhile our culture narrows the wage gap between hod carriers and engineers, between ditch diggers and professors. *Who's Who* and similar honors lists are still retained as harmless indicators of achieved status, but they are valuable only to the individual who gets into them. Society couldn't care less. At U.C.L.A. it is more important to carry a coffee cup than the key of a scholastic honor society—the key identifies you as an antisocial individualist, but the coffee cup proclaims your membership in the caste of graduate students who, unlike the undergraduate untouchables, are permitted to sup in the faculty coffee room. So, in the corridors and classrooms of the Anthropology Department at U.C.L.A., students go about with the indispensable coffee cup in one hand, like the *chapeaux bras* that amused Ben Franklin two hundred years ago.

Our whole society is becoming one-handed. The coffee-cup graduate student moves out of the classroom into the cocktail-party set, where he takes up a cocktail glass, whether he drinks or not (and, as a good conformist, he will drink). In the far-off days of the American family, one couple visited another on terms of warm familiarity, even intimacy; now an invitation to an evening's visit means a gaggle of fifty pleasant Hollow Men, each in his

conformist stretch socks, each with his cocktail glass and his in-
nocuous conversation that never essays a gambit but always keeps
the draw in hand.

THE IMPLEMENTATION OF MORALITY

Whether in the cocktail lounge, on the stony wastes of Judea, or
the red sands of Australia, man is a bad lot, on whom culture
must keep a sharp eye. It is not true, as Plato naively contended,
that social order and law come about because man recognizes his
enlightened self-interest and gives up a small measure of freedom
for the greater freedom and good of all. What man does for his
collective good he is forced to do. They do it better on the primitive level, again because of the small size of the social groups. As
a member of a forty-person, stark naked Australian horde, a thief
cannot prosper. He can steal a boomerang, but what would he do
with it? He couldn't even throw it away.[2] He is equally restrained
from offenses against the person; since all deaths are thought to
be the result of sorcery—a capital crime—any enmity between two
men that precedes, even if it does not cause, the death of one is
prima facie evidence of murder on the part of the survivor. In such
a society, it is expedient to be the smiler with the knife, and over
the millennia this internalized, indirect coercion toward amicable
relations has resulted in the Australian aborigines' acquiring a
genuine good nature, which almost every observer, early and late,
noticed. Unfortunately for the good people that still believe that
the meek shall inherit the earth, there is some doubt that, in the
unlikely event of such a legacy, they will be able to keep their
inheritance very long; certainly, the gentleness and guilelessness of
the aborigines resulted in their extermination in areas the white
man thought worth the taking.

[2] This is not strictly true. The returning boomerang was a great rarity in
aboriginal Australia; it was used only to imitate the flight of duck hawks to
frighten birds into traps, and it was used for this purpose only in two small
sections of the country.

As Sir Henry Maine stated a century ago, the dissolution of the family is paralleled by the growth of individual obligation; the trend of society is the replacement of the family by the clan, the clan by the tribe, the tribe by the state, and so on to 1984. As the internalized suasions toward good conduct weaken, the impersonality of law takes over.

There is a superficial progression toward humaneness in law; as civilization grows, corporal punishment declines; with us it is a private matter within families, never used in major crimes, never marshaled for general offenses. But this advancement is a very recent phenomenon. Only a century and a half ago in England, the most civilized country in the world, a person could have been executed for any one of two hundred different infractions. One is not surprised to hear that in Melanesia the proper method of holding a captive is to break his legs, but, as Judge Curtis Bok summarized it in *Star Wormwood*, it is somewhat unexpected to find torture in Europe:

> . . . in the Middle Ages society had a considerable catalogue of tortures, including the Iron Maiden, drawing and quartering, breaking on the wheel, bone-crushing, tongue-extraction, blinding, flesh-ripping, nail-pulling, burning at the stake, crushing by increased weights, smothering in ashes, strangulation by water, smearing with honey and spread-eagling over red-ants' nests, hanging by the thumbs, flaying, burying alive, exposure to wild animals, and so on. King Edward II of England was killed in such a way that was intended to leave no obvious mark upon his skin. His bowels were burned out by red hot irons passed into his body through the anus. This was the sentence that was passed on Sir Walter Raleigh in 1603, following his conviction for treason: "That you shall be had from hence to the place whence you came, there to remain until the day of execution. And from thence you shall be drawn upon a hurdle through the open streets to the place of execution, there to be hanged and cut down alive, and your privy members cut off from your body, and your body

shall be divided into four quarters, to be disposed of at the King's pleasure. And God have mercy on your soul."

We can only hope for Sir Walter's soul that the god into whose mercy it was conveyed by his executioners was not the Semitic Jehovah, who, judging from the 21st chapter of Exodus, would have applauded the imagination of the British judges.

Raleigh's justices were not Puritans, but the Puritans were no better in these things, and in fact devised unique punishments in the New World. The most humane sect in early America was the Quakers, whose chief social invention was the solitary prison in Philadelphia, established on Walnut Street in 1790, of which Charles Dickens painted so horrifying a picture several decades later. England by that time was more humane; after the unpleasantness with her American colonies, she lost a good place for the disposal of handkerchief stealers, potato filchers, loom breakers, wage conspirators, and hare poachers, and established the colony of Australia to which to transport these unfortunates. Poor unfortunates—they moved down into Tasmania in 1803 to displace a handful of French, and stayed to exterminate the Tasmanian natives through such means as Sunday aboriginal-hunting excursions, killing them for dog meat, and cutting off fingers for tobacco stoppers. As we said, a bad lot.

One can posit a First Law of Freedom, paralleling the First Law of Thermodynamics. The freedom of action of an individual is absolute in quantity, capable neither of diminution nor of augmentation, but only of transfer from one entity to another. If a person loses through societal action a unit of decision-making, that unit does not disappear, but moves into the province of another receptor of authority, and in this process social organization grows through the phases we have seen—from the individual (hypothetical) through the family through the clan through the tribe to the state. Every regulation, ordinance, or law is an example—even the most innocent, even the most necessary. Traffic regulations are accepted, in principle at least, by everyone as necessities in the modern state. Without them, utter chaos would result, as anyone can demonstrate on a small scale by trying to drive around a supermarket parking lot. But if you have to stop for a traffic light, your freedom of action is impinged upon, and that unit of freedom you have lost goes into the possession of the state. As organization increases in size and impersonality, its coercive powers decrease; even Nazism, with its medieval tortures implemented by modern technology, could not approach the effectiveness and thoroughness of control the Australian social organization had over the ignorant native squatting under the blue-gum tree, contemplating his duty to his uncle's aunt.

The coercion of law is very much less effective than the suasion of the mores, not only for the reasons we have examined, but because it is not continuous. Law—that is, the dictates of the state—is effective only when it is implemented by physical force. Where force does not exist, law does not exist, and the true state does not exist, Plato notwithstanding. The Supreme Court can pass decisions about integration until the cows come home, but until soldiers are sent to Mississippi to shoot segregationists, there will be no compliance and the state flag will fly over that of the United States. On the broader scene, we have the "space lawyer," Andrew G. Haley, who warns the Russians against flinging missiles into the Pacific because they are thus pursuing a dangerous program—they could violate international law. "International law" is the modern oxymoron; it is hard to tell which is more illusory—international law or One World.

The futility of the One World idea is part of the corollary deriving from the principles of state organization. The external physical force of the state is no match for the internalized moral force of society, since it is inherently divisive rather than cohesive. Because of this characteristic divisiveness of the state, organization of people on a higher level is, so far as we can see, impossible, however much our best people hope for a real United Nations. The instinctive human propensity for co-operating only by means of an in-group will prevent that consummation from ever being achieved. However weak it is, the largest in-group we have is the state, the nation; and since an in-group is inconceivable without an out-group, we will be at one another's throats until we are invaded by the Martians. The state does the best it can, but without social organization, internal cohesiveness and the forceful power of the superego are lost. The really terrifying thing about the Utopia of Orwell's Oceania—whose purpose, we should not forget, was to make its citizens (including such antisocial deviates as Winston Smith) happy—is that the tranquillity it sought will never be achieved.

The Unreal Americans

THE SOCIAL USES OF UNREASON

Although the foundation of the social order is stark physical force, no efficient society can afford to spend very much of its energy in making its members behave themselves. Guards and salt mines are effective means of assuring good conduct, but they are far too wasteful of social effort to be tolerated by a well-ordered government. This is why prison industries turn out little more than license plates and recidivists; this is why dictatorships are inferior to democracies in getting things done in any variety. The good society internalizes its coercions so that the people are their own police.

The means of internalization are various. When parents first withdraw affection from a crying infant, the Superego is born, a censor that grows stronger as directive prohibitions are acquired for the life of its host. By one means or other, culture protects itself by making sure we get our conscience before we get our knowledge, so that by the time most of us discover that crime pays excellently well, the still small voice has become a stentorian guard against our making any use of the discovery. By adulthood, the rampant Id has been so thoroughly intimidated that dissenters are not numbered in vast undergrounds of rebels, but consist of a minority of two kinds of criminal—those who have never acquired a conscience, and those who have risen above it. The first, who steal the goose from the common, fill the penitentiaries; the second, who steal the common from the goose, fill the stock exchanges. The inequity of law in punishing these criminals is not, as some suppose, a prejudicial discrimination against the lower classes, but a wise recognition that the mugger, unlike the swindler, does not understand the nature of social control and is therefore a threat to order.

Despite man's intellectual arrogance in calling himself *Homo sapiens* and insisting upon his Constitutional right to Free Will, the most changelessly dependable characteristic of man is his irrationality. Oscar Wilde declared for humanity when he said: "I can stand brute force but brute reason is quite unbearable. There is something unfair about its use. It is like hitting below the intellect." In his serious moments, Wilde would probably have denied that all men prefer to feel rather than to think, but culture understands man better than he understands himself. Like some misanthropic physical anthropologists, culture doubts that man's brain has yet evolved to the point where it works wholly by reason; consequently, culture places its confidence in the tried, true, and reliable unreasoning nature of man. Culture deludes man into proper deportment by giving him not something to understand but something to believe in—something to flatter him when he is good and frighten him when he is bad; in short, culture gives him religion.

There are many alternative explanations for this universal trait found in every human society since Neanderthal man began to bury his dead with equipment for the journey to the other world. Howells said: "We must all die in the end, and that is everyone's personal hell upon earth. The idea of an immortal soul fulfills our wishes, and there is no society, anywhere, that dares to disbelieve it." But some of our best people live reasonably happy lives without looking for any paradise beyond Miltown; as for the believers, one sees very few of them who are anxious to abandon this vale of tears for celestial bliss. The Druids would lend you money in this world to be repaid in the next, but they are understandably extinct. Max Müller and his fellow Solarists laid the origin of religion to nature, supposing that primitive man, waking one bright morning to the glory of the sunrise, invented religion to account for it; but, unfortunately for this romantic notion, real-life primitive man has no more interest in the origin of the sun than he has in the origin of his foot. Sir Baldwin Spencer, who should have known better, saw religion arising from the wish to revive dead and revered ancestors; but funeral rites everywhere are designed to convince the dear departed that, having made his grave, he must lie in it—permanently. There are other etiologies, all plausible but in some way unsatisfactory. The most convincing theory was propounded a half century ago by Émile Durkheim in his brilliant *Les formes élémentaires de la vie religieuse*: that religion was society deified, its fundamental rules apotheosized in order to make them into divine sanctions and render them therefore less liable to infraction. Thus, the purpose of social organization is to enable man to behave himself; the purpose of religion is to see that he does it.

Some authorities believe that Durkheim was wrong, that religions do not ordinarily intrude upon the secular life, but these scholars have been too apt to define morality in terms of the religion of their own culture. It is true that in Polynesia, for example, religion had nothing to say about the sin of alcoholic besottedness, how many gods a man might worship, or the immorality of killing; but in aboriginal Polynesia there was no hard liquor, there were no gods other than those worshipped officially, and no social harm would result from reducing the serious overpopulation. In those areas of conduct relevant to the stability of Polynesian society, Polynesian religion intruded with such force that just before the coming of the Europeans life in several parts of Oceania was nearly intolerable.

The fact that all religions are based upon the abrogation of reason has nothing to do with the case. Two hundred years before Christ, the Roman historian Polybius anticipated Durkheim when he wrote:

> It seems to me the most distinctive superiority of the Roman political and social order is to be found in the nature of their religious convictions; and I mean the very thing which other peoples look upon with reproach, as superstition. But it nevertheless maintains the cohesion of the Roman state.

Polybius was writing in a time of prosperity, when it might be assumed that society could well afford the luxury of unreason, but it is axiomatic that the harder the times, the more willing people are to submit to unsupported faith.

If Polybius had lived two centuries later, he would have seen another fact about religion rather more disturbing to him: that great social changes are always accompanied by the creation of a new religion. Arnold Toynbee is probably wrong in thinking that the new religion is a cause of the change; so far as we can tell by studying changes in culture and religion among primitive peoples after the shock of white contact, change comes first and religion follows to support the new system with the old unreason. This is true for social changes that are apparently secular—the Reformation, for example, and the myths arising from the Civil War and the Industrial Revolution. But perhaps the best example known to anthropologists of irrational religion growing out of social change is the phenomenon which Alfred L. Kroeber called the nativistic endeavor.

NATIVISTIC ENDEAVORS: UNREASON GONE MAD

Defeated people are mercifully the last to know their fight is lost. When hopelessness finally seeps into consciousness, it often pro-

duces a desperate last-ditch resistance rather than sensible submission. Typically, this nativistic endeavor arises in the poorest,
most oppressed segment of the people, beginning with one of the
poorest, most oppressed individuals among them. The pattern is
always the same: a prophet arises to announce that he has been
carried corporeally into the presence of the gods, who tell him
that they are dissatisfied with the way things are going, and that
if the prophet's people will signify their willingness to take up the
mantle of blessedness by performing a dance, by reciting a myth,
or just by returning to the ancient virtuous ways, then soon their
oppressors will be destroyed and the good old days will come
again. This prophet is often a thinking man rather than an acting
man, a John Ball rather than a Wat Tyler, a Preacher Casy rather
than a Tom Joad, ineffectual in convincing the people of their
imminent redemption. At this point the endeavor usually dissi-
pates, but if the prophet finds what might be called a St. Paul
(after the most famous example of the type), impatient, ebullient,
ruthless, irrational, unscrupulous, and bellicose, a man convinced
that God helps those who help themselves, the movement ex-
plodes into violence among all the people whom it reaches. In
almost all cases the endeavor drowns in the blood of its makers
and the prophet unwisely dies without making provisions for his
resurrection, but there are a few examples of success, or at least a
long postponement of defeat. The Jews have the endurance record; from 722 B.C., when they were conquered and scattered by
Nineveh, until the present, they have carried on an unflagging
rebellion against their myriad oppressors, and in so doing have
made possible the creation of many other nativistic endeavors—
Christianity and Islam, to name only the two most important—
each of which produced others, for a nativistic endeavor turned
against a nativistic endeavor is a heresy.

Though the endeavors of which we have historical record are
almost innumerable, they must be only an incalculable fraction of
the entire number resulting from clashes of culture through the

ages. Peter M. Worsley listed seventy-six nativistic endeavors in the southwestern Pacific alone. In our own history, there are such examples as the Seventh Day Adventists, Beekmanites, Campbellites, Wilderness Worshippers, Kentucky Revivalists, Heavenly Recruits, French Prophets, British Israelites, Fifth Monarchy Men, Quakers, Shakers, Ranters, and Jumpers. In the Colorado town in which this is being written, there are seven churches that were produced by nativistic upheavals of this sort.

Some of these have become quite respectable now that their early enthusiasm has run out. There is no more sober or dignified sect on earth today than the Quakers, but at the time of their origin the Quakers were a lively bunch indeed, and were in fact named after their frenzy. One Quaker lady in Puritan Boston tried, with some success, to distract the attention of the congregation from a sermon in a Puritan church by running up the aisle naked.

The extermination of the eastern Indians was accompanied by the appearance of numerous messianic cults, one of which indirectly elected three American presidents: Tenskwatawa, the Shawnee Prophet, used his brother Tecumseh as his St. Paul; Tecumseh set the frontier aflame and was defeated at Tippecanoe in 1811 by one William Henry Harrison, who was elected president by a political party which dug him up out of cider-guzzling retirement because there were no other successful generals around to satisfy the American demand for this type of candidate; Harrison died early in office and was succeeded by Tyler; and at the end of the century Harrison's grandson used his forebear's precedent as his strongest qualification for his own election to the presidency. There were other ramifications of poor forgotten Tenskwatawa's endeavor; imprisonment for debt in the United States was ended through the diligent persistence of Richard Johnson, who got into Congress on the strength of his boast:

> *Ripsy-rantsy, humptsy-dumptsy,*
> *I, Dick Johnson, killed Tecumsey.*

We see the name of another Indian St. Paul hundreds of times every day—Pontiac, who carried into bloody action the message of the Delaware Prophet.

Several of these nativistic endeavors are fascinating as evidence of the working of cultural processes. St. Anthony of Padua was an electrifying preacher in the twelfth century—so much so that his audiences and those who heard about his message began a religious peasants' revolt that swept across all of Europe for a century. The Church disapproved of the enthusiasm of these Flagellants, as they were called because of their practice of scourging their half-naked bodies with whips, and succeeded in putting out the fire, but not before the flaming spill had been carried to the New World in the first Spanish settlements. So now, though the movement has been long forgotten in the land of its origin, the Penitentes of the American Southwest carry on exactly like their medieval ancestors, except that they now use whips made of cholla cactus, and still the Church disapproves. Everyone is familiar with a number of examples of this phenomenon, from Joan of Arc's rebellion (noteworthy because Joan was her own St. Paul) to the Black Muslims, but few know, any more than the participants, that these movements follow a well-patterned socio-religious syndrome. Possibly there are even some folklorists who are unaware that the Irish interest in salvaging for scholarship millions of pages of Celtic lore in their absurd language is a manifestation of a nativistic endeavor. It is heart-warming for Americans to know that the messiah of one of these movements in the South Pacific (where they are known as Cargo Cults) was the "friendly king of America, Roosevelt."

The most significant, most bloody, most tragic, most widespread, and most interesting of all nativistic endeavors among primitive peoples was the Ghost Dance. Nearly half of all the Indians west of the Mississippi participated in the mania that surged over western Indian country in two successive waves in 1870 and 1890, ending so tragically in the Wounded Knee Massacre on the twenty-ninth of December in the latter millennial year. The prophecy of Short Bull, the Dakota (Sioux) shaman who led his people into the wintry wilderness at the running out of the Ghost Dance, contains the best brief statement of what the Ghost Dance meant to the Indians:

> In this world the Great Father has given the white man everything and to the Indian nothing. But it will not always be thus. In another world the Indian shall be as the white man and the white man as the Indian. To the Indian will be given wisdom and power and the white man shall be helpless and unknowing with only the bow and the arrow. For ere long this world will be consumed in flame and pass away. Then, in the life after this, to the Indian all shall be given.

The history of the Ghost Dance is a dreadful chronicle of unreason gone mad—of Indians slaughtered in their "ghost shirts," which they believed made them invulnerable to bullets; of fantastic perversions of the original gentle philosophy of the prophet Wovoka by an entire battalion of fanatic St. Pauls; of hopeless Indian heroism; of Wovoka ending up as an oddity in a San Francisco sideshow. The violent suppression of the Ghost Dance put an end to the American Indians as an independent people, but some Indians still quietly dance its rituals. Such is the power of faith.

If the Indian agent James Mooney, who reported the inception and growth of the Ghost Dance so magnificently, had been a man of action instead of an observer, he could have discouraged the movement without bloodshed, for reason applied before emotion takes hold can strangle a religion in its cradle; but if emotion is allowed to grow, there is literally no end to a faith. Had the Dead Sea scrolls been discovered at an earlier time in Christian history, they might have done more than the theory of evolution to bring about the melancholy, long, withdrawing roar of the Sea of Faith. But it does not matter now that a pre-Christian Jesus led a band of fanatical Jewish cultists in a last-ditch fight against both the invading Romans and the corruption of their own people, or that the figure of Jesus himself may have been entirely mythical. As one Christian commentator on the scrolls put it: "Christ is now too well established." Like the other iconoclastic discoveries in archaeology and folklore that rob the Bible of originality and divinity—Babylonian religion, Zoroastrianism, Mithraism, and the existence of other messianic prophets at the time of Christ such as Apollonius of Tyana—the Dead Sea scrolls will also be conquered by the pale Galilean. Already they have fallen entirely into the hands of religious translators, who are making the message of the scrolls more compatible with their beliefs. After all, to the disbeliever, no refutation of a faith is necessary; to the believer, none is possible.

FOLKLORE: THE CORRECTIVE FEEDBACK TO MORIBUND RELIGION

The trouble with religion as a societal device is that it defends the order that produced it with such tenacity that a serious, usually fatal cultural lag builds up as other aspects of civilization move into the future, leaving religion to guard an abandoned bastion. We have already seen examples of the conservatism of religion in some material things—clothing, architecture, and language. In immaterial things as well, the forms of religion are persisted in by churchgoers, but the meaning of religion must lose its force and vitality in fast-changing cultures like our own, and its unreasoning directive functions are taken over in part by folklore.

The socio-religious function of folklore is overlooked by nearly all laymen, who see it as the timeless philosophy of unspoiled people, and even by many folklorists, who see it merely as traditional oral artistry. In *Funk and Wagnalls Standard Dictionary of Folklore Mythology and Legend*, twenty folklorists give twenty different definitions of folklore, all of which miss the point in some way. For our purposes, folklore is a system of beliefs protecting the culture of the folk, who in turn can be defined as a homogeneous unsophisticated enclave living in but isolated from a surrounding civilized society by race, religion, economics, lack of education, topography, and the like. Folk culture is phasic; it represents an earlier, more general system of beliefs and values, just as superstition is the detritus of a once generally held religious system, and it is this phasic nature of folklore that enables it to supplement and even to supplant obsolescent social ideas, even among civilized people who believe they think realistically.

An example of the latter process is familiar to anthropologists in the character of the Culture Hero and the Trickster. Most peoples have the concept of the Culture Hero, a being more than human but less than divine who appears when the gods become too remote, a hanger-on at Olympus whose humanism makes him forsake his adjunctive divinity and become the benefactor of humanity, who starts mankind on its ambitious way by stealing fire and other good things from the gods, and who implants in man the rules, rites, and mores that prevent him from destroying himself through his animal nature. Too often for our ease of understanding, the Culture Hero is also the Trickster—and thus is a perfectly equivocal figure; and nearly always the Culture Hero, regardless of his purity, retains enough vestiges of a primordial nature for it to be argued that he derives from an earlier demigod, the Trickster. Prometheus is the classic example of the Culture Hero; the purest example is Jesus Christ—a being whose every act was virtuous, obedient, life-giving, and social; yet the early "apocryphal" legends which the Church in its mythogenic Councils tried to eradicate still survive in folklore after almost two thousand years of official disapproval, to suggest that in the beginning Christ was an exceedingly dangerous companion to mortal human beings. As the North American Indian Trickster kills people who slight him, so the Christ child in persistent folk ballads such as "The Bitter Withy" plays fatal tricks on playmates who slight him, though only one incident of this nature infiltrated the official canon—the story of his disobedience in the Temple. As a general rule, the more sophisticated the society, the fewer characteristics of the primitive Trickster are retained by the Culture Hero.

The Trickster is rather more difficult to understand. He is one of the most ubiquitous characters in world literature, and, after Satan (to whose creation he probably contributed), the most artful shape-shifter. He appears first as Enkidu in the oldest story in the world, the five-thousand-year-old Gilgamesh epic; in ancient Greece he concealed his true nature in Hermes and Heracles and Odysseus; in our medieval period he can be seen in the court jester and in this form still carries on a marginal existence in the circus clown and in Punch and Judy shows. As an anthropological problem, the Trickster is insoluble. His character and the incidents in which he participates are so alike in such widely separated parts of the world that they cannot be convincingly explained either by the process of diffusion or by the process of polygenesis. Everywhere he is like the Coeur d'Alêne Coyote, as Gladys Reichard described him—"greedy, sly, impudent, impatient, impulsive, stupid, suspicious, ignorant, imitative, cruel, ungrateful, interfering, boastful, vain, clever, and rarely, compassionate." These are his least repulsive qualities, for he is also crapulent, coprophilous, flatulent, incestuous, satyromaniacal, voyeuristic, and given to the most indecent exposure of his most remarkable genitalia. People profess to be outraged by him, and, in point of fact, would not tolerate in their society a real person with half the bad qualities of the Trickster, any more than Tennyson would have tolerated as neighbors persons with half the bad qualities of the knights in his *Idylls of the King;* but for all his peccadilloes, the Trickster is a delight maker. Since the Trickster is characteristic of a society whose religion is just beginning to show signs of cultural lag, he is hard to find in American lore, but he skulks behind the rip-tail roarers of the frontier such as Davy Crockett and Mike Fink, and endures in his clearest form in the Traveling Salesman jokes. If you look closely, you can see him metatactically in the children's cartoons on television, nicely cleaned up for our Puritanical society, as Yogi Bear, Hoagy Wolf, and Bugs Bunny.

It has long been recognized—in a general way ever since Aristotle advanced his cathartic theory to explain the attraction of tragic drama—that the Trickster in his anti-social acts has the important psychological function of enforcing the mores he violates by enabling people to share vicariously with him the pleasure of sinning. No one who has witnessed these outrageous stories being told among a primitive people doubts that the audience, for all its disclaimers, enthusiastically empathizes with the Trickster as he breaks clan and moiety laws, mother-in-law avoidance prohibitions, incest tabus, and other fundamental rules. This function of the Trickster is too nearly universal to be refuted; it appears wherever social and religious laws, however necessary, become oppressive. In medieval Europe, even the omnipotent Church had to tolerate grossly offensive practices such as the Boy Bishop, the Feast of Fools, the Feast of Asses, and the Foolish Pope, which remain with us as April Fool's Day, Mischief Night, and the office Christmas party.

ROBIN HOODS AND ROBBIN' HOODLUMS

Tricksters, Culture Heroes, and nativistic endeavors are more characteristic of primitive than of folk societies. Primitive societies are usually exterminated, but folk societies are merely exploited, so their reaction to oppression is protest rather than rebellion. Regardless of personal character or real motives, the man among them who succeeds in despoiling or even annoying the oppressive exploiters is elevated to a champion by his people, and becomes a Robin Hood. Almost none of these criminals ever presents any documentary proof of altruism, and some of them, like Robin Hood, probably never existed, but folklore has no more concern with reality than religion has with reason. An illustration is the prototype of the retaliatory hero, the original Robin Hood.

Robin Hood appeared first in literature in a snide reference in

Piers Plowman at the end of the fourteenth century, when Slob-bering Sloth admits ignorance of his Pater Noster, but says he can make up for it by reciting "rymes of Robin Hood and Randolf, erle of Chestre," another person of dubious morality. The antiquarian Bishop Stukeley in his *Paleographia Britanniae*, written about the middle of the eighteenth century, gives Robin Hood a noble pedigree by claiming him as the son of Waltheof, Earl of Northumberland and Huntingdon, and Judith, niece of William the Conqueror, thus making him sibling to Malcolm and Donalbain, of famous memory. Of this, Charles Parkin in his "An Answer to, or Remarks upon, Dr. Stukeley's *Origines Roy-stonianae*" said: "His pedigree of Robin Hood is quite jocose, an original indeed." Joseph Ritson's version of Robin's origin (1795) is more popular:

> Robin Hood was born at Locksley, in the county of Nottingham, in the reign of King Henry the Second, and about the year of Christ 1160. His extraction was noble, and his true name was Robert Fitzooth, which vulgar pronunciation early corrupted into Robin Hood. He is frequently styled, and commonly reputed to have been Earl of Huntingdon, a title to which in the latter part of his life, at least, he actually appears to have some sort of pretension.

Ritson actually appears to have some sort of pretension to verisimilitude, but his biographical sketch of Robin Hood is wholly imaginative. The turn of the eighteenth century was not a time of outstanding scholarly probity, but, as we shall see presently, folklore is not limited to the folk; there are, distressingly, many cases of irrational belief even in scientific bodies. It would be profitless to summarize the numerous pseudo-historical vaporings about the true life of Robin Hood; however, they all generally agree that he was a Saxon who took to the woods of eastern England after the Norman conquest and there he carried on a campaign of altruistic pillage. The western territory, meanwhile, was

held by another retaliatory hero, one Hereward the Wake, puta-
tive son of Lord Leofric, whose wife, Godiva, made a public
exhibition of herself in protest against her husband's tax policies,
an act which doubtless had some influence in shaping young
Hereward's later demeanor.

The most literate of contemporary iconoclasts, Lord Raglan,
does an admirable job of destruction on the historical Robin
Hood in his delightful book, *The Hero*. He shows that Saxons had
no surnames, and not before the sixteenth century did Normans
take herditary last names; that "of none of the families in which
earldoms were created from 1066 until 1442, when John, Lord
Talbot, became Earl of Shrewsbury, is there a legitimate descendant in the male line"; that there is no such place as Locksley
either in Nottinghamshire or Yorkshire; that the long bow did not
come into use in England until the end of the thirteenth century;
that the earldom of Huntingdon was held from 1185 until 1216
by David of Scotland; that there were no friars in England, Tuck
or other, until the year 1224; that "Little" as in "Little John,"
did not in Norman times refer to one's physique but to one's
character; and, as a final humiliation, that the names of Robin
(diminutive of Robert) and all his merry men (and his merry
maiden Marian) except the miller, Much, were Norman. Further-
more, he adds, "the first Wake to be christened 'Hereward' was
born in 1851." But come back two hundred years from now and
see who is better remembered—Robin Hood or Lord Raglan.

Because of the waves of immigration into America through
much of its history, which poured ethnic groups into backwaters
all over the continent, where they became folk enclaves, this
country has many more than the usual quota of Robin Hoods.
Most of these are local boys, tied closely to the neighborhood
which produced them, and so do not get into general currency.
But, even so, we have more than enough to go around on a
national circuit: Jesse and Frank James, Sam Bass, Billy the Kid,
Wyatt Earp, Wild Bill Hickok, and the other juvenile and senile

delinquents who have been unearthed, bathed, and absolved by television's Resurrection Men. Some of these characters, unfortunately, actually lived, but in real life they bore no resemblance whatsoever to their latter-day images. It is true they stole from the rich, for their intelligence was too low for them to understand, as did their contemporaries Jay Gould, Jim Fisk, Uncle Dan'l Drew, and the other robber barons, that it is much more profitable to rob the poor. It is also true that they gave to the poor, but charity, they believed, stopped at home. None of them will bear scrutiny on the claim of public generosity, but, for that matter, neither will Robin Hood. How the story that he distributed wealth got started no one can say, for of the thirty-nine Robin Hood ballads on which his entire legend is built, only one shows any indiscriminate altruism.

The real Billy the Kid was a nightmarish creature to look at, aside from his unpleasantness as a psychopathic killer, but a recent television series has a human female actually making love to him, if such a thing can be imagined. Jesse James shot children, but only in fact, not in folklore. Yet the factual James brothers. William and Henry, our great novelists and psychologists, get only nominal precedence in history over the legendary James brothers. The *Columbia Encyclopedia* tries to correct this by giving four and a half inches of space to Henry and only three inches to Jesse.

So long as we have an exploited folk, we will have Robin Hoods—or Robbin' Hoodlums. All that is needed for their appearance is an oppressive situation among a folk group, and a successful bandit. People who knew Pretty Boy Floyd called him a beast on two legs, but in Oklahoma the folk have a different opinion of him. The great Oklahoma composer of folk ballads, Woody Guthrie, wrote this song about him:

PRETTY BOY FLOYD

If you'll gather 'round me, children,
A story I will tell
Of Pretty Boy Floyd, an outlaw,
Oklahoma knew him well.

It was in the town of Shawnee,
It was Saturday afternoon,
His wife beside him in his wagon,
As into town they rode.

There a deputy sheriff approached him
In a manner rather rude,
Using vulgar words of language
Which his wife she overheard.

Pretty Boy grabbed a log chain
And the deputy grabbed his gun,
And in the fight that followed
He laid that deputy down.

He took to the trees and timber
And he lived a life of shame;
Every crime in Oklahoma
Was added to his name.

Yes, he took to the trees and timber
On that Canadian River's shore,
And Pretty Boy found a welcome
At many a farmer's door.

There's many a starving farmer
This same old story told,
How this outlaw paid their mortgage
And saved their little home.

Others tell you of a stranger
That come to beg a meal
And underneath his napkin
Left a thousand-dollar bill.

It was in Oklahoma City,
It was on a Christmas Day,
There come a whole carload of groceries
With a letter that did say:

"You say that I'm an outlaw,
You say that I'm a thief;
Well, here's a Christmas dinner
For the families on relief."

Now as through this world I ramble
I see lots of funny men;
Some will rob you with a six-gun,
Some with a fountain pen.

But as through your life you travel,
As through your life you roam,
You won't never see an outlaw
Drive a family from their home.

John Steinbeck in *The Grapes of Wrath* supports Guthrie's folk opinion of Floyd in the words of Ma Joad:

"I knowed Purty Boy Floyd. I knowed his ma. They was good folks. He was full a hell, sure, like a good boy oughta be." She paused and then her words poured out. "I don't know all like this—but I know it. He done a little bad thing a' they hurt 'im, caught 'im an' hurt him so he was mad, an' the nex' bad thing he done was mad, an' they hurt 'im again. An' purty soon he was mean-mad. They shot at him like a varmint, an' he shot back, an' then they run him like a coyote, an' him a-snappin' an' a-snarlin', mean as a lobo. An' he was mad. He wasn't no boy or no man no more, he was jus' a walkin' chunk a mean-mad. But the folks that knowed him didn't hurt 'im. He wasn' mad at them. . . ."

Even though the napkin in the eighth stanza of Guthrie's ballad is as unlikely as the thousand-dollar bill under it, one might be persuaded to believe this view of Floyd if the same stories were not told about every hoodlum in the new West, even Matthew Kimes. There even have appeared sentimental ballads about Caryl Chessman—but if the folk have made heroic songs about Lenin, Stalin, Huey Long, Ivan the Terrible, and Henry the Eighth, surely the Red Light Bandit is entitled to some posthumous attention. In folk heroes, the man is made to fit the need.

A subtle change of folk emphasis was detected by Marshall Fishwick in a recent article in *Western Folklore*. Fishwick noticed that the folk symbol of the Negro in literature until a short while ago was Uncle Remus, "the Negro who accepts life rather than revolt against it. With humor and cunning he makes the best of things, and finds many satisfactions in the world of wonder and comic retribution. Like Dilsey (his latter-day counterpart in the fiction of William Faulkner), Uncle Remus endures." "But," he continues, "another Negro sang a different song. John Henry refused to demur; he defied. He did not depend on cunning but strength to win his battles. And he died with his hammer in his hand." Fishwick's insight that John Henry has displaced Uncle Remus was substantiated, shortly after the appearance of his article, by the N.A.A.C.P.'s campaign to have Joel Chandler Harris's stories removed from school libraries. Uncle Remus had been driven out of the Negro folk mind, just as in real life Booker T. Washington had been displaced by W. E. B. DuBois.

THE FABRICATED HEROES

Those who chide the N.A.A.C.P. for initiating the change of a folk image should understand that this too is an inevitable process, going on in jerks and lurches. Right now the official journal of the N.A.A.C.P., *Crisis*, chooses its cover girls from very Caucasoid mulattoes. Throughout history, wise—or expedient—men have appreciated the social value of folklore and, recognizing its iron hold on the minds of its possessors, have directed it to their own purposes instead of profitlessly trying to uproot it. One of the wisest and most expedient men of the Western world, Pope Gregory the Great, at the end of the sixth century instructed his missionary to the Germans:

> Let the shrines of idols by no means be destroyed but let the idols which are in them be destroyed. Let water be conse-crated and sprinkled in these temples; let altars be erected . . . so that the people, not seeing their temples destroyed, may displace error and recognize and adore the true God. . . . And because they were wont to sacrifice oxen to devils, some cele-bration should be given in exchange for this . . . they should celebrate a religious feast and worship God by their feasting, so that still keeping outward pleasures, they may more readily receive spiritual joys.

And so we celebrate in Christian guise the pagan feasts of Christmas, Easter, Halloween, and May Day, among many others. It is amusing to note that in 1962 Christmas trees were banned in Massachusetts schools as a symbol of Christ; less than a century earlier, they would have been banned as a symbol of paganism. And the Puritans of the Massachusetts colony in 1625 did not need Freud to tell them what the maypole on Thomas Morton's property stood for.

After two generations of futile effort against religion, Soviet Russia produced in 1954 a standard reference work on folklore, which was re-edited in 1956 to make Stalin and a few others into unpersons. It is suspected also, by the folklorist Richard M. Dorson, that the establishment of a Folklore Center in Cairo shortly after the accession of Gamal Abdel Nasser was no coincidence.

But as in most other things, capitalist America creates "folk" heroes better and bigger than do Communist dictatorships, for here this is private and profitable enterprise. Take Paul Bunyan for a prime example.

When Carleton C. Ames published an article in *Minnesota History* in March, 1940, stating that he had spoken to hundreds of old lumbermen without finding one who had ever heard of Paul Bunyan, the states of Michigan, Wisconsin, North Dakota, South Dakota, Oregon, Washington, New Hampshire, New York, and California—all claimants of Bunyan's nativity—joined Minnesota in condemning the blasphemous Professor Ames. Other scholars supported the iconoclast, and the furor died down; but towns like Bemidji, Minnesota, went on constructing gigantic figures of Paul and Babe the Blue Ox to draw tourists to celebrations of Paul Bunyan's Day. Even Paul's most inveterate opponent among the historians, Dan Hoffman, admits that Paul Bunyan is displacing Uncle Sam as the anthropomorphic symbol of America.

Paul Bunyan seems to have been invented by a newspaper writer named James McGillivray in 1910, but as a hero Paul was an insignificant figure until 1913, when the Red River Lumber Company moved from Minnesota to California and hired William Laughead, a publicity man, to inform its customers of its new location. Laughead picked up a few of the Bunyan stories that were now beginning to circulate in lumber camps, expanded them with new incidents and with characters like Babe the Blue Ox, Shot Gunderson, Chris Crosshaul, Brimstone Bill, Big Joe the

Cook, and Johnny Inkslinger, and rolled them all into a series of brochures entitled *Introducing Mr. Paul Bunyan of Westwood, California.* Carl Sandburg, who was then inventing Abraham Lincoln, brought his People into it: "The people, the bookless people, they made Paul Bunyan and had him alive long before he got into the books for those who read. Paul is as old as the hills, young as the alphabet." Another poet, W. H. Auden, saw in him the archetypical American, a "projection of the collective state of mind of a people whose tasks were primarily the physical mastery of nature," a conclusion furthered by Marshall Fishwick: "Robust, uncouth, destructive, resourceful, friendly, when he moves into the forest he gets things organized and he gets results; he can't be very much concerned with who or what suffers in the process. Where others think in terms of tens or hundreds, he thinks in terms of thousands. He believes in the survival of the fittest."

And so the fabricated Paul Bunyan, made of less solid substance than his giant effigy at Bemidji, undergoes a transubstantiation from just another spurious hero created by professional writers[1] into a figure with more reality than many readers of this book. Fishwick, who has exposed many of America's manufactured heroes, sensibly concludes that "only a purist, convinced that 'the folk' are holier than specific contrivers, resents what has happened. A hero is a hero, no matter who creates him, or why. Too many folklorists think they are scientific when actually they are only sentimental. They deplore efforts of corporations or political groups to invent new symbols and characters, without realizing

---

[1] Some other fabricated folk heroes and their creators:
Pecos Bill—Edward O'Reilly
Bowleg Bill—Jeremiah Digges
Febold Feboldson—Paul Beath
Annie Christmas—Lyle Saxon
Joe Magarac—Owen Francis
Tony Beaver—Margaret Montague
George Washington—Mason L. Weems

that in our society these are the natural agencies to do such things. Like everything else, folklore and mythology are shaped by the culture in which they flourish." And William Laughead? "All I wanted to do," he said, "was to sell lumber."

The most elusive creation of commercial, corporate effort whom we suspect to have had reality as a human being is without question Henry Ford. In the claims made for him by himself and by others, he becomes a symbol of American inventiveness and efficiency, and is so recognized in *Brave New World* as the most important person since Christ. History, incidentally, is a subject it is not politic to mention in context with the name of Henry Ford. When the Chicago *Tribune* called him an "ignorant idealist," Ford sued the paper for libel; in the examination given him on the point of his ignorance, it was disclosed that he thought the American Revolution had occurred in 1812 and that Benedict Arnold was one of his employees. But, as he said, "history is bunk."

The legend that is Ford has been examined with incredulity by many historians in many books. As an extreme example of the personalization of invention and discovery that makes these complex events understandable to the human mind, Ford has no equal. In briefest summary—drawn largely from the books of Marshall Fishwick, Ralph H. Graves, Allan Nevins, Keith Sward, Allen L. Benson, and William C. Richards—here are the chief inventions, innovations, and decisions, some of which have been of inestimable importance to American life and economy, attributed to Henry Ford—and their actual genesis:

The automobile—The automobile as a self-propelled land vehicle dates from about 1800, according to Alfred Kroeber, but the invention was displaced for nearly a century by the locomotive, which overcame the main obstruction in the acceptance of the automobile, the lack of suitable roads. Gottlieb Daimler is usually given credit for the invention of the high-speed internal-combustion engine and its combination with a wheeled vehicle in Paris in 1886; simultaneous invention is claimed for Carl Benz, of Mannheim, Germany.

The first automobile made by Ford—This historic vehicle was actually built by Charles B. King, Ford's friend and fellow tinkerer. King's automobile, the first in Detroit (1894), and its plans were given by King to Ford when King, convinced of the superiority of the French automobiles, went to Paris to study them. He disappears from the automobile story at this time, for he abandoned tinkering to take up art. Ford did not build an automobile until 1896.

The Ford Motor Company—This organization was formed by a group who took Ford in because by this time (1899) he had built three cars and some reputation. The company failed within the year because of Ford's inability to design a practical car. His backers withdrew and formed the Cadillac Motor Car Company. Another company of capitalists, again including Ford, then formed the Ford Motor Company in 1903.

Mass production of automobiles—The first company to mass-produce automobiles in the United States was that of Ransom E. Olds—the Olds Motor Works—founded in 1899. Olds also produced the men who produced automobiles; more than a hundred of his associates and employees later became executives in other companies.

Construction of the first Ford cars—During the first year of operation, the only function of the Ford Motor Company was to attach tires and finishing touches; the rest of the car was being built by John and Horace Dodge at their machine shop.

Legend of the three Fords in London—Very nearly the only bit of truth in the Ford folklore is the tale of his taking three of his standardized cars to London and there dismantling them completely, mixing the parts, and rebuilding three cars at an industrial exhibition. The story is true, but the cars were Cadillacs and the builder was Henry M. Leland.

Standardization and interchangeable parts—This is the most famous and persistent invention attributed to Ford, but, as in the other instances, he had almost nothing to do with it. The first cars made by this process were those of Henry M. Leland, who had been an employee of the Colt arms plant, which shortly after 1850 had 400 machines turning out 24,000 revolvers a year, all with interchangeable parts. But Colt had borrowed the idea from Eli Whitney, who got it God knows where.

Theory of line production—The man who most influenced modern industrial method and theory was Frederick W. Taylor, known to economists as the "Father of Scientific Management," and unknown to everybody else. He is not mentioned in *Chambers's Biographical Dictionary*, which gives space to Jesse James. Taylor predicted (in print) in 1895 all the later production methods of the automobile industry; he had perfected some of these methods even earlier for the steel industry.

Mass production methods at the Ford plant—Walter Flanders introduced mass production at Ford in 1908, replacing the stationary construction methods used before that time.

Perfecting of the assembly line—Although the most important figures in the perfection of the assembly line at the Ford factory were C. W. Avery (an old high-school teacher of Edsel), William Klann, and Carl Emde, it is hard to attribute credit for the innovation precisely. William S. Knudsen said later that Emde was the important person in this development, but Knudsen himself was influential in it. However, the principle of the assembly line had been used for years by Chicago meat packers in carrying meat to a line of butchers.

Emergence of Ford as the real head of the Ford Motor Company—In a negative sense, credit for his ascendancy must go to Ford, for he was less foolish than his other partners, who were wiped out after investing their Ford profits in scatterbrained speculative ventures, such as gold mines in Canada. The measure of Ford's own perspicacity can be gauged by his willingness to sell out in 1908 to W. C. Durant, founder of General Motors, for three million dollars. The deal fell through because Durant could not pay cash, and Henry's mother told him never to sell any cows for bags of beans. Ford went on to make 200 million dollars clear profit in the fiscal year 1921–22.

The Ford trademark signature—C. H. Wills, the most important designer among Ford's early employees, printed the familiar Ford longhand signature with a child's printing set.

The first important Ford slogan—"Watch the Fords Go By" was coined by E. Leroy Pelletier, Ford's first advertising manager. Ford's perspicuity in this area may be seen in his decision to suspend advertising completely for five years.

Mass-production management—The human problems in mass production were solved temporarily by Charles E. Sorensen, C. H. Wills, and William S. Knudsen.

Development of the Model T—C. H. Wills, who invented the Ford engine, the Ford planetary transmission, and its alloy steels, designed and built the Model T.

Development of the Model A—The most eagerly awaited car in automotive history, the Model A (possibly the best automobile ever designed), was the work of P. E. Martin and Charles Sorensen.

Development of the Ford V-8—Charles Sorensen is the man chiefly responsible for the design and development of the Ford V-8.

Sales driving, dealer crowding, dealer financing—Though in perfect Henry Ford character, these devices to force dealers to assume responsibility for selling all cars arbitrarily alloted to them were the invention of James Couzens.

The Five-Dollar Day—The idea of the Five-Dollar Day, generated in the mind of James Couzens, was prompted by the 380 per cent annual labor turnover in the Ford plant, the agitation of the I.W.W., and the basically illusory nature of the "raise." An immediate result of the plan was higher production at less labor cost; as Ford himself said: "The payment of five dollars a day for an eight-hour day was one of the finest cost-cutting moves we ever made." "Probationers," who comprised a large percentage of the work force, continued to labor for $2.72 a day. Within five years, the cost of living in Detroit had risen 108 per cent.

Phantom freight charges—Still one of the main sources of automotive revenue, phantom freight charges were the invention of idea man James Couzens.

Ford's Peace Ship and his peace plans—Ford's naive ideas for bringing peace to Europe before our entry into World War I were set buzzing in his mind by the erratic social reformer Rosika Schwimmer.

Ford's writing—Ford's literary works—his four-volume autobiography, his life of Edison, "Mr. Ford's Own Page" in the *Dearborn Independent*, and other writings—were ghosted by William J. Cameron.

The idea for water-power sites and small village factories, the scheme that eventually prevented him from becoming president of the United States, was implanted in his head by his hero, Thomas A. Edison. As Ford's candidacy boomed through 1922 and 1923, his own interest turned almost obsessively to acquiring the entity which later became the TVA—so much so that after a secret meeting with Calvin Coolidge (from which Coolidge emerged with the recommendation that Muscle Shoals be sold to private capital and Ford emerged with an endorsement of Coolidge), Ford withdrew. However, Senator Norris cut through Ford's scheme, and in 1933 the TVA was created by Act of Congress.

The Lincoln automobile—The Lincoln, cited as evidence that Ford could design quality as well as quantity, was designed and built by Henry and Wilfred C. Leland.

Ford's anti-Semitic articles in the Dearborn Independent—Although Ford probably instigated and thoroughly believed in the anti-Semitic articles that appeared in his paper (though he denied both), they were cooked up by Ernest Liebold. The infamous

Protocols of Zion were translated into English, at Liebold's direction, by Boris Brasol.

The Ford folk image; Ford as a hero—Credit or responsibility for Ford as hero must go to William J. Cameron, though, on reading about the life of Henry Ford, one wonders whether, like Orwell's Big Brother, Ford ever really existed. Even his famous remark, "History is bunk," was probably quoted from Thomas A. Edison.

THE ILLUSORY HERO IN POLITICS

If the ultimate purpose of the educational process is to prepare the immature individual to take his place in his society and culture, the ultimate purpose of the materials and means of education—myth, religion, dogma, folklore, civics, and history, as these materials and means are variously called at different levels of social evolution—is to make the individual's culture and society acceptable to him. In order to do this, steps must be taken to prevent inconvenient truth—or, more accurately, inconvenient fact—from becoming obstructive. One of the best arguments for faith is that it is a necessary protection against unbearable reality. We are all like Willy Loman in this respect; we must form a shield of illusions against the lifelong buffeting of truth.

Even academicians, for all their wisdom, knowledge, and education, create delusions that are hard to distinguish from true folklore. The palpable nonsense of children raised by wolves was folklore in ancient Rome, but social science in modern America; articles supporting or at least conceding the possibility of wolf children appeared in textbooks of psychology and anthropology and in such sober periodicals as the *American Journal of Psychology, Science, The New York Times, Scientific American,* and *Science News Letter,* as well as such regular folklore journals as the *Reader's Digest* and *Time.*

The Jukes-Kallikak myth is still being used by sociologists, though anyone who has read the original Jukes report, Richard L. Dugdale's *The Jukes: A Study in Crime, Pauperism, Disease, and Insanity* (1875), should be ashamed to admit having read through such an insane work. In Russia we have seen the religion of Marxism producing the folklore of Lysenko. In Nepal, Sir Edmund Hillary goes hunting for Sherpa bogymen, sometimes known as Yeti. And there are some among us who believe that Darwin showed how species originate.

Cultures—or nations, as these entities are called in the political context—must make more frequent use of educational folklore than the individual person, for though nations do not behave according to the rules of individual morality, they must be represented as doing so. That is why, as La Rochefoucauld said, "history never embraces more than a small part of reality."

It is useful for a civilization that its heroes have some basis in reality, since literate people demand a modicum of documentation, but nothing more than the identification of a hero with some actual person is ordinarily required. If the actions and characters of these people accord well with the legendary purpose they have been selected to fullfill, this is welcome; but it is not necessary. Folklore can construct a man entirely by itself. The world will little note nor long remember what we say here about the real characters of the following brief selection of national heroes, and this is as it should be. The Father of His Country should have been a boy who could not tell a lie; he should have been a youth who could throw a dollar across the Potomac; he should have been a man of dignity, intelligence, wisdom, high-mindedness, compassion, magnanimity, and the other great virtues. It is quite irrelevant that the real George Washington had precious few of these qualities until the itinerant book peddler and occasional author, Parson Mason L. Weems, took it upon himself to construct a book which he promised his publisher would be "artfully drawn up, enlivened with anecdotes, and in my humble opinion, marvelously fitted *ad captandum gustum populi Americani!*"

History is so full of unreality that it is best considered as literature, to be evaluated and criticized on the basis of literary principles. Why did its anonymous author choose certain themes to be
emphasized? More interestingly, why did its author choose certain
persons to be protagonists and heroes?

The patriot Dawes, who carried the news to Concord after Paul
Revere was captured by the British, very probably missed out on
the immortality conferred upon his companion because "Revere"
rhymes with better words than "Dawes." Longfellow would not
have begun his poem with:

> Listen, my children, to your paw's
> Tale of the ride of William Dawes.

In this case, Paul Revere is simply a rhyme-induced hero. Stonewall
Jackson is another factitious hero who can be criticized from a
literary point of view, for his famous nickname is based upon later
misinterpretation of what General Bernard Bee meant at the First
Manassas. Bee called for Jackson's assistance, but Jackson hesitated,
and Bee complained: "Look at Jackson, standing there like a
damned stone wall." Captain Lawrence gets into folk history because only the first part of his story was told; less than fifteen
minutes after he uttered the immortal words: "Don't give up the
ship," he surrendered.

Folklore makes better literature than history. For one thing,
history is indiscriminate in its distortions, falsifying everything to
some extent. Folklore selects fewer subjects for distortion and so
is able to put more energy into the job. The legendary King
Arthur, the most famous political folk hero in Western history, is
the distillation of a mixture of hundreds of lesser figures whose
individual identities were sacrificed to make this Celtic captain
into an English king. Davy Crockett, on a less sublime level, is an
American example of the same process.

When history combines with folklore to create a hero, there is
no limit to the distortions possible. Henry Adams in *The Forma-*

tive Years (the first part of his great history of the Jefferson and
Madison administrations) tells us that under Jefferson

> the government had suffered no change in principle from
> what it had been under President Washington; that not a
> single Federalist measure, not even the Alien and Sedition
> Laws, had been expressly repudiated; that the national debt
> was larger than it had been before, the navy maintained and
> energetically employed, the National Bank preserved and its
> operation extended; that the powers of the National Govern-
> ment had been increased to a point that made blank paper
> of the Constitution as heretofore interpreted by Jefferson,
> while the national territory, vastly more than doubled in
> extent, was despotically enlarged and still more despotically
> ruled by the President and Congress, in the teeth of every
> profession the Republican party had ever made. Had this been
> the work of Federalists, it would have been claimed as a
> splendid triumph of Federalist principles.

The other great democrat before the second Roosevelt was
Theodore, who waved the Big Stick at home and abroad against
evil, oppression, and exploitation. Thomas C. Cochran and William Miller in *The Age of Enterprise* summarize the work of his
administrations:

> Under pressure from him Congress in 1903 created the De-
> partment of Commerce and Labor, the Hepburn Act enlarg-
> ing the jurisdiction of the Interstate Commerce Commission,
> and the Pure Food and Drug Act in 1906—but all these were
> sops to the need for real effective legislation in these areas.
> Yet with these toothless bills, and the eight-hour day for
> federal employees, that is the paltry record of Roosevelt's two
> "Progressive" administrations. Big Business had learned early
> that as Elihu Root reputedly said of him, Roosevelt's "bark
> is worse than his bite."

. . .

Taft in his one term got more real progressive legislation through than Roosevelt in both of his terms—parcel post, postal savings banks, Bureau of Mines, Children's Bureau; made the Labor division of the Commerce Department a separate Department; the 17th Amendment (providing for direct election of senators); the Income Tax Amendment, and the Man Elkins Act, which put teeth into the Interstate Commerce Act.

Until the Great Depression, no event in American history was more traumatic than the Civil War, and consequently no event in American history was able to produce a greater hero than Abraham Lincoln. Purely as a centripedal force in folklore, Lincoln had no remote rival. Davy Crockett swallowed all the native humorists who came before him, but Lincoln as a humorist alone —a minor occupation in his legendary career—swallowed humorists who came after him as well. Almost every aspect of his biography as written by retired Midwestern clergymen and People's poets would, like his famous rathole, bear looking into by the folk iconoclast. Yet, when all the false images of Lincoln are broken, one can always say: "Well, he freed the slaves."

Did he, now?

Here are a few quotations rarely publicized, from the lips of the Great Emancipator, as collected by Ralph Korngold:

I will say, then, that I am not, nor ever have been, in favor of bringing about in any way the social and political equality of the white and black races; that I am not, nor ever have been, in favor of making voters or jurors of negroes, nor of qualifying them to hold office, nor to intermarry with white people. I will say in addition that there is a physical difference between the white and black races, which, I suppose, will forever forbid the two races living together upon terms of social and political equality; and in as much as they cannot so live, that while they do remain together, there must be the position of the superiors and inferiors; and that I, as much as any other man, am in favor of the superior being assigned to the white man.

Judge Douglas has said to you that he has not been able to get from me an answer to the question whether I am in favor of negro citizenship. . . . He shall have no occasion to ask me again, for I tell him very frankly that I am not in favor of negro citizenship.

Free them and keep them among us as underlings? Is it quite certain that it will better their condition? . . . Free them and make them politically our equals? My own feelings will not admit of this.

General Butler, I am troubled about the negroes. We are soon to have peace. We have got some one hundred and odd thousand negroes who have been trained to arms. When peace shall come I fear lest these colored men shall organize themselves in the South, especially in the States where the negroes are in preponderance in numbers, into guerilla parties, and we shall have down there a warfare between the whites and the negroes. In the course of the reconstruction of the Government it will become a question how the negro is to be disposed of. Would it not be possible to export them to some place . . . ?

[Clay] did not perceive, as I think no wise man can perceive, how it [slavery] could be at once eradicated without producing a greater evil even to the cause of human liberty itself.

[Count Gurowski, speaking of Lincoln to Governor John A. Andrew of Massachusetts] He considers that general emancipation will smother the Free States. Such are his precise words.

I yield to all that follows from necessity. What I would desire would be a separation of the white and black races.

[In reply to a request for instructions from Major General Benjamin Butler as to what should be done with fugitive slaves that took refuge in Butler's camp] It is the desire of the President that all existing rights in the States be fully respected and maintained.

[In 1862, in a proposal to Congress for gradual emancipation by the purchase of slaves] Such a proposition on the part of the Federal Government sets up no claim of a right by the Federal authority to interfere with slavery within State limits—referring as it does the absolute control of the subject, in each case, to the State and the people immediately interested. It is proposed as a matter of perfectly free choice to them.

[In 1862] What I do about slavery and the colored race, I do because I believe it helps to save the Union, and what I forbear, I forbear because I do not believe it would help to save the Union.

This is not to say that the great humanitarian ideas attributed to Abraham Lincoln did not exist. They did, and they were expressed. There was in truth and fact an Abraham Lincoln, but his name was Thaddeus Stevens.

It was Stevens who was the implacable enemy of slavery, the caustic wit, the energizer of the nation, the great believer in human equality. "There is not the scintilla of a doubt," the Bourbon historian Claude Bowers wrote of him in horror, "that he pushed to the utmost limit his ideas of absolute equality, socially and politically, between the races." His steadfast support of this unpopular idea can be seen in the epitaph he provided to be carved on his headstone:

I repose in this quiet and secluded spot, not from any natural preference for solitude, but, finding other cemeteries limited by charter rules as to race, I have chosen this that I might illustrate in my death the principles which I advocated through a long life, Equality of Man before his Creator.

Stevens had only contempt for the devious policies of Lincoln, and suspected—as later historians have suspected—that Lincoln issued the Emancipation Proclamation as a device to keep Stevens ineffectual until after the war, when it would obviously be ruled unconstitutional. Even Steven's enemies were prepared to concede that he was far more intelligent and far-seeing than Lincoln. He predicted the failure of the Fourteenth Amendment, almost as if he foresaw that, by 1912, out of 604 Supreme Court decisions based on the Amendment, only six would be successful suits brought by Negroes for civil rights. Yet he voted for the Amendment because, as he said: "I live among mortals and not among angels." Why then is Lincoln the great American hero rather than Stevens? Because Lincoln had qualities which Stevens and the great mass of mankind lack but which mankind values the more for their scarcity: true charity, humility, and compassion; and because, most importantly, he did not

> swell the rout
> of lads that wore their honors out.

Even Stevens appreciated this when speaking of what he considered the infamous and absurd plan for Reconstruction bequeathed to the unfortunate Andrew Johnson. "Well for his reputation," he said of Lincoln, "that he did not live to execute it. From being the most popular, he would have left the office the most unpopular man that ever occupied the executive chair."

A Postscript on the Latest Candidate for Folk Heroism, Offered Without Comment to Those Who Doubt that Unreality Is the Common Denominator of All Folk Heroes

THE TRIAL OF FRANCIS GARY POWERS

In the stately Hall of Columns, nineteen sixty was the year,
When young Francis Gary Powers stood before the Russian
    bear.
They were trying him for spying, o'er the Soviets he flew
In the famous plane, U-2.

> CHORUS: *Glory, Glory, he's a hero!*
> *Glory, Glory, he's a hero!*
> *Glory, Glory, he's a hero!*
> *Who flew for Uncle Sam.*

Far across the foreign waters in the state USSR
O'er the Lubyanka Prison shines a bright foreboding star.
In that Godless land of Russia, in that vale of endless tears,
They gave him ten long years.

In the future page of hist'ry in the ages yet to come,
When free men speak of heroes and the deeds that they have
    done;
They will sing of Francis Powers and the famous plane he
    flew,
For the great "Red, White, and Blue."

> *Glory, Glory, he's a hero!*
> *Glory, Glory, he's a hero!*
> *Glory, Glory, he's a hero!*
> *Who flew for Uncle Sam.*

☆ VI ☆

The

Acquisitive Americans

Lincoln Steffens came down to Los Angeles from San Francisco in 1907 to see whether that vigorous city had learned anything from the public shaming of its unfortunate sister municipality in the graft prosecutions just concluded. Steffens, in his day the greatest journalistic commentator on government, friend and advisor to several presidents, and the most feared of the muckrakers, had observed the course of the San Francisco scandal from the inside, as a confidant of the leaders in the prosecution, Joseph Worster and Fremont Older. There were others on the side of righteousness whom Steffens knew intimately—Rudolph Spreckels, who had cleaned up the city gas company after buying control for two cents a proxy vote; Hiram Johnson, who cashed in politically on the affair to become a reform governor of the state and a

United States senator; and William J. Burns, who was to become the head of a great national detective agency when those he had helped to prosecute realized his value and became his clients. The corruption in San Francisco was one of the worst in American history. So many were involved that none were convicted, except the merest representation of scapegoats. Not the worst of the revelations was that the attention of the city had been deliberately diverted from the investigations by the head of the transit company, Patrick Calhoun, who had bribed the leaders of his employees' union to call and direct a bloody class-war strike against him.

Steffens was then beginning to formulate his theory of inevitable corruption, and he wanted to find out whether the clergy, businessmen, lawyers, and other good people of Los Angeles had advanced in their political education. He found they had not. Some actually believed that Los Angeles was a virtuous city. Steffens told them that the only difference between it and San Francisco was that San Francisco had been caught. But San Francisco had a labor government, they protested; of course it was corrupt. Steffens reminded them that the "labor" government was financed by business, which found it more useful than an open business government. They continued to shift the blame until Steffens proposed that the important people of the city allow him to speak to them in assembly. They agreed—as he said: "They would have a little dinner and eat me up."

Steffens was not eaten. He began his lecture by saying that he once thought as they did, that bad men caused bad government. But he had met many crooked politicians and found them to be pretty good fellows. They in turn blamed the businessmen, but Steffens had met them, too, and found them to be pretty good fellows also. And so on.

But the ever-recurring question that night was Who? Who is to be blamed and—punished? And at last, the Episcopal bishop of that diocese stated it in a form that suggested an answer. I was emphasizing the point that society really offers a prize for evil-doing: money, position, power, "Let's take down the offer of a reward," I said. "Let's abolish—privileges."

The bishop rose and very kindly, very courteously said that I was not meeting the minds of my hearers. "What we want to know," he said, "is who founded this system, who started it, not only in San Francisco and Los Angeles, in this or the last generation, but back, 'way back, in the beginning."

"Oh, I think I see," I said. "You want to fix the fault at the very start of things. Maybe we can, Bishop. Most people, you know, say it was Adam. But Adam, you remember, he said that it was Eve, the woman; she did it. And Eve said no, no, it wasn't she; it was the serpent. And that's where you clergy have stuck ever since. You blame the serpent, Satan. Now I come and I am trying to show you that it was, it is, the apple."

Anthropologists have traced the pursuit of the apple back through the labyrinth of social evolution to the time when man was not yet Man. For all man's million-year history, from the time he was a man-ape killing baboons in South African cave shelters until he evolved into an atomic physicist, man has always put his greatest energy into making implements of predation, the better to rob his fellows with.

Acquisitiveness has taken many forms in its long evolution, but it has left no fossils; every species still exists. On the earliest level, acquisitiveness is territoriality. Clarence Ray Carpenter took a colony of rhesus monkeys to an island in the Panama Canal and turned them loose in their brave new world. Within a short time, they had established tribes and tribal regions bound by invisible, but no less real, borders. Carpenter found also that the tribes were not always at peace; when one group produced a male of great dominance, it expanded politically, with much the same consequences that history has shown for human societies. The same sort of territoriality has been discovered among other primates—howler monkeys, red spider monkeys, orangutans, gibbons, baboons. And not only among primates, but among lesser animals as well; the birds that sing in the spring are warbling assertions of ownership, not love.

This ancient form of acquisitiveness has not weakened as other forms developed out of it. For human beings, territoriality is a cultural universal. The only significant exceptions are the Jews and the gypsies, and the Jews are not thought to be overly pleased with their homeless state. The most propertyless people on earth, the Australian aborigines, are bound by every force within their culture to hold and to remain within their horde boundaries, so that, even when one horde dies out, another does not take its land, at least not until their mythology has had sufficient time to construct a religious charter for its possession, something that does not happen overnight.

The fact that many primitive peoples hold land in common has been noticed by proponents of sophisticated socio-economic philosophies. The Communists maintain that community of property, by virtue of its antiquity, is the natural state of things, and therefore capitalism is decadent. The capitalists maintain that community of ownership, by virtue of its primitiveness, is an unnatural state of things, and therefore communism is an evolutionary reversion. Assuming the validity of the premise, the capitalists are probably right, but the question is begged. Where primitives hold land in common, it is because they cannot do otherwise. In a hunting and gathering society, a man cannot be assigned a few square feet at the corner of a parking lot to have and to hold any food that intrudes upon his property. The primitive view of land ownership differs from ours, moreover, in that only the usufruct is recognized at the hunting-gathering level. One social division, and none other, is entitled to the use of the land for exploitation. Though it is sometimes customary for a group that holds hunting rights to land to permit a visiting horde to gather vegetable foods upon it, the concept of ownership as we know it is as alien to their thinking as it was to that of Henry George. This confusion of proprietary concepts in land led to much of the trouble between the whites and the Indians in early American history, generally to the disadvantage of the Indians. But not always. When the Indians sold Manhattan Island to Peter Minuit for $24, they swindled the Dutchman, because they did not recognize any absolute rights to real estate. Moreover, they were Indians from Canarsie, just visiting Manhattan for the day.

As we shall see, as soon as a society can abandon community of ownership for private property, it does so.

Probably the next step in the evolution of acquisitiveness is the concept of the ownership of chattels; some zoologists say that mother love, exhibited in most of the mammals, is just a rudimentary form of the ownership drive. Certainly the proprietary concept is quickly and eagerly learned by some animals. The dog has thoroughly absorbed the proprietary inclinations of man, says Alexander Goldenweiser. "When it comes to the master's property, which in a sense is *his* property, the dog is an unmitigated egotist and an incurable snob. Man himself, with the possible exception of the landed proprietor, seldom equals in virulence of his proprietary sense the corresponding behavior of the watchdog." What man has taught the dog to do is to conceptualize its ancient relationship to the bone.

At the Institute of Human Relations at Yale, a device called the Chimpomat was introduced. Resembling the Automat of eastern American cities, in which at one time in economic history a person could insert a nickel and obtain automatically a piece of pie, the Chimpomat dispensed bananas, which are coveted by chimpanzees the way Americans are said to covet dollars. Refinements of the Chimpomat provided various kinds (denominations) of coins and a selection of foods. The chimps quickly learned the absolute and comparative value of the coins which the banker dispensed to them at the beginning of the game, and surprisingly learned also the supposedly exclusively human and characteristically Amercan trait known as deferred gratification. They saved their coins against a hungry future. The situation became more human and more ridiculous, until a visitor to the acquisitive chimpanzees could see them silent in their cage, each sitting covetously huddled over his coins, furtively watching the others and their hoards. When one chimp had to leave the room, another stole his money.

The chimpanzees learned still another lesson in what it means to be human, when the Chimpomat was removed: that society giveth and society taketh away. There is no "exclusive right of use," as the judiciary defines property. Property is the creation of society—or culture—which retains all rights. Jeremy Bentham extended this truth in blowing away the vaporings of John Stuart Mill on his Natural Rights of Man. "Rights of man, nonsense," said Bentham; "absolute rights of man, nonsense on stilts." Mill and Jefferson and other idealists were deluded by the fact that society seldom abrogates the illusion of property rights, since this illusion is extremely useful to make man do the things best for all concerned. Culture evolves by augmentation, and the object of man's acquistiveness is augmentation; them as has, gits. For Americans especially, it is easy to be overcome by the illusion of permanence of ownership, since this is the basis of the American system. After the complex of status and prestige, which is a further development of the acquisitive sense, the concept of permanence of ownership is the most important force among us, even stronger now than the love of life. In the last war, young men were taken away from their parents and some of them were killed. The parents grieved, but did not protest—but what do you suppose would have been their reaction, had the government exercised its equal right to take away their property?

TRADE IN THE PRIMITIVE WORLD

Perhaps the most common misconception in the folklore of capitalism is that trade did not begin until agriculture and its conse-

quent civilization gave man something to sell. Archaeology is daily
revealing amazing networks of trade routes in the prehistoric
world: in Paleolithic Europe, sea shells were traded from the
Mediterranean; amber from the Baltic was traded to Egypt for
faience beads; sealskins were traded between the troglodytes of
Spain and France; a unique kind of flint from Grand-Pressigny
penetrated much of Neolithic Europe; obsidian from Yellowstone
Park reached many distant Indian tribes; Cyprian copper carried
the Bronze Age to northern Europe; Ulster axes radiated out over
most of Europe; Cornish tin was exported to the Mediterranean
while the Celts and Picts were still fighting for England. In these
distant times, nothing so united mankind as the impulse to give
one thing for another, and common to all in this most human of
all activities down to the present is the unquenchable delusion in
the mind of every tradesman that he got the better of the other
fellow. Very often both were cheated, as in the case of a used-car
dealer trading with a real-estate mover. Primitive peoples carried
on a lively exchange of homemade weapons; not many warriors
had confidence in something they had made themselves. A native
at one end of a trading route would send off a weapon he would
be afraid to use against a jackrabbit, and receive in return an
implement of similar quality from another man with an equal
sense of inferiority. Value is the most illusory factor in economic
exchange. In an absolute way no economic act is perfectly equal,
for difference *ipso facto* means inequality. And to paraphrase
Ruskin, the value of a dollar in my pocket depends entirely on
the absence of a dollar in your pocket, and this holds true whether
the trader wears a gray flannel suit or no trousers at all.

A curious feature of trade in all periods of history and all levels
of culture is that the function of an artifact is determined almost
as much by the really irrelevant factor of the use of the article
generally traded for it as by the artifact's intrinsic purpose. Thus,
the *didgeridu*, the drone pipe trumpet of the Arnhem Landers,
was traded nearly a thousand miles south to the Aranda people,

who in turn traded boomerangs north—which were used by the northern tribes only as musical instruments (tapping sticks).

Judging by the slanders heaped upon our innocent heads by the rest of the world, one would think that Americans invented the middleman, the fellow who squeezes the excess value out of an object as it passes from the horny hands that make it to the grubby hands that buy it, but as is the case with everything else American, we have just improved on an idea that was old long before the New World was discovered. The Yir Yoront tribe of the northern Cape York Peninsula in Australia at the coming of white man vested all material wealth in stone axheads, which meant immeasurably more to them than something to chop trees with, as we will see in a few moments. Yir Yoront country is stoneless alluvial land, so the Yir Yoront had to trade some 400 miles south for their axes, offering in exchange spearheads made of the barbs of the sting ray, considered by their southern rayless neighbors to be excellent anti-personnel weapons. The exchange was effected through a series of trading partners, who formed a kind of economic bucket brigade down the peninsula. In Yir Yoront country one had to give six spearheads for one stone axhead—but, at the quarries to the south, one had to trade six axheads for one spearhead—with the middlemen taking off the viggerish of 1,200 per cent profit.

Everyone knows, too, that Americans invented commercial dishonesty, but we can find a few examples of quite delightful rascality in the primitive world. The *kula* ring involves the circle of islands off the eastern coast of New Guinea dominated by Dobu and the Trobriands. On every island and in every village, men engage in an extensive, complex, intertribal exchange of what we would call junk jewelry, mainly white shell arm bands (*mwali*) and red shell necklaces (*soulava*). *Soulava* are always traded in a clockwise direction around the ring of islands; *mwali* are always traded in a counterclockwise direction. The objects are not of equal value, for some are almost priceless heirlooms which bring their temporary owners great prestige (ownership is only temporary; the *mwali* and *soulava* must after a specified time be traded along, like a sports trophy held by the winner for one year only). Each man deals with a distant partner, but in an indirect way by means of representations (like a sample case), and always around the circle of islands in the prescribed direction. The whole affair is indescribably complicated, like the business of a stock market; all sorts of impossible promises are made, all sorts of dodgery, falsifications of the product, dishonest advertising; the traveling salesman tidies himself up as best he can, dressing in his Sunday clothes, perfuming himself, fortifying himself with commercial magic, and so forth. He does not carry his trade goods with him.

The successful Dobuan trader is one who has mastered the craft of *wabuwabu*. He visits one of the islands on his route, meets his trading friends, and says he is ready to exchange an heirloom necklace. The particular item he has for barter is famous all over the *kula* ring, and so he is able soon to move on to the next island with an armload of arm bands, having promised the necklace to the man who gave them to him. All along the circle he goes through the same ceremony, always offering the same necklace but collecting different *mwali*, and eventually he arrives back home, laden with treasures and prestige. Some time later, the men with whom he traded begin to arrive, looking for their necklace. The first man gets it; the others are met with empty hands, a shrug of the shoulders, and a philosophical remark about *caveat emptor* and the toughness of things all over. Dobuan hospitality is too uncertain for them to protest very much, so they gnash their teeth, stamp on their hats, and go off to work magic against the man who got the necklace. Our man accumulates large amounts of *mwali* and a reputation for being pretty smart. He may even run for congress, for he is a successful businessman.

Before you ask why anyone in his right mind would continue to do business with such a crook, examine your own record with regard to your television repairman. If any further elaboration of the point is needed, let us read what Charles Dickens wrote more than a century ago about the essence of American economic activity, "smart dealing," which was our term for *wabuwabu*. "The following dialogue I have held a hundred times," he recorded in his *American Notes for General Circulation*:

> "Is it not a very disgraceful circumstance that such a man as So and So should be acquiring a large property by the most infamous and odious means, and notwithstanding all the crimes of which he has been guilty, should be tolerated and abetted by your Citizens? He is a public nuisance, is he not?"
> "Yes, sir."
> "A convicted liar?"
> "Yes, sir."
> "He has been kicked, cuffed, and caned?"
> "Yes, sir."
> "And he is utterly dishonourable, debased, and profligate?"
> "Yes, sir."
> "In the name of heaven, then, what is his merit?"
> "Well, sir, he is a smart man."

In other areas of trade as well, the primitives seem to be making a travesty on our economics. Ruth Benedict used as her single example of Apollonian behavior the Zuñi Indians, one of the Pueblo group, all of whom are identified in anthropological imagination as unassuming, unaggressive, uncompetitive, unacquisitive people. The Taos Indians are also members of the Pueblo culture, but they are learning. Go down to Taos to see their remarkable pueblo; the governor, wrapped in a Sears Roebuck blanket, will approach you with his great ledger. "Will you see our pueblo?" he asks. "Yes, I'd be delighted!" "Fifty cents." With just a little disillusion, you pay the fifty cents, which transaction he records in the ledger. "Are you going to take pictures?" "Yes," you say, hesitantly. "One dollar for still camera, two dollars fifty cents for movie camera." Well, you ought to have some pictures, so you take out your still camera and pay the dollar, which, after looking about to see if any of his council members are watching, he puts in his pocket but does not enter in his ledger. You go into the village. You may see, as other visitors have done before you, a little Indian child leading a white lamb with a red ribbon around its neck; your camera goes up to catch this colorful native scene—but a fat Indian woman swarms out of the nearby house and rushes in front of the camera, her great arms waving. "Well," you think, "at last someone who does not appreciate tourist exploitation; ah! the sheer spirituality of the noble savage!" But no; all the old lady wants is ten cents for the right to photograph the child.

Nothing stops trade, not even war. Relations between the Malays and the Australian natives are as bad as one could imagine, and traditionally always have been so; yet trade has been going on between these two peoples for centuries—just as our products manage somehow to get into Red China, even though, as in the Korean War, they are used against us. While China is in mind, we might mention the infamous Opium War, begun because of frictions generated over the British introduction of opium as the only trade item that the infuriatingly self-satisfied Chinese of the early nineteenth century could be taught to covet. There is some unwelcome irony in the belief of the head of the United States Bureau of Narcotics that China is returning the favor now.

South of China, the Australian natives traded the narcotic *pituri* over most of the continent. Though the aborigines, like most primitive people, were quarrelsome rather than warlike, it was very dangerous for a man to wander out of his tribal territory, unless he were literally on business. All the world welcomes the tradesman, even if it does not love him.

Where political relations are unfriendly in the primitive world, silent barter is often carried on. Pygmies, the displaced aboriginal inhabitants of the tropical regions, live on sufferance and in bad terms with their larger, more dangerous neighbors, but trade persists, regardless of the race of the intrusive enemies. In Africa the pygmies leave game before the huts of their Negro masters at

night, and pick up ironware in return. In Malaya, the same exchange goes on between the pygmy Semang and the Mongoloid
Sakai. In Kentucky,

> Down the road not far from me there's an old hollow tree
> Where you lay down a dollar or two;
> You go round the bend and when you come back again
> You find a jug full of that good old mountain dew.

Some few primitive people have the grace to issue a warning to
those who think to do business with them. Rattray in his study
of the Ashanti describes the "proverb weights" used by gold-
smiths in their trading. Intaglio symbols are cut into the weights,
obviously affecting the honesty of their measure; but, to warn the
customer, the symbols refer to proverbs applicable in the transaction, such as: "A chief's weights are not the same as a poor
man's weights"; "The bird caught in the trap is the one to sing
sweetly"; "The beetle has fallen among the fowls"; and, most
fetching of all, "A man does not rub bottoms with porcupines."

In spite of the adumbrations of modern acquisitive techniques
among the primitives, most economic activity on the precarious
levels of human culture is so very different from our own practices
that the two systems are incompatible. The giving of food and
other necessities of life to one's relatives, real or arbitrary, to satisfy
the demands of one's social organization, exists in modern life
only in the rites of Christmas and birthday gifts, but in hunting
and gathering societies it is a continuous operation that serves
many purposes besides survival. This motivation for the exchange
of goods was perhaps strongest in aboriginal Australia, where the
kinship pattern intruded upon every activity of life. The lot of the
old people in the polar world is hard, for, when they are no longer
able to contribute to the common support, they are killed. Life is
almost as brutal in Australia, but there the system of reciprocal
obligations is used to elevate the status of old and useless men,
and, through them, the status of their aged wives. With each suc-

ceeding phase of religious initiation, a young man incurs a debt
to his older clan sponsor, a debt that is not easily amortizable, so
that, no matter how hard the initiate works, he owes his soul to
the company store. The system is quite foreign to our culture
(though, in view of the rapidly dropping status of old people in
the United States, it might be worth consideration by the senior
citizens), but it works for the aborigines, and has been interfered
with by do-gooding whites always to the natives' sorrow. A most
memorable example of the danger of imposing advanced economic
and technological concepts upon primitive people was found by
Lauriston Sharp among the Yir Yoront, the tribe mentioned
earlier as incipient capitalists.

One of the most basic things in Yir Yoront culture before the
coming of the white man was the stone axe. This was exclusively
a man's tool—only men could own one, though the women did
the work with it. Women therefore had to borrow the axe that
they used, and the borrowing had to be done according to the
regulated patterns of their social organization. A woman would ask
her husband first for an axe; if for some reason he did not lend it
to her, she went to her older brother; then her father; and so on,
in the strict channels of social relationship. The avoidance rules
of her society would prevent her from approaching her mother's
brother. Youths who had not been initiated also were forbidden
to own axes; they also had to borrow in a prescribed order from
other male relatives, and they also had to avoid certain men, such
as their mother's mother's brother's son (potential father-in-law).
The stone axe thus became a working symbol of the Yir Yoront
structure of kinship behavior, a means of exercising and thereby re-
newing it daily. So well did each person know his rights and duties
that work bosses were unimaginable. There was no social equality;
everybody had his assigned place in the hierarchy. Even in the
trading line described above, there was no equality—an older man
would be considered the superior of a younger, if no other factors
determined their relationship.

Even more fundamental to Yir Yoront society than the axe was the patrilineal totemic division of clans. If, as Lauriston Sharp illustrates it, a man was named Dog-Chases-Goanna-Up-a-Tree-and-Barks-at-Him-All-Night, and had a wife with a crippled leg and a left-handed son, it was because in the mythological Dreaming there was an *alchera* ancestor named Dog-Chases-Goanna-Up-a-Tree-and-Barks-at-Him-All-Night, who had a wife with a crippled leg and a left-handed son. Everything that the Yir Yoront had or the Yir Yoront were, had its origin in the Dreaming. Conversely, the Yir Yoront have no canoes, although their neighbors have canoes and the principle of the canoe is well known to them, because there is no warrant in their mythology for canoes; therefore, the Yir Yoront must paddle across rivers while clinging to logs.

Then came the steel axe.

Missionaries antagonize most anthropologists by their destruction of all the things primitive people live by. In this respect, however, the Anglican mission that established a post just outside Yir Yoront country in 1915 was nearly unique. The mission kept from the Yir Yoront almost everything in the way of material culture that the white man possessed, and, without a material lure to draw the aborigines to the mission station, not very much of the European immaterial culture infiltrated. But of the few things permitted to the natives, one item, the steel axe, destroyed the tribe.

There was almost no technological change, for the axe was not used for any new activity, and although it performed the old tasks more efficiently, the advantage was not sufficient to make any marked advance in the material culture of the Yir Yoront. But the sociological changes which it worked were catastrophic. Immediately the trading line broke down, and with it the socially-cohesive trade meetings and festivals. At the same time the intricate pattern of intratribal borrowing collapsed, and with it the system of social relationships. No longer was the stone axe the symbol of masculine superiority; a woman could own an axe by simply hanging around the mission station until axes were passed out. Axes would also go to the fawning, expedient men who had been unable to make a way for themselves under the old system but whose toadying subservience endeared them to the missionaries, who called them "good blackfellows" (naturally their tribe called them "bad blackfellows"). Even worse, a man might now prostitute his wife to strangers for steel axes. To get the new tools, men began to frequent the mission and work in gangs for the missionaries, who, in their ignorance of Yir Yoront ways, appointed bosses to direct the labor. The old system of independence was replaced by the soul-destroying leader-group relationship of the white man. Religiously also, the steel axe was disastrous. Theoretically, anything that the Yir Yoront did not have, they could not have because there was no accounting for it in the mythology. But the people obviously had the steel axe, so religious doubt began to stir in the minds of the Yir Yoront, and it was not long before the mythology and the religion crumbled altogether. This was the end. As Sharp sums it up:

> Without the support of a system of ideas well devised to provide cultural stability in a stable environment but admittedly too rigid for the new realities pressing in from outside, native behavior and native sentiments and values are simply dead. Apathy reigns. The aboriginal has passed beyond the reach of any outsider who might wish to do him good or ill.

Sharp records an ironic epilogue: while living at the mission station, he discovered that his toothpaste was vanishing mysteriously. He investigated, and found that the old men, whom missionaries ignore, were stealing it for use in a new toothpaste cult— the old materials of magic having failed, they pathetically were trying to regain some of their lost power and prestige through the mystic substance of the white man.

A recent case, to the shame of white Australia in its relations with the native peoples, is that of Albert Namatjira, the most famous and accomplished aboriginal in the history of the country. Albert, one of a group of partly tribalized natives cadging off the Hermannsburg Mission in the Aranda country west of Alice Springs, learned watercolor painting in the late thirties from the well-known Australian artist Rex Battarbee. Soon he had surpassed his teacher in skill and was selling extraordinarily fine landscapes of his tribal homeland for hundreds of pounds. When some of this money trickled through the mission to Albert, the pastors were dismayed to see that he "squandered" it, and precautions were taken to discourage his tendency to lapse from the Christian economic virtues of thrift and providence. Albert was forced into providence by his pastor, who deplored what he called Albert's "spenditis"; Albert could not, as he had done previously, support his numerous relatives. These relatives were "bludgers" to the missionaries, who, after nearly three quarters of a century of close acquaintance with the Aranda, evidently did not understand that in preventing Namatjira from fulfilling his rights and duties to his kinship group they were putting him, in the opinion of himself and of his people, precisely in the position of a man in our culture who would not support his wife and children. For this and other, simpler reasons, Albert took to drink; but in spite of this vice, his eminence as a painter earned him citizenship, not granted to many aborigines. This meant that he could buy liquor. Surreptitiously he gave his relatives a drink, as traditional white hospitality and Aranda social obligations require him to do. He was arrested for supplying liquor to the aborigines and sentenced to six months' imprisonment. Three months after his probationary release, this greatest of all Australian natives died in a tin-and-canvas shack on the banks of the Finke River; his body was sent to his fathers with appropriate Christian rites and expressions of *de mortuis nil nisi bonum*, which was nice.

Modern economics, with all its paradoxical characteristics of acquisitiveness and thrift and charity and providence and *laissez faire* and government subsidies, is the basis of the greatest civilization the world has ever had, but it is difficult to live in unless one is oneself the product of the same long evolution from Yir Yoront exchange to American enterprise. Primitive people cannot be thrust into it naked.

ANCIENT ORIGINS OF THE ACQUISITIVE SOCIETY

For at least ninety-five per cent of human prehistory it was man's way to live literally from day to day on what he could take from nature—without houses or clothing or other possessions beyond what he could carry without interfering with his hunting ability; without chiefs or government, or priests, or taxes, or enough children to guarantee him a secure middle age. Then for some people came the discovery of agriculture—how, no one tries seriously to determine any longer. Often this was a dead-end agriculture, the primitive kind called *milpa*, or *Brandwirtschaft*, or "slash-and-burn," which provided some security but no real surplus, as these "farmers" moved into an area, burned off the trees and brush, and worked the land until, in three or four years, soil exhaustion drove them on to fresh woods and pastures new. For these people life did not change appreciably; their evolution was arrested on a safe but uncomfortable ledge on the mountain of culture.

In the direct history of our own acquisitive society, true agriculture was discovered somewhere near the Biblical Garden of Eden about ten thousand years ago, though the oldest settlement yet found is the town of Jericho on the north shore of the Dead Sea, the oldest continuously occupied town on earth. This agriculture was sedentary, based upon cereal crops. Man could now stay in one place, and the great changes began.

He already had a dog, which as a scavenger was lured to his side and under his feet by being thrown morsels. As a *milpa* farmer, man picked up the pig and other sedentary scavenging animals. As a sedentary farmer, he acquired cattle.

The first true farmers acquired other things as well. First, children. Hunting peoples limit their progeny by sex tabus, contraception, abortion, and infanticide, for a woman cannot continue the inescapable duties of subsistence with more than one child in her arms. But, on a farm, even the smallest child can be put to work. Property in the form of houses, storage chambers, barns, tools, and furniture; social organization of a higher type than the clan, evolving to hereditary chieftains through classes and castes; chattel possessions, priesthoods and temples; specialization of labor; craftsmen and artists; and, perhaps most important, writing, which began as a means of keeping tax accounts in the temples of Mesopotamia—all these quickly follow the discovery of cereal agriculture. About this time man discovers that his domesticated animals are gregarious creatures who follow a leader, and, extending this discovery to himself, man invents slavery. His children grow up and take land of their own, usually most conveniently in their own country, but also inevitably, in the country of their neighbors. So begin theft and true war and conquest and exploitation and the acquisitive society.

THE ACQUISITIVE SOCIETY IN THE DARK AGES

The history of acquisitive societies holds nothing more difficult to explain than how the Western world achieved its unparalleled ascendancy despite the handicap of a thousand years and more of utter stagnation, a millennium of total cessation of its economic evolution. Christianity contributed nothing at all to the effort. Its great men poured their genius into spiritual channels, accumulating vast reservoirs of barren learning that still threaten to drown the fruition of materialistic economy. The holiest of the philosophers, the ascetics, demonstrated with overweening pride their contempt for the world and its possessions by living on the tops of columns, in narrow boxes, or immured in walls. In the Middle Ages the spark of acquisitiveness was kept alive by the great lords—almost by accident, since, like the clergy, with whom they shared the spiritual and secular oppression of the culture, they were not engaged in economic activity. In fact, the credit for preserving the small flame of acquisitiveness should go to the institution of war, for war, and war alone, was the proper occupation of a secular lord, and it cost money to fight great and useless battles. So, as Seignobos in his classic study, *The Feudal Regime*, quotes a protesting peasant of Normandy:

Tenants must fetch stone, mix mortar, serve the masons. Toward the last of June, they must mow and turn hay and draw it to the manorhouse. In August they must reap the convent's grain, put it in sheaves, and draw it in. For their tenure they owe the champart; they cannot remove their sheaves until they have been to see the assessor of the champart, who deducts his due, and they must cart his part to the champart barn; during this time their own grain remains exposed to the wind and rain. On the eighth of September the villein owes his pork-due, one pig in eight. . . . On the ninth of October he pays the *cens*. At Christmas he owes his chicken-due; also the grain-due of two setiers of barley and a quart of wheat. On Palm Sunday he owes his sheep-due and if he does not pay it on the day set the seigneur fines him arbitrarily. At Easter he owes corvée; by way of corvée he must plow, sow, and harrow. If the villein sells his land, he owes the seigneur the thirteenth part of the value. If he marries his daughter to anyone outside the seigneury, he must pay a marriage right. . . . He is subject to the mill-ban, and the oven-ban. . . .

The peasant complained about other assessments: the *taille*, *redevances* or charges on circulation (movement through or off the domain), bridges, roads, rivers, ports, sale of wheat, salt, meat, merchandise; taxes on fairs and markets, and so forth; *banalities* (monopolies); rights of justices; *pretestations* (irregular charges and services, of which the most frequent was the right of entertainment of the lord at any peasant house—the sort of thing which set the scene in *Amahl and the Night Visitors*, but which could be disastrous to a peasant); and the poll tax, or *capitation*—poll meaning head, not voting franchise, which was unknown.

Employers generally had not more than one employee, which severely restricted their exploitation of the working class. There were few free entrepreneurs, such as financiers or tradesmen on a large scale, to help the seigneur preserve exploitation in the Dark Ages, and it is seldom that one is heartened by the discovery that some traditions of acquisitiveness survived this period. One such is found in John Arderne's advice to "The Successful Surgeon," quoted in Ross and McLaughlin's *The Medieval Reader*:

> . . . if he sees that the patient eagerly pursues the cure, then according to the status of the patient let him ask boldly more or less; but always let him be wary of asking too little, for asking too little sets at naught both the market and the thing. Therefore, for the cure of *fistula in ano*, when it is curable, let him ask sufficiently of a worthy man and a great one hundred marks, or forty pounds with robes and fees of one hundred shillings for term of life by year. Of lesser men let him ask forty pounds, or forty marks without fees. But let him take not less than one hundred shillings. For never in my life did I take less than one hundred shillings for cure of that sickness.

The physician escaped the restrictions of the Church because he was a laborer, and moreover a laborer whose work had a spiritual conclusion, usually in a literal sense, considered officially to be the sole purpose of any activity. Usury was officially defined as taking interest of any kind on the loan of money, so, in spite of the laws which excluded them from England and other European countries, Jews had to be imported to carry on this necessary function.

Richard Henry Tawney, in his great history of this critical era, *Religion and the Rise of Capitalism*, describes Europe in the early Middle Ages as a circle, closed at the Mediterranean by ignorance.

"Tapping the resources of the East by way of the narrow apertures in the Levant, it resembled in the rigidity of the limits imposed on its commercial strategy, a giant fed through the chinks
of a wall." By the fifteenth century, the pressure inside the closed
sphere of Europe had become intolerable. Just as man now is
making his first attempts to break out of the closed sphere of the
earth itself, so medieval man made his first efforts at economic
release by means of the great voyages of discovery.

But the real escape was not to come so logically through the
navigators. It was the hand of religion that held down the safety
valve, and it was the hand of religion that had to be blown off.

THE PURITANS

Edmund Burke was to say much later, of another irrepressible
movement: "If a great change is to be made in human affairs, the
minds of men will be fitted to it; the general opinions and feelings will draw that way." But when great changes have to be
made, the minds of men make the changes tolerable by boundless
self-delusion. The Reformers thought that their revolt against the
Church was a religious rebellion—indeed, not a rebellion at all,
but a reformation in the mildest sense of the word. Luther wanted
to move the Church backward to the old virtues, not forward to
the new vices. He wanted to rid it of avariciousness. He was a
tropismatic reactionary who said that the protesting peasants
should be cut down by the bloody civil sword; he urged a curb on
the Fuggers, the Rothschilds of his time, to whom most of the
great men of Europe, from king to Pope, were in debt; and he
opposed the Pope himself because the Pope had given his tacit
sanction to the traffic in monetary interest. And yet, by taking
power from the corrupt Church to deliver it to what he naïvely
thought was the virtuous state, Luther accomplished quite the
opposite of what he intended. He freed the mind and hands of
medieval man, but in the process he destroyed Christianity.

Luther was too inflexible to conduct the inevitable changes, and so the leadership of the Reformation went to John Calvin. In Tawney's words: "Calvin did for the bourgeoisie of the sixteenth century what Marx did for the proletariat of the nineteenth," though he intended that consummation no more than Luther. Like that other great religious reformer (Marx) who lived to say: "I am not a Marxist," Calvin could have turned on his followers and perverters with the declaration: "I am not a Calvinist." He was not, however, adamantly opposed to the economic changes that were pushing through the door he had opened in religion, since a philosophy built upon the idea of predestination must believe that whatever is, is right; all Calvin seemed to demand was that economic activity, like other activities, must come under the purview of his theocracy. In Calvin, no more than in any other great man, was there consistency, but in Calvin's paradoxes one can now see, as he did not, the forces that were impelling him. He burned heretics in Geneva, yet his religion fragmented into hundreds of heretical sects; he beheaded disobedient children, yet the rebelliousness of his philosophy spawned centuries of dissidents; he dealt, as a contemporary English churchman said of him, "with usurie as the apothecarie doth with poyson," yet Calvinism produced the most successfully acquisitive people history was ever to know—the Puritans and their descendants.

From the straining by restrained trading classes of the cities, and from the country towns disrupted by encroaching industrialism, rose the Puritans, or "Unspottyd Lambes of the Lorde," as they liked to call themselves. It was obvious to these people that a system that suppressed competence and virtue was corrupt. No one knew any economics in the sixteenth century—there were no words for such a concept until after the American Revolution— so the Puritans thought and acted within religion, believing with all their minds that theirs was a religious protest. After suffering for years under oppressive restrictions, they came out into the open in 1588 with the Marprelate Tracts, addressed to the "proud,

Popish, presumptuous, profane, paultrie, pestilent, and pernicious prelates," demanding the separation of the state from *their* church. There was no historical precedent for their democratic views—society and religion having been ordered throughout the history of England in a rigid hierarchy—and no genealogical justification for their existence—they were all from the nameless classes. They had to find authority for both from some other source, and Calvinism gave them what they needed in its philosophy of predestination. According to Calvinism, God had arbitrarily chosen some people to be blessed and others to be damned, not through any deed or fault of the people themselves, but just because He wanted it that way. But how was one to know whether one was Elect or Reprobate? The Quakers said that such knowledge came through the heavenly suffusion of an Inner Light, and for this blasphemous nonsense the Puritans cut off Quaker ears. It stood to reason that those whom God had favored with a future in heaven would prosper on earth, and they would be successful in their earthly work—or as successful as the corrupt Church would permit them to be. The orientation of the Puritans to the world, as Tawney said, was in the second verse of the 39th chapter of Genesis, in their Bible as translated by the martyr William Tyndale: *And the Lorde was with Joseph, and he was a luckie felowe.* Conversely, the poor were damned, and the saints would fly in the face of God by helping them. Well through the nineteenth century, visitors to America noticed that the streets were singularly free of the sturdy beggars that infested the thoroughfares of Europe. And today no virtue is so conspicuously lacking in the American character as charity, though we long after it pathetically. Only the most unfeeling American can read the fifteenth chapter of *The Grapes of Wrath* without tears welling in his eyes for his lost charity.

With the accession of the Scot, James the First, to the English throne, the Puritans expected the elevation of the righteous and the overthrow of the damned. But James was having none of that.

"Presbytery," he said, "accords as much with monarchy as God with the Devil. I'll make them conform, or I'll harry them out of the land."

The radical Puritans, the Separatists, were harried out of the land to Holland, there to become, in the words of the orthodox, "Amsterdamnified." But it was to Leyden that the group who were to be our Pilgrims took their trade and their religion. At Leyden they lived with increasing restlessness for more than a decade, suffering the harassment of the Dutch Reformed Church, the discrimination of the Dutch tradesmen, and the sight of their children's growing indifference to their "pure and stainless religion."

At Leyden they were approached by one Thomas Weston, representative of seventy Merchant Adventurers, who had a proposition for the Puritan colony. His company would send them to the New World and provide them with the necessities of settlement in return for their group indenture for seven years. John Smith, in his *Generall Historie of Virginia*, estimates that Weston's adventurers advanced £7000, an enormous sum in those days, and eventually, after many discouragements, the former wine transport *Mayflower* landed its passengers in America.

As James Truslow Adams put it, the backers of the Pilgrimage had invested a lot of money into a distinctly unpromising commercial venture, not into a subscription for foreign missions. The Puritans thought otherwise; in fact, they began with a fine set of convenient misconceptions. They set up a civil government before they left the ship—a memorable precedent for the business government America was to become. They also conceived the strange idea that they were to work two days a week for their own profit, though the practice of emigration in the seventeenth century was that anyone who borrowed money to leave for "Virginia" bound himself over as a completely owned indentured servant for seven years. Moreover, they sent nothing back on the first ships to their sponsors, and Weston complained in a letter to them: "That you sent no lading in the ship is wonderful and worthily distasted. I know your weakness was the cause of this, and I believe more weakness of judgment than weakness of hands. A quarter of the time you spent in discoursing, arguing, and consulting would have done much more. . . ." The Pilgrims finally loaded the *Fortune* with beaver and otter skins and clapboard and sent it on its way—into the hands of a French warship, which captured it and its cargo. Weston, having received nothing for his investment, let the Pilgrims know that no more provisions would be sent until some return was made. This, remarked Governor Bradford in his *Journal*, was "cold comfort to fill their hungry bellies."

Meanwhile back in England Archbishop Laud set up a genuine persecution of the troublechurch non-Separatist Puritans, and in 1629 they began a mass migration to the Massachusetts colony, again under the guise of a commercial venture. These were a rather tougher bunch than the gentle Plymouth folk, and they set about immediately by perverting their commercial charter into the instrument for a totalitarian theocracy. They believed in tolerance, as American folklore tells us, and so they did in fact, but of a peculiar Puritan kind. Nathaniel Ward, the "simple cobler of Aggawamm," wrote in 1647:

I dare take upon me, to be the Herauld of *New-England* so farre, as to proclaim to the world, in the name of our Colony, that all Familists, Anti-nomians, Anabaptists, and other Enthusiasts shall have free Liberty—to keep away from us.

They also instructed the Plymouth Pilgrims to keep away from their trapping territory on the Kennebec, and when they did not, violence and the death of one Hocking followed. The Massachusetts Bay people were distressed at this killing, not so much for the unfortunate Hocking, but because of the possible consequences—that England would send over a royal governor (which it eventually did, after a half century of provocation)—and because, as Governor Winthrop recorded his concern in his *Journal*, the act "had brought us all and the gospel under a common reproach of cutting one another's throats for beaver."

But the colonies survived the Hocking incident and business went on as usual. By this time the Puritan theologians had incorporated economic activity solidly within the religious framework in treatises like *Husbandry Spiritualized, The Religious Weaver, Navigation Spiritualized,* and the important book by Baxter, *Christian Directory, or a Summ of Practical Theologie and Cases of Conscience.* They might have written also a manual on Slavery Spiritualized, for slaves, both Indian and Negro, were regular items in Puritan bills of lading. Slavery was not profitable in New England itself (except at Narragansett, where it was well established), though some fortunate individuals owned personal slaves. Cotton Mather publicly attributed his acquisition of a Negro slave to the favor of Providence. Even Samuel Sewall, who wrote the first American tract against slavery, had an otherwise undescribed servant named Scipio, a name not common among Caucasoid Englishmen. There were slaves of their own color, too; the children of two banished Quakers, Daniel and Provided Sothwick, were ordered sold into slavery in Virginia.

But a product is after all a product, and, what with one thing and another, the Puritans steadily prospered in worldly things while their religion steadily declined. When the revocation of their charter became imminent, the Puritan divines gloomily admitted that "God hath spit in our faces"—which, if such a thing were possible, would certainly be probable. As the Bible prophesied, the evening drew nigh and the wolves were loose upon the world, and the Puritan theocracy died valiantly fighting the witches in Salem Village. Before the end, the ministers desperately exhorted their people to remain steadfast. Thomas Wertenbaker in *The Puritan Oligarchy* recalls the churchman who journeyed from Boston to a reprobate fishing village. Assembling the congregation, he reminded them that the main end of their coming to America was to build a new Jerusalem. One of the men in the democratic assembly rose and shouted: "Sir, you are mistaken; our main end was to catch fish." And so it was.

THE ACQUISITIVE COLONY BECOMES
AN ACQUISITIVE NATION

Just as the Puritans in sixteenth-century England couched their economic reformation in religious language for want of economic terminology, so the Americans of the late eighteenth century couched their economic revolution in political terms. It was not political oppression, however, that infuriated the patriots as the Revolution began to simmer and boil, but economic repression. England's Mercantile Theory was an excellent idea, logical and fair—and was doomed, like all logical and fair concepts. Implemented by the Navigation Acts, it organized all parts of the Empire into a co-operative community, each part of which helped itself by helping England and the others. The East Indies produced spices and tea; the West Indies supplied sugar; Africa contributed the labor; Virginia and Maryland grew tobacco, the product that England was using to push her influence into the farthest East. From each according to his ability, and to each the protection of England. Private planters who began growing tobacco in England were forced with bayonets to put their energies into more legitimate enterprise. But poor New England had nothing of its own to give, so it went into the business of business —on its own hook. An epitome of early American commercial behavior is the Boston Tea Party, immortalized in our folklore as a daring political protest, a preliminary exercise for revolution. The facts of this folklore are that at the end of the third quarter of the eighteenth century the East India Company was in precarious financial straits because of the competition of the Dutch smugglers. Faithful to her responsibilities under the Mercantile Theory, England assisted the faltering company with a huge subsidy of more than £4,000,000. The East India Company was able to cut its prices in half and cut the market from under the Dutch. The objection from the point of view of the American merchants, as the cheap tea moved toward the American consumer, was that the American merchants were part of the smuggling ring. So, under the cover of resisting a purely nominal tax, and with the blessing if not the assistance of the smuggling governor of Massachusetts, the Americans boarded a ship of the East India Company in the immemorial year of 1773 and threw £100,000 worth of competing tea into the bay and the fat into the fire.

The commercial background of the making of the American nation is well known through Charles A. Beard's influential book, *An Economic Interpretation of the Constitution of the United States*, first published sixty years ago. Not so well known is the importance of Alexander Hamilton in manifesting the destiny of the United States as history's great acquisitive society. His resounding but cynical statements set the course of the new nation, but they do not find their way into elementary history books, which look for more comfortable things to remember from this gestative period, such as Washington's probity in the cherry orchard. But consider the abiding truth of these remarks of Hamilton:

That power which holds the purse strings absolutely must rule.

The only plan that can preserve the currency is one that will make it the immediate interest of the moneyed men to cooperate with the government in its support.

Every duty on imports is incorporated with the price of the commodity, [and] is ultimately paid by the consumer, with a profit on the duty itself as compensation to the merchant for the advance of his money.

A national debt if it is not excessive will be to us a national blessing. It will be a powerful cement of our union. It will also create a necessity for keeping up taxation to a degree which, without being oppressive, will be a spur to industry.

Hamilton also understood that the people were "a great beast" that had to be pampered and deluded, since it could not be coerced. Men, he contended, will always work for what they think is their best interest, and the wise politician will work upon this natural cupidity. He accordingly planned a distilling system of elections by means of which each level of representatives voted for the membership of political bodies above them, and thus purified the ultimate governors of the people of any proletarian contamination. There is still very much of Hamilton's invention in American government today.

People do not love men who give them truth, but rather men who give them illusions. Jefferson, whose ringing oratory reverberates through the heads of Americans until they cannot hear the inconsistencies and impracticality that characterize most of it, became the American hero, and Hamilton the American ogre. Not even dying young and dramatically could do much for Hamilton.

Though eighteenth-century Americans listened to Jefferson, they obeyed Hamilton, as the testimony of nearly every foreign traveler shows. Mrs. Frances Trollope, whose distaste for American acquisitiveness permeated her *Domestic Manners of the Americans* to such a degree that its publication was delayed in England until the work could be used as propaganda against the Reform Bill of 1832, relates, among similar stories, her conversation with a young capitalist in the fowl business. The boy, identified as Nick perhaps because of his satanic ancestor, made rather a good thing out of his chickens.

"And do you give the money to your mother?"
"I expect not," was the answer with another sharp glance of his ugly blue eyes.
"What do you do with it, Nick?"

His look said plainly, What is that to you? but he only answered, quaintly enough, "I takes care of it."

Probably Nick will be very rich; perhaps he will be President.

Captain Frederick Marryat, who came to the United States in 1837 for the purpose of correcting jaundiced appraisals of America such as those of Mrs. Trollope and Miss Martineau, was finally constrained to agree with them, but his observations are ameliorated by his fine sense of humor. He writes in his *Diary in America*:

> I was amused by a reply given me by an American in office here. I asked him how much his office was worth, and his answer was $600, besides *stealings*. This was, at all events, frank and honest; in England the word would have been softened down to "perquisites."

He was intrigued by the genius of Americans in commercial enterprise, even when they had no money. He admired the two ladies he saw swapping hats, and, as he says:

> I heard of an American who had two sons, and he declared that they were so clever at barter that he locked them both up together in a room without a cent in their pockets, and that before they had swopped for an hour, they each had gained two dollars apiece.

Marryat's book is not given the attention that de Tocqueville's *Democracy in America* receives, though, beneath its humor, it is a wiser and less erroneous analysis of American civilization. Marryat, for instance, excused the Americans' incessant pursuit of the dollar on the grounds that, since status is the great force in social effort, and since, in a democracy where everyone wants equality unless he has it, titles and other non-monetary honorifics are absent as goals for the ambitious man, he has nothing left but to make his way in the world through the accumulation of money.

This question of status-seeking, since it has been so influentially criticized by Vance Packard in *The Status Seekers*, as if it were another pernicious American invention, warrants an anthropological digression.

The most important thing to man as a social animal is prestige. Though the twentieth-century American is supposed to revere wealth above all other possessions, wealth is merely a means to the achievement of prestige. And power, which some others desire above money, is merely the result of prestige. Conversely, deprivation of prestige is the thing most feared by man as a social animal. In primitive societies there are no penal institutions for the punishment of criminals—those who violate the proper patterns of behavior. What usually happens is that the culprit is deprived of prestige, and this is often tantamount to a death sentence. In some societies, both civilized and primitive (for example, the Japanese and the Shilluk of the Anglo-Egyptian Sudan), a publicly ridiculed man commits suicide. The calypso, now an entertainment, was one of many examples in primitive and folk societies of the song of ridicule, whose record of ensuring good conduct is a good deal better than our houses of correction.

Prestige is status, and status is the prime mover of human society everywhere. On the primitive level, like other things in the early stages of cultural evolution, status-seeking is poorly developed. Its real development began with the "predatory barbarian economy" (in Lewis Henry Morgan's division of human progress) of sedentary agriculture, whose analysis Thorstein Veblen made into one of the great books of economic scholarship, *The Theory of The Leisure Class*.

Veblen's felicitous phrases "Conspicuous Consumption," "Conspicuous Leisure," "Vicarious Consumption of Goods," and others, and his shrewd differentiation between Industry and Exploit were ostensibly devised to show the workings of society as it moved from savagery to barbarism, but they describe his own time so well that no one ever supposed that he was talking about any other.

The nineteenth century in America was, as many books have described it, the age of the savagely leisure class—except that they were too frantically busy most of their lives to put the devoted effort into leisure that Veblen said was necessary. There was Uncle Dan'l Drew, who made his first fortune feeding salt to his cattle on their way to New York, so that each had several hundred pounds of water aboard when it got on the scales. Later Uncle Dan'l adapted the same technique to market shares, giving the language the term "watered stock." Uncle Dan'l took his only leisure in bouts in a hotel room with whiskey and the Bible. There was also Rockefeller's capable assistant, Henry H. Rogers, who began his career like so many of our economic heroes, as a newsboy, selling papers in a New England whaling town. One day as he received his newspapers he noticed an item telling of the sinking of a ship carrying the large cargo of whale oil the town was expecting. You or I would have rushed on the streets shouting: "Extra!" Not young Henry. He burned all the papers and bought up all the sperm oil in town, cornering his first market.

Similar tales of Yankee resourcefulness could be told of all the great robber barons who established the fortunes that now control the nation—Jay Gould, Jim Fisk, Cornelius Vanderbilt, John D. Rockefeller, Andrew Carnegie, Edward Henry Harriman, Jim Hill, Theodore Dehone Judah, Collis Potter Huntington, Henry Flagler, William Andrew Clark, Charlie Schwab, Andrew Mellon, the duPonts, the Guggenheims—but they have all been told too well in many books to justify retelling here. Some of the stories are not very funny—the *Crédit Mobilier*, for instance, which built the Union Pacific Railway at a hundred per cent profit through the corrupting of representatives, senators, cabinet officers, and the Vice President. The $44 million *stealings* of the *Crédit Mobilier* were nothing, really, compared to what was given outright to the railroads then pushing—uselessly, at first—across the frontier. One might think that thirty yards on either side of the tracks might be a fair average land grant to encourage the construction of a railway across the plains, but the actual average was closer to thirty miles. According to Thomas C. Cochran and William Miller in *The Age of Enterprise,* the railroads were given one fourth of Minnesota and Washington; one fifth of Wisconsin, Iowa, Kansas, North Dakota, and Montana; one seventh of Nebraska; one eighth of Califorma; and one ninth of Louisiana.

Most of the Moguls were too busy making money to talk about the philosophy of making money; this function was left to admirers on the outside, such as Horatio Alger, whose little primers of acquisitiveness sold 200 million copies. It is fashionable to laugh at Alger, but his message was only sublimated in the pragmatic philosophy of William James. Andrew Carnegie, who had other eccentric habits, did take pen in hand to write the gospel of wealth. Occasionally he drew upon the anthropology of his day to make his point:

> When visiting the Sioux, I was led to the wigwam of the chief. It was just like the others in external appearance, and even within the difference was trifling between it and those of the poorest of his braves. The contrast between the palace of the millionaire and the cottage of the laborer with us today measures the change which has come with civilization. This change, however, is not to be deplored, but welcomed as highly beneficial. . . . But whether the change be for good or ill, it is upon us, beyond our power to alter, and therefore to be accepted and made the best of. It is a waste of time to question the inevitable.

This is our thesis. It does no earthly good to whine about the inevitable or to make demands that something be done. One can only look beneath the bushel for the shining virtue that is certainly there, and make use of it—as the Japanese, the Americans of the Orient, did years ago when they invited the great social evolutionist Herbert Spencer to come and tell them how to take a short cut through the processes of the inevitable.

After a lifetime of exposing corruption in the United States and much of the rest of the world, changing his opinions and theories constantly as knowledge drove out preconceptions, Lincoln Steffens, who told us about the apple, concluded:

> If in Europe, as an outsider, I could see that there was an economic drift to merge industrial trusts into one combination of all business and that that tendency, encountering old, liberal laws passed at a time when we all believed in competition, had to corrupt its way through politics and government and become "true" government, then—it was time to go home and look again and see, and let my boy Peter grow up where he might see, that maybe—maybe bribery and corruption are acts of God, and his father and muckrakers in general the agents of the Devil.

☆ VII ☆

The

Dissident Americans

If young Timothy Root hadn't sneaked behind a barn with a dirty book one March day two hundred years ago, his name certaintly would not have entered the story of American dissent, and probably the career of one of this country's greatest philosophers would not have ended so tragically. For Timothy it was behind the barn, into church, and into history; for Jonathan Edwards it was a short while of cowering behind the protection of his patron, Colonel John Stoddard, then expulsion to the frontier, where it was devoutly hoped the Indians would get rid of him, and finally a call to Princeton to die of a smallpox inoculation while waiting to take up the presidency of the college from his son-in-law, Aaron Burr.

When the newly ordained Reverend Jonathan Edwards came

to Northampton, Massachusetts, in 1727 to inherit the ministry from his grandfather, "Pope" Solomon Stoddard, he received not only a church, but the harvest of Stoddard's expedient liberalism. It was Stoddard's thought that since there was no logic on God's part in the election or damnation of mankind and no certain way to ascertain one's destination in eternity, the church might as well be opened to all applicants, giving everybody the benefit of the celestial doubt. But Jonathan came to this backwoods parish with his mind full of the new science and the old theology, two apparently contradictory systems which he reconciled, to the bewilderment and discomfort of his congregation.

By the middle of the eighteenth century, the latter-day Puritans had managed to remove their practices a safe distance away from their ideals. Then came Edwards with his difficult sermons, bringing Locke and Newton to justify Calvin, making Puritanism into a system of empirical psychology, telling the people that their purpose on earth was not to be happy but to be blessed. He even brought the intolerable paradox of predestination into a frame of reason, arguing that, with a true love for God, man can love God for his own damnation, the unnaturalness of such a love proving its supernaturalness and accordingly its limitation to the elect. Without such a love, a man did not belong in Edwards's church. His rustic parishioners did not know what in heaven he was talking about, but they did know that he had made Calvinism once again impossible to live with.

Edwards unwittingly postponed, but made more certain, the reaction against him by drawing from Locke further support of his theology. Locke had taught that intuition was an illusion, that all knowledge was sensible, and Edwards extended this idea to say that even man's perception of salvation was sensible. Some extremely effective sermons to this point in 1734 resulted in explosive conversions. Soon the Great Awakening was on and spreading through the entire frontier. Edwards brought in from England (via the Wesleys) the most spellbinding preacher of the century,

George Whitefield, to accelerate the movement he had begun in the north. Thus the dour intellectual, the distruster of unthinking emotion, became the father of American revivalism—another in the endless series of philosophers who engendered the direct opposite of their intention. In his research into theology, Edwards should have given some attention to the medieval Church from which Calvin revolted. He would have learned the danger of enthusiasm and perhaps have saved himself. But by the time he began to suspect the excesses of revivalism, his town had been blown asunder by Ids exploding away from Superegos. His own uncle committed suicide in a religious frenzy. Resentment surged against him; and then Timothy went behind the barn.

The book that Timothy and his pubescent companions studied was a handbook for midwives known to the adults of Northampton as the "Granny Book." The study session in obstetrics was observed by another survival from the Puritan past, a "tithing man," whose duty it was to keep an eye on the behavior of his neighbors. This fellow, one Moses Lyman, reported to Edwards, who had the boys indicted before the church on a charge of moral treason. One can imagine the confrontation: a sniveling crew of shamed boys, towered over by the most fearsome of the Puritan divines, the man whose "Sinners in the Hands of an Angry God" is easily the most harrowing hell-fire sermon in the annals of Christendom. Probably never was a more awesome wrath threatened against more hapless human beings since Jehovah cursed Sodom. But Timothy Root defiantly replied with what oft was thought in Northampton but ne'er so well express'd, the defiance of tyranny that would be echoed in less forceful words a generation later by Patrick Henry. Lumping Edwards together with his holy peers and predecessors, Timothy declared: "I won't worship a wig. They are nothing but men moulded up of a little dirt. I don't care a Turd, or I don't care a Fart, for any of them!"

The significant thing here is that Edwards was the dissenter, not Timothy. Timothy was impudent, uncouth, and probably not overly bright, but he was eminently sane. One does not need to know that there was ordinary insanity in Edwards's immediate ancestry, and two psychopathic killers (one an axe murderer, the other a killer of her own child), to realize that for all his brillance Edwards was a deviate.

THE DEVIANCY OF DISSENT

Although, in the progress of culture, situations often occur which of themselves produce dissent and even revolution, the reason for protest is usually in the individual rather than in his society. He may be eccentric, or he may be quite mad, but the true dissident is a congenital misanthrope, who hides his dislike for himself and his society behind a cause to which he is only tenuously attached. Consistency is the hobgoblin of dissident minds. After the "Granny Book" trouble, Jonathan Edwards barely decided against accepting an offer for a Scottish appointment which would have required him to abandon his Congregationalism. Roger Williams, too, moved steadily along a gamut of deviancy; he was in turn a Calvinist, a Congregationalist, a Baptist, and a Seeker. Orestes Brownson was a supernaturalist, a rationalist, a Universalist, a Deist, a Unitarian, a Transcendentalist, a socialist, a free-thinker, and a Catholic, in that order; and in two of these religions he served as an ordained minister. The first man dragged from a Freedom Riders' bus and beaten had earlier been arrested on the Pacific Ocean for sailing a boat into the atomic-testing area in protest; other than protest, the only common feature of this man's dissidence was that it expressed itself in transportation. The important thing for the true dissident is that he must be Against whatever most people in the community he enters are For.

If his mania anticipates the future direction of his culture, the deviate frequently becomes a martyr. A cultural movement that is itself dissident will refurbish a quite unworthy real person or even invent one to provide a symbol around which more passive dissidents can gather. John Brown is the classic instance in American history; in recent memory there are Joe Hill, Nicola Sacco, and Bartolomeo Vanzetti. If these symbols have been well chosen for their messianic drama, the minds of their followers become blind to reality in the area of dissent. Many people who read this paragraph will be angered by the suggestion that Joe Hill and Sacco and Vanzetti actually committed the murders for which they were executed; it will not occur to these people that the facts of these cases can easily be obtained. There will even be some who have looked into these *causes célèbres* and who still believe that these martyrs were innocent victims of capitalism, though it is not unlikely that these same people ridicule Fundamentalists for believing that the whale swallowed Jonah. In such situations as these, there will also be the users of dissidence, the people who know that the martyrs as well as the martyrdoms are fictitious, but who suspend their disbelief because these men are symbols that the dissent of radicalism requires.

Though any of scores of genuine martyrs could have been chosen to be the symbol of labor heroism, Joe Hill had a necessary quality that such men as Harry Simms and Wesley Everest lacked —consummate drama, even in death. The photograph taken of Hill after he had been shot by the firing squad and the blood wiped from his chest shows him looking more like the image of Christ in the minds of Christians than any iconographer's painting. Hill was a criminal and not a true dissident, who differs from the criminal in that he openly and persistently defies society for reasons other than personal gain. But the difference is slight, for both are deviates if they are serious about their business, and culture can make either into the other if it is needful.

Like almost everything else in human behavior, dissidence is the product of culture working upon genetics. Heredity produces the eccentric; culture directs him how to express his eccentricity. Reo Fortune, in his *Sorcerers of Dobu*, describes in that paranoid society a native who commended himself to the anthropologist by his personal qualities. He was good-natured, cheerful, kind, help-ful, co-operative, altruistic, industrious, honest, trusting, and trust-worthy. Fortune liked the man, but to the normal Dobuans he was the village lunatic, and dangerous at that. The normal Dobuan had a great store of black magic which he used indiscriminately and often; had the reputation of poisoning his neighbors' chil-dren; was habitually unfaithful to his wife and magically thwarted her household labors; went berserk whenever it was unexpected; would cut his brother's throat—literally; and returned thanks—if a situation requiring an expression of gratitude could be imagined on Dobu—with the locution: "And if you now poison me, how shall I repay you this present?" On Dobu, as in the United States, the good and normal man is the one who conforms; the deviate is the nonconformist.

Human nature does not change, but culture often changes away from human nature. Today Michael Wigglesworth would be put under forcible restraint; in his own time he was not only sane, but sane to the point of dullness. Even crime, which is deviancy that immediately threatens the stability of a community, differs as time and the cultural situation change. Businessmen in modern America are so highly regarded that success in their line of work can often be exchanged directly for high political office, even though the ethics of the two professions are entirely different. The politician in whom such private enterprise would be grounds for impeachment is often the businessman who rose to eminence by successfully and illegally working for his own pocket. In 1949 E. H. Sutherland published a definitive study of *White Collar Crime* in which the police dossiers of seventy large American cor-porations were examined. He found a total of 980 convictions among them; ninety per cent were recidivists; sixty per cent had at least four criminal convictions. More recently, the Kefauver com-mittee investigating the drug industry disclosed that one thousand ethical drug manufacturers conducted a two-billion-dollar annual business by methods that would have put them away as habitual criminals if the Fourteenth Amendment, which defined business concerns as legal persons, had provided some way of putting corporations into jail.

The ethical drug manufacturers and the businessmen and the politicians may be subversive of the outmoded ideals of their society, but they do not qualify as true dissidents because they lack the deviate's characteristic irrational emotion. The genuine dissident is an eccentric. Charles Chauncy, pastor of the First Church in Boston for most of the eighteenth century, the opponent of Calvinistic fundamentalism in general and of Jonathan Edwards in particular, wrote of the deviate as a religious fanatic, as if he were a sociologist analyzing a Black Muslim:

> . . . the Enthusiast is one who has a conceit of himself as a person favored with the extraordinary presence of the Deity. He mistakes the workings of his own passions for divine communications, and fancies himself immediately inspired by the Spirit of God, when all the while, he is under no other influence than that of an overheated imagination.
>
> The cause of this enthusiasm is a bad temperament of the blood and spirits; 'tis properly a disease, a sort of madness, and there are few, perhaps none at all, but are subject to it; though none are so much in danger of it as those in whom melancholy is the prevailing ingredient in their constitution. In these it often reigns, and sometimes to so great a degree that they are really beside themselves, acting as truly by the blind impetus of a wild fancy, as though they had neither reason nor understanding.

How the "enthusiast" is treated depends on his time and his culture. In Northampton in 1744 the normal person spoke rudely to the deviate. In the early days of Christianity he would be made into a saint. In primitive cultures and in folk America he becomes the shaman, the individualistic religious practitioner, subversive of organized religion, the person of unstable personality, prone to self-hypnosis and visitation by the spirits, the healer-by-laying-on-of-hands, the speaker-in-tongues, the direct mediator between God and man, the entertainer who can literally roll them in the aisles. No civilized society on earth will put itself into the hands of its deviates, but civilized societies often make use of deviates and always provide them with the materials to express themselves. The American Psychiatric Association in 1959 agreed that, despite the notorious suffering of the wives of alcoholics, these women often married habitual drunkards knowingly, divorced them only to marry other alcoholics, and prevented their husbands from overcoming their addiction if possible; and if they failed in that endeavor, they developed psychic troubles themselves, frequently becoming alcoholics. Drug addiction is also a social phenomenon. Bingham Dai's *Opium Addiction in Chicago* showed that 61–5 per cent of opium eaters learned the habit in social situations and another 27.2 per cent became enslaved as a result of medication; only 11.3 per cent become addicted for the popularly accepted reasons. It is probable that all marihuana users came by their pleasure socially, for marihuana is not a drug, does not cause addiction, and produces effects that usually cannot be perceived without instruction.

Society can also make overt deviates by withholding interference and authority. The concept of *anomie*, introduced by Émile Durkheim a half century ago, describes a state of being in which the individual has no standards of value to guide him in either evil or virtue. The anomic person is merely futile; his life is meaningless. He has no norms of behavior for himself and cannot recognize any in others, so that he sinks into apathy and disorganization. He is prone to suicide, as are all members of social groups that do not sufficiently make their people behave. As in Orwell's world, totalitarian dictatorships make their subjects happy; democracies drive them to suicide—and dissent.

Anthropologists do not concern themselves much with deviant individuals in the primitive societies they study; such societies in their pristine state are often so well integrated and coherent that deviant individuals do not manifest themselves in any significant numbers. The really troublesome deviate may be speared, as was the unlucky boy in Tindale's motion picture of initiation surgery in Australia, or he may be ordained a shaman, in which office he can perform a necessary service to his community, but he does not ordinarily form associations of dissent, as he does in the United States.

Widespread or organized dissent is characteristic of two kinds of culture: the primitive or folk society which is breaking up in collision with advanced civilizations, and the advanced civilization that is progressing very rapidly. Homer G. Barnett has included a fine study of the first of these situations in his *Being a Palauan*, about a group of islands where a person's greeting may be in Palauan, German, Japanese, or English, depending on his age.

The United States is the outstanding example of the second type of massive deviancy—that produced by a civilization that is progressing too fast for many of its citizens. It is the belief of Thorsten Sellin that crime grows out of conflict in "conduct norms"; the individual is a member of several groups, each of which has conduct norms peculiar to itself, as for instance business and politics. Carrying Sellin's suggestion further, we might say that the more elevated the culture, the more norms and therefore the more crime—so that crime is the measure of the advancement of a civilization. Enormous cultural lags develop out of the friction of a runaway technology and an inert society, which yield as byproducts the kind of people with whom the remainder of this chapter is concerned. Life in a progressive culture can be hard on people who cannot progress with it, and the culture, as a kindly compensation, tolerates more dissent than it logically should. American culture is uniquely permissive to its dissidents— almost as if it understood that their variety and number were evidence of its superiority among nations. This is admittedly a difficult idea to accept when one must suffer the annoyances of beatniks and more conventional juvenile delinquents, associations for the advancement of retrogressive racial separation, Black Muslims and white Citizens' Councils, unions, nativistic endeavors, and a myriad of eccentrics on the extreme political right and left—the former besotted with a dead past, the latter besotted with an unborn future. But we are not alone in failing to see the real significance of dissent; so far as we know, no Russian has written an appreciation of the rise of hoodlumism in the Soviet Union, although this is one of the more hopeful signs of genuine advancement in that benighted country. We need not worry about the Soviets on this account, however; they have a long way to go before they catch up with our production of eccentrics.

A SAMPLE ASSORTMENT OF AMERICAN NUTS

Thomas Wentworth Higginson, abolitionist, woman suffragist, organizer of the first Negro regiment, first serious collector of Negro folksongs, and general advocate of dissident causes, had a quality rare in dissenters—a sense of humor. He recalls in his *Contemporaries* an abolitionist meeting presided over by Wendell Phillips, the chief orator of the abolition movement. One of the assembled dissidents was Abby Folsom, a young lady whose store of wrath was great enough to embrace both slavery and capitalism. At this meeting she chose to interrupt proceedings with a tirade against the Goulds and the Fisks and she was promptly carried out, kicking, by Wendell Phillips and another man. Higginson notes that Phillips was embarrassed because he realized that he was engaging in "the petty discrimination of putting out only the craziest."

They hustled Carry Nation inhospitably from the premises, too, but it was rather more dangerous to throw out a lady armed with a two-foot hatchet. Carry's first husband died in delirium tremens, which those who did not know Carry supposed was brought on by drink, and Carry seized upon liquor as her primary object of dissent, though she also opposed smokers ("horrid, nasty" men whose fate would be "an eternal smoking"), paintings of women

who "ain't got a thing on," corsets (which she said made "hearts
and livers into one solid lump"), and "wicked, riotous, rum-
soaked, bedeviled Republicans." The Kansas Smasher erupted
from the presidency of the Barber County Women's Christian
Temperance Union in 1900, to carry her "hatchetation" to New
York. And the weakness of the American masculine character
where women are concerned prompted men to applaud Mrs.
Nation's mania, ultimately to the point of accepting as the law
of the land the grandest dissident lunacy in history, the Eighteenth Amendment. In her own time Carry was admired by all.
Police who arrested her did so with cheers for their prisoner, and
bartenders who managed to disarm her before she liquidated their
stock, hung her beribboned hatchets over their bars as trophies.

Ronald M. Deutsch has given us a bookful of delightful eccentrics in his *Nuts Among the Berries,* beginning with "the first
great American quack," Dr. Elisha Perkins, who in 1796 put an
end to ill health for all time with his "tractors," two small metal
cylinders that drew poisonous vapors from the body like lightning
rods. "Of course," says Deutsch, "action was taken by the authorities at once. President George Washington immediately bought
tractors for his entire family." Perkins, by the way, discovered that
vinegar was the universal panacea, thus anticipating our own Dr.
De Forest C. Jarvis, whose honegar you may have in your cup-
board and *Folk Medicine* on your bookshelf.

No portable volume could begin to list all the nuts in American
history, so Deutsch limits his survey to the food faddists, who
created a peculiarly American industry. Its two-billion-dollar annual monkey business is the funniest, if not the least harmful,
result of dissident mania. There was, for example, Sylvester
Graham, contemporary of Dr. Perkins and inventor of "setting
up exercises," Ladies' Physiological Reform Societies, hard beds,
Saturday night baths, and the graham cracker. Graham put bran
back into the cracker (like putting shells back on nuts) by analogy
with the farmer who blew the cobwebs out of lethargic horses by
mixing a little straw in with the hay. Evidently Graham's own

colon throve on the bran cinders, for he grew in health until 1851, when he changed his diet to rice and quickly succumbed.

The most famous of all the health-food eccentrics was John Harvey Kellogg, a Seventh Day Adventist hired by Sister Ellen White at her Western Health Reform Institute at Battle Creek, Michigan. Sister White was a fugitive from the heavenly laundry baskets when the Second Coming failed to meet the Reverend William Miller's schedule. But she persevered in the faith, fortified by visions in which she saw 144,000 Adventists dining at the Lord's table on fruits, manna, and, appropriately, nuts. On divine direction, she opened her sanitarium and conducted it without trained medical help for ten years, until she found an Adventist physician to serve for Adventist pay, that is, for nothing. Dr. Kellogg was the man, a possessor of a genuine mid-century M.D. degree (he served his internship under himself), a vegetarian, upright and cleanly (he took a daily enema)—a sound mind in a flushed body, so to speak.

Dr. Kellogg took on his brother William as clerical assistant, instituted an ideal diet of vegetables, graham crackers, and water. If you had a specific ailment, there were special diets. A two-week regimen of grapes was excellent for bringing down high blood pressure. Water was a plentiful commodity at Battle Creek, and Kellogg's patients got their fill at both ends, for one of the doctor's early inventions was an enema machine that could pump fifteen gallons of water through a person in less than no time. These were the positive benefits at Battle Creek. More important, as might be expected among professional deviates, were the negative innovations. It need hardly be recorded that smoking and drinking were forbidden. Coffee too was prohibited, for it caused diabetes. And tea, which brought on insanity, an ailment the Kelloggs understandably feared. Dr. Kellogg married, but, perhaps because he remembered that chicken pie and lewdness caused cholera, he never consummated the marriage. However, the happy couple adopted in time a total of forty-two children.

In 1895, a patient demanded compensation for her shattered

teeth after chewing on Dr. Kellogg's prescribed zwieback crusts. He then invented the food rumored to be the most profitable in the history of mankind—cereal flakes. But, as we have seen, the great ideas of Promethean minds are instantly perverted by their mundane followers. The purpose of Kellogg's wheat flakes was to strengthen the teeth, and they were designed to be eaten dry. They were *not* delicious with strawberries and cream. Meanwhile, the dyspeptic Henry D. Perky invented shredded wheat, which, he instructed, had to be eaten with soup.

Like other worthy prophets of note, Kellogg was displaced by a less worthy man. His unpaid clerking brother Bill quietly bought up shares of stock in the sanitarium and its enterprises—John had strewn stock among the Adventist laborers in lieu of wages—and moved out with the cereals. It is Bill's famous signature you see on the product on your breakfast table.

Kellogg was to have some fairly eminent patients in his time, such as Henry Ford, John D. Rockefeller (who retired on milk and graham crackers), and Upton Sinclair (who probably frightened himself away from real food with his novel *The Jungle*), but few were so influential in the development of America's uniquely fanatic dietary ideas as Charles W. Post. After nine months in a Kellogg wheel chair, which he left only for enemas, Post found himself internally clean but sick and broke. He left the sanitarium, took up Christian Science, cured himself, wrote a book (*The Road to Wellville*), and invented the corn flake, to which he gave the happy name ELIJAH'S MANNA. This was not his only invention in breakfast foods; possibly at the suggestion of Kellogg's hypertension diet, he perpetrated Grape Nuts in 1898. The product most closely associated with his name is Postum, invented after his horrifying discovery that coffee would not only give you diabetes—it would make you blind as well; and on the positive side, it was good for nothing. Postum, on the other hand, was good for three quarters of a million dollars profit in its first year.

And there was Horace Fletcher, who found himself rich, fat, and tired at forty, and worried about his health. Then a truth was revealed to him that not even Aristotle (who also had some strange ideas about teeth) had noticed: that there were thirty-two teeth in the human skull because each morsel of food had to be chewed thirty-two times. Fletcher improved the posture of mastication as well as its frequency. "Hold the face down," he directed, "so that the tongue hangs perpendicular in the mouth." For a generation nearly everybody tried Fletcherism, even William James. "It nearly killed me," said the philosopher. Fletcher wore himself out chewing; near the point of expiration from mandibular exhaustion, he went to see Dr. Kellogg, who tried desperately to save him with bran and enemas. Fletcher was unluckier than William James. He promptly died.

What Americans worry about determines their areas of dissent. Since Squanto introduced turkeys to Pilgrims, it has been part of the national character to worry about food and its effects, and so the food faddists will always be with us. Fortunately, other eccentrics in dissent are less chronic. Even war may not always be our chief worry; in 1937 the fear of war ranked eleventh among the *Paramount Problems of the United States* as determined by a poll taken by the National Economic League, ranking just ahead of "Merit System in the Civil Service." At this moment the impending doom, according to the Keep America Committee of Los Angeles, centers on the evil triumvirate of Fluoridated Water, Polio Serum, and Mental Hygiene, though the Committee does not want us to overlook the threats of the Jews, the Negroes, grants to mothers with illegitimate children, federal aid to education and to other things, the United Nations, and Christmas seals. It is good, in these parlous times, to know that the ramparts are still being watched.

THE REVOLUTIONARIES

Revolutionary dissenters are not very funny in America. They are not especially funny anywhere, except perhaps in Latin America, but in a nation unused to taking life seriously, the thought of individuals and groups willing to kill and be killed for an idea is shocking. Shocking too is the knowledge that there were conditions even in recent United States history that drove ordinary men and women into extraordinary protest. As an individual example not known to many Americans, take the case of Aunt Molly Jackson, who died on the first of September, 1960, after eight decades of violent dissent against oppression of her Kentucky coal-mining people.

Aunt Molly's family was old in America. For seven generations the Robinsons and the Garlands worked the land of Clay County, Kentucky, with the self-reliance and resourcefulness of virile pioneers. Then the coal mines were opened, and along with the other small farmers, her people became, in a literal sense, industrial slaves. Aunt Molly might have had a difficult time proving to others in Kentucky that she "had more trouble than any other poor woman who has ever been born," though her brother, husband, and son were killed in the mines; her father and another brother were blinded in mine accidents; her mother died of tuberculosis when Molly was six years old; and her sister's child starved to death. For seventy-five of her eighty years, one force drove Aunt Molly Jackson: justice for the working man. When she was five, she walked picket lines with her father, a miner and preacher. Violence was the man's part in those hard days when Mary Magdalen Garland came quickly of age in the coal-blackened, blood-reddened Kentucky hills, but even a young girl could not escape the elemental savagery of men in continuous war. She went to jail first at the age of ten, was married at fourteen, and while still in her teens became a nurse with the job of making as easy as she could the death of children taken by the diseases of poverty. She early learned a fact of life that Ma Joad in *The Grapes of Wrath* never learned: the fight was so desperate that only a completely unselfish union would win it. A mother could not favor even her own children. Ma Joad told the hungry children of the

Hooverville that they could share what was left of the stew after her "fambly" had eaten; Aunt Molly, as custodian of the communal soup kitchen in a long strike, told her own little son to "go and fare as the rest fares."

Aunt Molly Jackson was one of the greatest composers of folk-songs ever found by American scholars. At the age of four she began composing songs that became more bitter and more sorrowful as she came to knowledge of the world of the mines. Let her tell how she came to write the poignant "Dreadful Memories."

In 19 and 31 the Kentucky coal miners was asked to dig coal for 33 cents a ton and they had to pay the company for the carbide to make a light and the coalite to shock the coal. And they had to pay for their picks and augers to be sharpened— the coal company took one dollar from each man's wages every month for having their picks and augers sharpened. And each man paid two dollars a month for a company doctor even if he did not have to call the doctor once. All we had to make a light in our shacks was kerosene lamps, and after the miners was blacklisted for joining the union March 5, 1931, the company doctor refused to come to any one of the coal miners families unless he was paid in advance. So I had to nurse all the little children till the last breath left them, and all the light I had was a string in a can lid with a little bacon grease in it. Kerosene was five cents a quart, and I could not get five cents. Thirty-seven babies died in my arms in the last three months of 1931. Their little stomachs busted open; they was mortified inside. Oh, what an awful way for a baby to die. Not a thing to give our babies to eat but the strong soup from soup beans, and that took the lining from their little stomachs, so that they bled inside and mortified, and died. And died so hard that before we got help from the other states my nerves was so stirred up for four years afterward by the memory of them babies suffering and dying in my arms, and me sitting by their little dead bodies three or four hours before daylight in the dark to keep some hungry dog or cat from eating up their little dead bodies. Then four years later I still had such sad memories of these babies that I wrote this song.

Aunt Molly fought back. She carried two pistols "fer my pertection in them hills," as she explained, and she used them more often than she was willing to admit.

Other labor dissidents relied on more efficient weapons of retaliation than revolvers. The most violent dissenting group in American history, the Industrial Workers of the World, had an overriding motto:

DYNAMITE. THAT'S THE STUFF

and a philosophy for using it:

> The working class and the employing class have nothing in common. There can be no peace so long as hunger and want are found among millions of working people and the few, who make up the employing class, have all the good things in life.
>
> Between these two classes a struggle must go on until the workers of the world organize as a class, take possession of the earth and the machinery of production, and abolish the wage system.

The I.W.W. was a true dissenting group, composed mainly of the deviant sub-society of itinerant workers (hoboes), itinerant nonworkers (tramps), and sedentary nonworkers (bums). Their protest was not really against capital, but against organized society, and with nothing to hold them together except indiscriminate hate, they began to disintegrate after a few bloody strikes. The weakest of them went over to Communism, which the dominant "syndicalistic" faction despised as a compromise with capitalism; the stronger, now old men, still sit in their union hall on North Halsted Street in Chicago, remembering the golden days when Mac MacClintock and Harry Orchard were alive—Haywire Mac, who knocked out Stanley Ketchell, the light-heavyweight champion of the world, with a beer bottle when the pugilist tried to boondoggle his uncertain income with a little scabbing. And good old Harry Orchard, who had about thirty labor-capital killings to his credit when he blew up former Governor Steunenberg of Idaho and finally made it into prison.

THE BURDEN

The hard core of the I.W.W. were true revolutionaries, but the culture in which they lived did not give them the ferment of a dispossessed proletariat to work upon. De Tocqueville perceptively observed in 1835:

> Not only are the men of democracies not naturally desirous of revolutions, but they are afraid of them. All revolutions more or less threaten the tenure of property; but most of those who live in democratic countries are possessed of property—not only are they possessed of property, but they live in the condition of men who set the greatest store upon their property.
>
> I know of nothing more opposite to revolutionary manners than commercial manners.

De Tocqueville went on to predict America's only genuine revolution:

> If ever American undergoes great revolutions, they will be brought about by the presence of the black race on the soil of the United States, that is to say, they will owe their origin, not to the equality, but to the inequality, of conditions.

Whenever two peoples distinguishable by real or imagined differences live contiguously, race prejudice exists. There are no exceptions, not even in the three countries often held up as cynosures of egalitarianism—Brazil, Hawaii, and New Zealand. Samoans had pre-white race prejudice against the Negroid Fijians.

The British had to hook the Chinese on opium before the celestial race would have anything to do with the inferior Caucasoids from the West. New York Negroes look down upon immigrant Puerto Rican Negroes. The Japanese have the effrontery to be prejudiced against the Caucasoid Ainu. Normal grackles buffet and peck albino grackles, and other birds are taught by their parents which groups in their species they must not associate with. Liberia, the one nation founded upon principles of human equality, is still a notorious slavocracy that paradoxically restricts citizenship to Negroes. The people of Israel, who one would think had their fill of race prejudice, similarly restrict citizenship to Jews and forbid marriage between Jews and Gentiles.

When the Pharaoh Sesostris nineteen centuries before Christ erected on the southern border of Egypt the first monument to race prejudice—a stele excluding Negroes from the kingdom— Isaac had already warned Jacob against marrying into the contemptible Canaanites. While these first civilized people opened the four-thousand-year literature of discrimination, the primitive tribes of the world went on with their half-million-year tradition of eating one another. Eating stops and exploitation begins when the economic forces of civilization show the dominant classes that the worst use one can put a man to is eating him. He is much more productive as a slave.

Slavery in America did not begin, as elementary history books tell us, with the importation of Negroes to Jamestown in 1619, the year before the Pilgrims settled at Plymouth. Real chattel slavery began with Columbus, who tried to barter some Indians to Spain for supplies, but Isabella voided the deal, possibly in repentance for having financed Columbus's voyage with the proceeds of her confiscation of Jewish property in Spain.

The Jamestown Negroes were, like their white brethren, indentured servants, a status which held a fine distinction from genuine slavery. The first slave settlement in what was to become the United States was, ironically, the place where the first slave revolt occurred—at the mouth of the Pedee River in what is now South Carolina. There half a thousand Spaniards founded a colony with a hundred Negro slaves in 1526. The Negroes almost immediately rebelled, and although it would have been possible to repress the rebellion, the conspiracy of enmity on the part of the Negroes, the Indians, the snakes, and the alligators made the Spaniards give up in disgust. The Negroes remained with their native allies, to become the first permanent settlers on the continent.

Other slaves were tried as the American colonies grew. The Indian, lying nearest to hand, was the first, but his primitive way of life made him antagonistic to the master-slave relationship. In the later West, the Indians were no more reasonable about these things, and so Chinese were imported; the first pair arrived on the *Eagle* in San Francisco in 1848. By 1870 there were 71,000 of them, too many to be kept busy with the laundry of the miners, and the irrepressible result was widespread persecution of the Oriental immigrants.

If the culture of the Indian did not suit him for slavery, quite the opposite was true of the imported African. Though this fact is not well publicized by the Emergent Nations, slavery was an almost universal characteristic of the African tribal states, and also other things one would be well advised not to write about on post cards. The millions of slaves that came to the New World, many of them gathered up and sold by their own chiefs, did not descend from freedom into slavery, but merely changed masters for the better. But improvement in conditions encourages rebellion, as the slaveholders understood very well. Since rebellion cannot occur without conspiracy, and since conspiracy cannot occur without communication, the slaveholders put a stop to communication. First they applied the lesson taught by the Bible on the sabotaging of construction work at Babel. The American slavers, unlike their neighbors to the south, repressed their personal preference in slaves. The West Indian English liked Ashantis, the French liked Dahomeans, the Spanish liked Yorubas, and the

Portuguese liked Senegalese, but the Americans, more wisely, bought only assortments, so that their purchases had to communicate in the paltry language allowed them. They also prohibited gatherings of slaves, except in church under the observation of a white man. And their anthropological knowledge was sufficient to apprise them of the ability of the Africans to communicate by message drums, so this recreation was denied them as well. We can see the results of these impositions on Negro culture today; there are only about half a dozen words of African origin in American English; the chief respectable occupation of Negroes, in the view of many whites, is religious singing; and the superb drumming of Africa has been lost by the American Negro. Jazz is a musical genre created by the Negro and is suffused by the complex rhythms of African culture; yet not until the swing era in the development of jazz was there any significant number of outstanding Negro drummers. In early jazz, only Baby Dodds was as well known as any of several score Negro pianists, trumpeters, clarinetists, and trombonists, and Dodds's fame came principally through his association with Louis Armstrong. The great names in drumming in the United States are still whites—Dave Tough, Tony Sbarbaro (Spargo), George Wettling, Gene Krupa.

The American slaveholders had reasonable grounds for suspecting that the loyalty of the Negroes to Ole Massa was not adamant. For one thing, there was an uncomfortable number of Negroes; it is not generally known that at the time of the American Revolution the Negro constituted twenty per cent of the population of the country. For another thing, they were not all given to standing with a respectable bend in their backs and hats in their hands.

Herbert Aptheker has identified at least 250 open rebellions of slaves in the United States. Most of these were local and insignificant, but some involved thousands of Negroes. An estimated 50,000 slaves participated in Gabriel's Conspiracy of 1800. Then there were the frightening revolts led by Cato in 1739 and Denmark Vesey in 1831. The worst of all was Nat Turner's Rebellion, the revolt that convinced the South, as an anonymous Virginian expressed it, that "if we will keep a ferocious monster in our country, we must keep him in chains."

Nat Turner was a constitutional deviate in just the situation that encourages such people to fullfil themselves. His fanatic religiousness spurred him on with visions whose images had their earthly origin in William Lloyd Garrison's *Liberator*. The solar eclipse of February 12, 1831, gave him the final clearance from heaven, and he planned his rebellion for the following Fourth of July. But he was ill that Independence Day, and had to wait for another celestial signal—which came on August 13, the day when the sun appeared to turn greenish blue. He set out with six companions in a band that grew quickly to seventy; by the time they had traveled twenty miles, they had slaughtered fifty-seven white men, women, and children.

All the eccentricity was not on the side of abolitionists such as Phillips, Garrison, and Higginson. The only real difference between them and their opponents was that eccentricity persisted longer in the mind of the Southern white. As late as 1929, one renowned Southern historian—Claude Bowers, in *The Tragic Era* —seriously offered this origin for the Ku Klux Klan:

> The night before Christmas in 1865, six young men, who had seen service in the war, were seated about the stove in a small brick building in Pulaski, Tennessee. Penniless, with poor prospects, with poverty and depression all about, a pall of sadness rested on the little town that Christmas eve. "Boys," said one of the young men, "let's start something to break the monotony and cheer up our mothers and girls. Let's start a club of some kind." It was agreed, and plans were made to be perfected at another meeting. This was held in the home of a leading citizen, where many merry initiations were to be had that winter. In considering a name for the club, some one suggested "Kuklio," from the Greek word meaning a band or circle; another proposed adding "Klan," because all the members were of Scotch-Irish descent; and a third offered Ku Klux

Klan. Since the object was fun, why not costumes to deepen
the mystery? Agreed—and the young men joyously raided the
linen closet and brought forth stiff linen sheets and pillow
cases. It was a period of much masquerading and the costuming was a natural instinct. And why not ride horses? and
disguise these, as well, with sheets. Yes, and ride out into
the black night and call at the houses of parents and sweet-
hearts in a silent serenade?

Thus for the first time the Ku Klux rode, and every one
was merry for the moment, every one but the freed-men,
who being superstitious, thought they had seen ghosts from
the nearby battlefields. Many of these, who had been idling,
hurried back contritely and subdued to their old masters'
fields.

The racial problem does not conduce to rationality in this
country or any other, and it is prejudicial to require rationality
of Claude Bowers. James S. Coleman, in his article "Community
Disorganization," tells of the English mathematician in Chicago
who was accosted by a gang of Negro youths threatening him with
a knife. He protested that he was a visitor from England and did
not regard this as a proper way to be treated. The boys said: "Oh,
we thought you were one of those white guys," and left him with
his wallet. And J. C. Furnas, in *Goodbye to Uncle Tom*, remembers that his wife, while investigating the racial situation at an
Eastern coeducational college, was told by the dean that there
was no prejudice at the school, but racial mixing between the
sexes was not allowed. Mrs. Furnas in bewilderment said she had
just seen Negro boys and white girls together in a lounge. The
dean explained: "Oh, those boys aren't Negroes; they're Haitians.
They speak French."

THE RELIGIOUS DISSIDENTS

The best place to look for irrational behavior is in an area of
irrationality. The first century of American colonization was a
time of nearly unanimous unreason; the rational man was the

deviate. Michael Wigglesworth dealt, in *The Day of Doom*, with the complaint of the damned children "Who died in infancy And never had no good or bad Effected personally," by having God reply:

> You sinners are, and such a share
>   as sinners may expect,
> Such you shall have, for I do save
>   none but my own elect.
> Yet to compare your sin with their
>   Who lived a longer time,
> I do confess yours is much less
>   though every sin's a crime.
>
> A crime it is; therefore in bliss
>   you may not hope to dwell;
> But unto you I shall allow
>   the easiest room in Hell.
> The glorious King thus answering,
>   they cease and plead no longer;
> Their consciences must needs confess
>   his reasons are the stronger.

He was perhaps a bit unkind, but he was quite reasonable within the Puritan ethos.

The Puritans had a little trouble with secular dissidents, such as John Billington, one of the Mayflower Old Comers, whom they hanged for murder in 1630 (the first criminal executed in American history), and Thomas Morton, the atheist, lecher, roisterer, manumitter of indentured slaves, seller of liquor and guns to the Indians, poacher on Plymouth's trapping grounds, and erector of the horrid maypole on Merry Mount, a device the Puritans had had some acquaintance with in England:

> . . . of fourtie, threescore, or a hundred maidens going to the woods amaying, there scarcely the third part of them returned home againe as they went.

They got rid of Morton for a while on a framed murder charge, but the religious dissidents were not so easily eliminated, since they were driven by the same selfless spiritual energy as the orthodox Puritans. The American Puritans were only one (or actually several, though they were not fully aware of their internal disharmony) of a myriad of religious protestants that included Brownists, Precisians, Separatists, Semists, Calvinists, Congregationalists, Presbyterians, Antinomians, Arians, Anabaptists, Sebaptists, Familists, Fifth Monarchy Men, Levellers, Arminians, Diggers, Quakers, Seekers, Catholics, and Atheists, to name only the English denominations. Many of these were sent by the Devil to the colonies to plague the Saints; others developed locally. Anne Hutchinson came in 1654, by direct inspiration from God, with prophecies to impart to the Massachusetts colony. Like her distant descendant, Aimee Semple McPherson, Anne was a convincing preacher, and she very nearly seduced—figuratively speaking—the great John Cotton into Antinomianism before the Puritans came to their senses and exiled her to the frontier, where the Indians got her, thus vindicating the judgment of the Puritans.

The Quakers came in 1651 as missionaries to Boston, a piece of impudence that in itself condemned them. They were whipped and run out of town. They came back with augmented forces. They had their ears cut off. They came back again; and so the hanging of Quakers started in 1659, and did not stop until King Charles the Second ordered it stopped and sent over a Quaker to enforce his ruling.

In 1631 Governor Winthrop recorded in his *Journal* that "one Philip Ratcliff, a servant of Mr. Cradock, being convict, ore tenus, of most foul, scandalous, invectives against our churches and government, was censured to be whipped, lose his ears, and be banished the plantation, which was presently executed." In this entry Winthrop notes also the arrival of a "godly minister" and his wife, with the tacit satisfaction that thus was the vile Phillip Ratcliff overbalanced by Providence. He would learn better, for the "godly minister" was Roger Williams, who was to cause the Massachusetts Puritans more trouble than anyone else in their history.

Through the good offices of Winthrop, whom Williams had met in England, Williams was offered the position of teacher in the leading church in Boston, but he declined upon finding the congregation "unseparated." He was called to a pastorate in Salem, where he expressed publicly his opinion that the clergy did not have secular authority under either the Covenant or the charter. The Boston theocrats proved him wrong by preventing his installation. He went then to Plymouth, which was beginning its fatal decline, but once again his advanced views got him into trouble. Somehow he was taken on at Salem as assistant pastor. He behaved himself for a while, muttering only against such things as the wearing of veils by women and the eradication of the cross from the ensign, but before long he was again attacking the royal patents and the Boston authority. This time he received support from his Salem congregation, which was beginning to chafe under the Bay Tyranny, but after a good deal of vicious infighting, the General Court on October 8, 1635, banished him from the colony. It was the intention of his judges that either the Indians or the cold weather should remove him even further from their provinces. Fortunately for Williams, he was one of the very few Englishmen who had made friends with the Indians, and they kept him alive until spring, when he was joined by other dissidents. After losing their harvest at Seekonk, Williams and his companions moved into the territory of the Narragansetts and founded the first truly democratic settlement in America, the community of Providence. Exactly three hundred years after Williams's banishment, in 1935, the Massachusetts legislature officially rescinded the decision of the Boston General Court— and in the same session passed legislation to require a loyalty oath for teachers.

At Providence, regarded during all its colonial history as the sewer of the New World, Williams wrote some of the most embarrassing attacks on established Puritanism which that harried sect would ever suffer, but he was big enough to send back to Boston advice that could have saved the Puritans, had they been sufficiently wise to understand it. Regarding religious and political dissidence, of which he was his time's chief representative, he said in a letter:

> As concerning these quakers (so called) which are now among us, we have no law among us, whereby to punish any for only declaring by words, etc., their minds and understandings concerning the things and ways of God, as to salvation and an eternal condition. And we, moreover, finde, that in those places where these people aforesaid, in this colony, are most of all suffered to declare themselves freely, and are only opposed by arguments in discourse, there they least of all desire to come, and we are informed that they begin to loath this place for that they are not opposed by the civill authority, but with all patience and meekness are suffered to say over many here to their way; surely we find that they delight to be persecuted by civill powers, and when they are soe, they are like to gain more adherents by the conseyte of their patient sufferings, than by consent to their pernicious sayings; and yet we conceive, that their doctrines tend to very absolute cuttinge downe and overturning relations and civill government among men, if generally received.

Williams's message has not been received by later suppressors of dissent, nor was it received by the Massachusetts theocracy, which continued severe repression until Puritanism died in the shambles at Salem Village in 1692 with the execution of twenty-six of the three hundred card-carrying witches in the area. Deputy Governor Stoughton expressed himself bitterly when Governor Phipps finally ordered the witch hanging stopped: "We were in a way to have cleared the land of the witches! Who is it that obstructs the course of justice I know not. The Lord be merciful to the country!"

In the eighteenth century a new delusion supplanted Puritanism—the idea that men were rational creatures. The Puritans presumptuously called themselves the Saints; the 18th century presumptuously called itself the Age of Reason. The state of mind that produced Newton and the scientific revolution turned the religious thinkers to "natural religion"—Deism—a logical derivation from Puritanism, though its intellectual forerunners are more usually identified as Lord Herbert of Cherbury, Locke, Shaftesbury, Pope, and Bolingbroke. Puritanism obtained its authority by subjecting the Bible to legal scrutiny; the next logical step was to carry doubt into dissent.

In the intellectual atmosphere of the Age of Reason, the merest suggestion could turn a Puritan into a Deist. On the American frontier there was Ethan Allen, a rip-tail roarer of a Deist, though he swore he did not know what a Deist was. His *Reason the Only Oracle of Man* is a hilarious demolition of the Bible, with the iconoclasm of Lord Raglan written in the inept language of Dreiser. Like Raglan, he was concerned with the reliability of legendary history, and as Raglan might have done, Allen expressed his admiration for Moses, who, he said, was the only historian of his acquaintance to give a detailed account of his own funeral.

Like all Deists, Allen rejected revealed religion, retaining only the most natural of the natural laws of morality, such as "Thou shalt not kill," and the idea of a God of some sort too intelligent to communicate with man through clergymen, who, being totally depraved, were the best evidence of the condemnation of mankind. Allen went further than other Deists in accepting a Hell, but he had personal reasons for this heresy. As a captive of the British during the war, Allen insisted: "There must be a hell for the punishment of Tories!"

Ethan Allen was a simple product of a theological tradition crumbling in a backwoods environment, but Elihu Palmer was a Deist of an entirely different kind. He was an intellectual who began life conventionally as an ordained minister, as every edu-

cated poor man had to do at the end of the eighteenth century.
It is said that one evening, while reading from Isaac Watts the
good Puritanical reflection:

> *Lord, I am vile, conceived in sin*
> *And born unholy and unclean,*

he closed the book, turned to his wife, and said flatly that he did
not believe a word of it. When he expressed this opinion in his
church he was thrown out. The rest of his career is a tragic
chronicle; he was flung out of church after church, and, for his
sins, lost his wife and his sight in the great epidemic of yellow
fever in Philadelphia in 1793.

Palmer's *Principles of Nature, or, a Development of the Moral
Causes of Happiness and Misery among the Human Species* is
probably the bitterest attack on revealed religion ever publicly
printed in this country. Among the mildest of his indictments are
statements like this:

> Moses, Mahomet, and Jesus can lay as little claim to moral
> merit, or to the characters of benefactors of mankind, as any
> three men that ever lived upon the face of the earth. They
> were all of them imposters; two of them notorious murderers
> in practice, and the other a murderer in principle: and their
> existence united, perhaps, cost the human race more blood,
> and produced more substantial misery, than all the other
> fanatics of the world.

Almost as unfortunate as Palmer, but more famous for his earlier political rebelliousness, was Thomas Paine, the intellectual
leader of the American Revolution, without whose *Common Sense*
and *The Crisis* the independence of the United States might not
have been achieved. This consummate patriot lost some of his
American adulation when he went to France to help the French,
as Franklin said, "set up shop for themselves," but he was at least
tolerated until his Deistic book *The Age of Reason* was published
at the end of the century. Jefferson, not appreciating the extent of

public opinion against Paine, invited him to return to the country
he so very much helped to make, but the outcry against Paine was
so great that Jefferson was afraid to meet him. The welcome given
Paine by the Baltimore *Republican* was typical:

> Thou lilly-livered sinical rogue, thou gibbet inheriting slave,
> thou art naught but the composition of a knave, beggar,
> coward, pander, and the son and heir of some drunken she-
> devil.

The poetaster William Coleman wrote a poem in estimate of
Paine beginning "Detested reptile! wherefore hast thou come. . . ."

Time, as we know, alters the perspective of things. A few years
ago a statue of Paine was offered to Roger Williams's city of
Providence. The mayor refused to allow its erection on the ground
that Paine was still a "controversial figure."

Jefferson himself was a Deist, but, like Franklin, he was cautious
enough to keep this knowledge from the common people, to whom
he swore resounding promises "on the altar of God." The artist
John Trumbull had another view of Jefferson at a dinner at which
Senator Giles of Virginia got off some sharp hits against Christianity. Trumbull recalled later:

> Jefferson, in the meantime smiling and nodding approbation
> on Mr. Giles, while the rest of the company silently left me
> and my defense to our fate; until at length my friend, David
> Franks, took up the argument on my side. Thinking this a
> fair opportunity for evading further consideration on this
> subject, I turned to Mr. Jefferson and said, "Sir, this is a
> strange situation in which I find myself; in a country pro-
> fessing Christianity and at a table with Christians, as I sup-
> posed, I find my religion and myself attacked with severe and
> almost irresistible wit and raillery, and not a person to aid in
> my defense, but my friend Mr. Franks, who is himself a Jew."

The Deists were considerably ahead of the Transcendentalists,
who, for reasons hard to appreciate, are considered by some historians to be important in the intellectual development of the

United States. The leader of this philosophy, a temporizing phase in the deterioration of the vestiges of Puritanism, and imported from Germany, England, and India, is now taken to be Ralph Waldo Emerson. The writings of Emerson appealed to the young nation, then held in contempt by its fellow communities in the world for its utter lack of "culture," just as they appeal now to sophomore students suffering from the same delusion. But Emerson and Thoreau and the other Transcendentalists elected Amos Bronson Alcott as their superior; Emerson noted in his *Journals* that for "pure intellect" he had never known the equal of Alcott.

In view of this estimation, it is worth looking into the behavior of this chief philosophical dissident of his time.

As a boy, he was a vegetarian, a turn of mind that made him receptive to the ideas of Sylvester Graham, he of the cracker, when Bronson's brother invited the great dietician to Dartmouth. Another early friend of Alcott's was William Miller, he of the laundry baskets and the Second Coming. By 1835 Amos was failing in his chosen profession of peddling, and he had given up, besides meat, such derivatory animal products as butter, eggs, and cheese, eating at each of his three meals potatoes, unleavened bread, apples, and ice water. He had another use for ice water that deserves noting: he used to pour it over his daughters in the morning—perhaps this is why Louisa May's sisters, the Little Women, did not grow up to be big women.

Amos had some good ideas for his time about education, and these, together with his association with the Transcendentalists, who were making a big splash in the tiny intellectual pool at Boston, provided for his reception by their idol in England, the crotchety Thomas Carlyle. But Carlyle stalked disgustedly from the dinner table when he saw Amos mixing his strawberries with his potatoes. It probably gave the irritable Scot second thoughts about the genuine profundity of Alcott's Orphic Sayings published in the *Dial*, such as "Love globes, wisdome orbs, all things," and "Alway are the divine Gemini entwined."

One of the products of Alcott's pure intellect was the communal

farm of Fruitlands, on which no exploitation of animals was permitted—that meant no honey, because honey-gathering exploited
bees, and no woollen clothing, because wool-clipping exploited
sheep. Alcott had to have his potatoes to go with his strawberries,
but he and his socialistic companions preferred to plant aspiring
vegetables, ones that reached for the sky, like beans.

The Fruitlands people did not believe overmuch in sex, and
safeguarded their ladies by putting them into bloomers.

It would not have been profitable for dissenting masculine
inmates of Fruitlands to go down the road to the nearby Shaker
community at Niskayuna, for the Shakers did not believe in any
sex at all. We can say for them that in consequence of their
opinions on procreation they had the goodness to extinguish themselves. They made some of the most excellent folk furniture this
country has ever produced, and we are glad to have it instead of
their dissident religion. It is a far more welcome survival into the
present than vestiges like Wilbur Voliva, pastor of the Christian
Apostolic Church of Zion (Illinois), who lived on milk and nuts,
went around the world seven times, and died insisting that the
earth was flat.

☆ VIII ☆

The
Playful Americans

Spitting was the first gift truly their own that Americans offered the world of sport, but it was a contribution rejected with disgust. "The time has come," wrote Charles Dickens in 1842 after his visit to Washington,

> when I must confess without any disguise that the prevalence of those two odious practices of chewing and expectorating began about this time to be anything but agreeable, and soon became most offensive and sickening. In all the public places of America this filthy custom is recognized. In the courts of law, the judge has his spittoon, the crier his, the witness his, and the prisoner his; while the jurymen and spectators are provided for, as so many men who in the course of nature must desire to spit incessantly. In the hospitals, the

students of medicine are requested, by notices on the wall, to eject their tobacco juice into the boxes provided for that purpose, and not to discolor the stairs. In public buildings visitors are implored through the same agency to squirt the essence of their quids, or "plugs" as I have heard them called by gentlemen learned in this kind of sweetmeat, into the national spittoon, and not about the bases of the marble columns. But in some parts, this custom is inseparably mixed up with every meal and morning call, and with all the transactions of social life. The stranger who follows in the track I took myself will find it in its full bloom and glory, luxuriant in all its alarming recklessness, at Washington. And let him not persuade himself (as I once did, to my shame) that previous tourists have exaggerated its extent. The thing itself is an exaggeration of nastiness.

Spitting began in America as a necessity, progressed to a simple pastime, and ended in regularized competition that still can be seen along many tobacco roads where amber-drooling farmers assemble to bespatter the landscape.

The first white man to have tobacco in his hands, if not in his mouth, was Christopher Columbus, who was given a few cigars by the Carib Indians, a people shortly to commend themselves to his attention by their equally noisome habit of cannibalism. Columbus and his followers apparently did not appreciate the basic purpose of tobacco among the Indians, for the plant was introduced to Spain first as an ornamental flower and then as a medicine—the latter use a curious one in view of recent medical indictments of tobacco as a carcinogen. The English, though they came across tobacco later, among the pipe-smoking tribes of Virginia, caught on more quickly to its real use, probably because Sir Walter Raleigh was an accomplished *viceur*. Raleigh seems to have been the man who took tobacco into England in 1586, for which some people believe God in His infinite mercy will in time forgive him. By 1615, over the violent opposition of decent people (including King James, who took time off from his research into witchcraft to write a tract against it), some £200,000 worth of tobacco was being imported annually—this at a time when a man could get drunk for a penny and dead drunk for two. In volume this was not a large amount of tobacco by modern standards, since the sotweed was then literally worth its weight in silver, and was accordingly smoked in pipes with tiny bowls.

The plague of 1666 and the rationalization that tobacco was nasty enough to be salubrious broke open the market. The English spread a pall of smoke over western Europe through the agency of both traders and soldiers. The traders found it an excellent item to barter for Negro slaves (anticipating the use of opium in business dealings with the Chinese two centuries later), and the British soldiers in the beginning of colonial expansion spread tobacco the way their American posterity were to spread cigarettes, chocolate, nylons, and chewing gum in a later war. Laws were passed against tobacco smoking—or "drinking," as inhalation was first called—but about as effectively as the Eighteenth Amendment. The Thirty Years' War took pipe smoking to Bohemia; the Bohemians in turn carried the favor into Austria and Hungary. Before the end of the century, pipe smoking had penetrated into the gateway to the Orient—Constantinople (Istanbul)—through the offices of the English Levant Company. The Turks fought the Persians in 1636, passing along the pipe-smoking habit in the course of military operations. Meanwhile the English pushed forward directly into the Orient; in 1698 Sir Thomas Osborne acquired the monopoly of the tobacco trade in Siberia, whose nomadic tribes carried the pipe and its contents northeast, passing them along across the Bering Strait and home again to the New World—so that the Alaskan and northern Canadian tribes got the nicotine habit not by the logical short route a few hundred miles to the south, but by the long way around the world.

There were other lines of diffusion, of course, but they had much less influence than that of the expansive British. The Spaniards and Portuguese introduced tobacco to western Oceania and the southern Orient in the seventeenth century, but since their American contact had been with cigar- and cigarette-smoking Indians, the more widespread English method of taking tobacco can be identified by the incidence of pipe smoking among native peoples. One way, for example, of certainly distinguishing a male from a female South Australian aboriginal skull laid down in the early nineteenth century is by recognizing a slight separation of the mandibular premolar from the first molar, for the fashion in pipe smoking, then limited to men, was to grasp the clay pipe tightly between these teeth. In the Torres Strait islands, a native adaptation of the pipe is a large crab claw with the ends opened.

Since World War II, the earlier extent of pipe diffusion has been hidden by the introduction of cigarettes by the millions of American soldiers who swarmed over the world from 1942 to 1945, inculcating American habits, good and bad, to friend and foe. The modern American cigarette, incidentally, is a re-invention, rather than a direct descendant of the Aztec cigarette. The Aztecs and their Maya neighbors, for all their mathematical competence, could not have conceived that the wild country to their north would in one year consume about half a trillion cigarettes.

The process of diffusion so well illustrated by the eastward spread of tobacco is an absorbing one for anthropologists. Inter-tribal contact in the savage world is not friendly; if one tribe has another in for dinner, the guests are the ingredients. Yet very inconsequential things will move freely even among the bitterest enemies. In the area of art, so closely allied in form and purpose to sport, the extent of diffusion is hard to believe. A complex story collected in central Australia may be nearly identical to another found in South America, though, on the basis of all other evidence, the Australian aborigines have been isolated from the rest of the world since the Ice Age. In South America, the diffusion of games and tales is difficult to conceive, since relations among these tribes were mostly cannibalistic. The only convincing explanation is that these people took so much pleasure in their food that the victim was encouraged to whet the hosts' appetites by entertaining ante-prandially. There was not much after-dinner speaking on his part.

A brief analysis such as that given in the preceding paragraphs about the ways of tobacco could as well be made for every game, sport, or pastime enjoyed by human beings anywhere in the world. The spinning top (which for no apparent reason suddenly fell from popularity in the United States during the last three decades) moved into the Orient from the West, and China gave in return the kite, which the great anthropologist A. C. Haddon, in *The Study of Man*, in 1908 did not see as an unmitigated blessing; he feared that an enemy, by means of a parcel of kites, might be able to "detonate over our cities several dozen pounds of nitroglycerine." And what hidden force makes the first boy bring out the first kite in spring? Or the first marbles?

Sometimes neither diffusion nor its alternative, polygenesis, seems to be an adequate explanation of the presence in separate cultures of the same game. Before the coming of the Europeans, the Aztec of Mexico played a game called *patolli*, a board game with at least six major features (and many more minor ones)— flat dice, a cross-shaped board, several men or counters, the idea of "killing" an opponent's man, penalty and safety stations—in common with the famous game of India, *parcheesi*. The complexity of the games eliminates any reasonable possibility of independent invention, but on the other hand no contact between India and Mexico in prehistoric times has yet been established with certainty by the common occurrence of other cultural items.[1]

Many things have come to us by way of India (*parcheesi* is the direct ancestor of Monopoly and similar games), but tobacco chewing and spitting is our own—or, more honestly, it became our own after we took it from the Indians of the eastern woodlands. The British thought this method of taking nicotine disgusting

[1] Excavations at Teotihuacán, near Mexico City, in 1963 have revealed certain other very probable borrowings from India and the Orient before the coming of Columbus.

enough in the sixteenth century, and their opinion did not change thereafter. In the hundreds of volumes written about American manners by visitors from the Mother Country in the Victorian period, when our national character had firmly established itself, nearly the only writers who did not revile the habit were those whose constitutions were too delicate to allow even a mention of it.

Mrs. Frances Trollope was in almost continuous nausea, starting with her trip up the Mississippi in the steamboat *Belvidere*. "We found the room destined for the use of the ladies dismal enough," she began, "as its only windows were below the stern gallery; but both this and the gentleman's cabin were handsomely fitted up, and the latter well carpeted—but oh! that carpet! I will not, I may not describe its condition; indeed it requires the pen of a Swift to do it justice. Let no one who wishes to receive agreeable impressions of American manners commence his travels in a Mississippi steamboat; for myself, it is with all sincerity that I declare that I would infinitely prefer sharing the apartment of well-conditioned pigs to being confined to its cabin."

English gentlemen, trained to a hardier life, were able to stomach American traveling better than their ladies, though perhaps the most disgusted of the travelers in regard to tobacco spitting was the journalist and businessman Alexander Mackay. In his book *The Western World, or, Travels in the United States* (1847) he tells of being spat upon, as well as being near-missed by expectorators who hit between his feet and over his shoulders. He said he once saw a chewer take the quid out of his mouth and use it to draw pictures on a windowpane.

John Melish, a Scottish textile exporter, did not write with much greater pleasure, in retrospect, in his *Travels in the United States of America in the Years 1806 and 1807, and 1809, 1810, and 1811*. At a tavern outside Geneva, New York, he recalls:

> The fire was not lighted in the parlour, and I sat down at the fire in the bar-room, and began to write my notes. But I did

not long enjoy repose in this situation; a man came in and lighted his segar, and, turning his back-side to me, he whiffed away, at the end of every two or three puffs squirting a mouthful of saliva through the room. He was soon joined by a second and a third, when they made a little circle round the fire. They all had segars, and I was soon enveloped in smoke, and obliged to shut my papers. Three others came in and joined the party. One took a large roll of tobacco out of his pocket, and taking an immense quid, he rolled it about in his mouth, and squirted about the saliva in all directions, without paying much regard to who might come in contact with it. Another pulled a pipe out of his pocket, and the third joined the segar-smokers. I like to see singular scenes occasionally, even though they should be rough ones; but this scene of smoking, and chewing, and spitting, was *too* rough. The smokers were also nasty in the highest degree, and seemed to pay no attention to where they spat, in the fire, on the hearth, or on the floor; the face, the neck, or the pocket; it was all *one*. I withdrew from the scene, and albeit it was a very cold night, I was fain to sit down in the furthest corner of the room, by a broken window. But this did not secure me against the smokers; two of them got up and marched through the floor, smoking and spitting, and I was finally obliged to abandon the scene and seek refuge elsewhere. By this time there was a fire in the supper-parlour, and, soon after, supper was announced. After supper, I began to write up my notes, when two of the smokers lighted their segars beside me, and began to smoke and spit almost in my face. At last one of them perceived me making wry faces, and said, "I'm afraid the smoking disturbs you." "A little," said I, my face sufficiently indicative of my feelings, on which they very civilly withdrew, and left me in possession of a good clean parlour, the value of which was enhanced by the dirty scene I had endured.

Dickens's experience on a riverboat had a more pleasant conclusion:

On board this steamboat there were two young gentlemen, with shirt collars reversed as usual, and armed with very big walking sticks, who planted two seats in the middle of the deck at a distance of some four paces apart, took out their tobacco boxes, and sat down opposite each other to chew. In less than a quarter of an hour's time these hopeful youths had shed about them on the clean boards a copious shower of yellow rain, clearing by that means a kind of magic circle within whose limits no intruders dared to come, and which they never failed to refresh and re-refresh before a spot was dry. This being before breakfast rather disposed me, I confess, to nausea; but looking attentively at one of the expectorators, I plainly saw he was young in chewing, and felt inwardly uneasy himself. A glow of delight came over me at this discovery, and as I marked his face turn paler and paler, and saw the ball of tobacco in his left cheek quiver with his suppressed agony while yet he spat and chewed and spat again in emulation of his older friend, I could have fallen on his neck and implored him to go on for hours.

No matter what mode of transportation Dickens tried in America, he found no respite. On the train from New York to Philadelphia, he watched the brilliant sunset from the window, but he was soon distracted by

a remarkable appearance issuing from the windows of the gentlemen's car immediately in front of us, which I supposed for some time was occasioned by a number of industrious persons inside ripping open feather beds and giving the feathers to the wind. At length it occurred to me that they were only spitting, which was indeed the case, though how any number of passengers which it was possible for that car to contain could have maintained such a playful and incessant shower of expectoration I am still at a loss to understand, notwithstanding the experience in all salivatory phenomena which I afterwards acquired.

If Dickens had come over during the California gold rush, he

could have experienced the same situation on the stagelines. A
popular song of the time says that on these close coaches

> *The ladies are compelled to sit*
> *Their dresses in tobacco spit,*
> *The gentlemen don't seem to care*
> *But talk on politics and swear.*

Mrs. Trollope had her worst time at the theater, where the
American men

> sprawl about the benches, throw their feet up on the seat in
> front of them, spit, take off their coats, spit, roll up their
> sleeves, spit, exhale stifling odors of whiskey and onions, spit,
> and applaud by stamping their feet and yelling and spitting.

This vice was not all on the part of the men. In the South,
ladies encouraged their gentlemen friends in the pastime by carrying ornamented tobacco boxes in their purses to supply their
escorts in emergencies. And back in 1782 St. Jean de Crèvecoeur
in his *Letters from an American Farmer* writes about the manners
of Nantucket:

> A singular custom prevails here among the women, at which
> I was greatly surprised, and am really at a loss how to ac-
> count for the original cause that has introduced in this primi-
> tive society so remarkable a fashion, or rather so extraordinary
> a want. They have adopted these many years the Asiatic cus-
> tom of taking a dose of opium every morning; and so deeply
> rooted is it, that they would be at a loss how to live without
> this indulgence; they would rather be deprived of any neces-
> sary than forego their favorite luxury. This is much more pre-
> vailing among the women than the men, few of the latter
> have caught the contagion. . . .

The "headquarters of tobacco-tinctured saliva," according to
Dickens, was the national capital. In the senate he met several
gentlemen "who in the course of conversation frequently missed

the spittoon at five paces, and one (but he was certainly short-
sighted) mistook the closed sash for the open window at three."

The direction of culture is rarely changed by the criticism of
foreigners, but in the matter of spitting, the unremitting censure
of our British cousins did succeed in channeling the mandibular
exercise of Americans into more acceptable lines. An American
invented chewing gum in 1869, and so, instead of chewing Indian
tobacco, the people of the United States began chewing Indian
chicle, whose essence did not have to be constantly ejected,
though the disposal of the rubbery, adhesive quid involved a different kind of annoyance. Go into the bookstore at U.C.L.A., one
of our largest and greatest universities, and you will see the janitor
scraping the sticky discs off the floor with a special tool consisting
of a spatula and a broomstick. You think he is removing the accumulation of years of mastication; you ask him how often he cleans
up the gum. "Oh," he will reply disinterestedly, "every day."

When a cultural item moves into obsolescence, the anthropologist finds it persists longest in the marginal areas, among folk
groups which have not fully accepted the behavior of their sophisticated countrymen, and also in areas where tradition is revered.
Thus, city billboards advertise chewing gum, but rural billboards
advertise chewing tobacco. Fortunately, the United States is not
bound too tightly by the retarding drag of tradition, except in
government's hallowed halls. It was a surprise to most Americans
the year before last when Senator Kenneth B. Keating of New
York, prodded to his duty by a constituent, initiated a disconcerted effort to have removed the blue spittoons that since
Dickens's time reposed at strategic places on the senate floor.

A more fundamental early American sport that attracted the
unfavorable attention of foreign tourists was whittling. Captain
Marryat tied this aimlessly destructive activity of the pioneers to a
congenital tension:

It is a habit arising from the natural restlessness of the
American when he is not employed, cutting a piece of stick

or anything else, with his knife. Some are so wedded to it from long custom that if they have not a piece of stick to cut, they will whittle the backs of chairs or anything within their reach. A Yankee shown into a room to await the arrival of another has been known to whittle away nearly the whole of the mantelpiece. Lawyers in court whittle away at the table before them, and judges will cut through their own bench.

Several anthropological principles are embedded in Marryat's observation on whittling besides the recognition of the nervous tension of Americans which is manifested in other nationally characteristic activities. Perhaps the most fundamental is the destructiveness of primitive play, a trait that is possibly biologically determined. In primates other than man, it is only with great persistence that play can be directed into constructive endeavors; chimpanzees, the most tractable subjects for experimentation below the human level, can be taught rudimentary play, such as stacking blocks, but if left to themselves they greatly prefer knocking blocks down. The more intelligent simians can be instructed to perform tricks that give the illusion that the mind rather than the body is at play, but they take much more delight in the brute exercise of their muscles.

Human beings took a long time to progress appreciably beyond the level of chimpanzee activity. It is true that man was qualitatively more intelligent, that he used language and fire and tools, but nearly all of his history on earth shows that he used these things to make himself more efficiently destructive. During the whole of the Paleolithic period, which lasted for most of a million years, man demolished the things that nature had constructed. He made his few tools by fracturing, breaking, and chipping stone, and he used these artifacts to increase his powers of destruction— to prey upon animals rather than to domesticate them, to dig pit "houses" rather than to build structures, to burn forests and grass- lands rather than to plant crops, to kill other men rather than to co-operate with them in building civilization. All the evidence we have, archaeological and ethnographical, shows that man's first games were violent.

Wrestling, the most fundamental of all sports, is perhaps the most nearly universal unproductive activity of mankind. We have no evidence to prove it, but running may be more ancient; Professor Gordon Hewes suggests that man's bipedalism began not when he started using tools, but when he stole meat from predatory carnivores and outran them to the trees.

In sport as well as in the process of biological evolution, ontogeny recapitulates phylogeny, to misquote Haeckel once again; the history of the individual reflects the history of the race, and, moreover, it reflects the history of the culture which directs his behavior. The subhuman chimpanzees do not ever progress naturally beyond muscular, destructive sport. Human children, trailing behind them, not clouds of glory as Wordsworth romantically supposed, but clouds of subhuman mischief, begin their play activity in destructiveness, and only with increasing maturity beyond the reach of the lesser primates do they turn to mental play. So also in the history of culture the earliest sports of a people are violent, muscular, unruly, unintellectual. As maturity comes to a culture, physical sports decline in popularity, and are replaced by less spectacular but more humanly satisfying intellectual competition. Over the long millennia of evolution, *Australopithecus* with his skull-crushing club evolves to man with his electronic computer, and wrestling evolves to the boundless mathematical vista of von Neumann and Morgenstern's Game Theory. Even the apparently fundamental physical sports that hang on and remain popular involve more mentality than many of their supporters realize. A football game to an American, whose interest and tension have been built up through knowledge of the strategical and tactical intricacies of the game as well as personal involvement with the competing teams and players, can be an absorbing experience; but to the uninitiated Englishman football is as exciting as a dripping faucet. And watching a cricket match, for an American, is like watching a man collecting stamps.

In the evolution of American history, the Cavaliers who fled the English Puritans a decade before the Puritans fled the Cavaliers, established in the southern part of this country a civilization outwardly healthy but inwardly moribund, a preservation of medieval aristocratic society and culture that had to fall before the mercantilism and democracy of the New England settlers. It is not at all surprising to anthropologists that, in the South, blood sports persisted longest, from goose pulling (in which horse riders at full gallop competed at pulling the head off a goose) to dueling. The nineteenth-century tourists had something to say about this, too. Dickens cites an account of an "Affair of Honour" which appeared in a Southern newspaper:

> We have just heard the particulars of a meeting which took place on Six Mile Island, on Tuesday, between two young bloods of our city: Samuel Thurston, aged 15, and William Hine, aged 13 years. They were attended by young gentlemen of the same age. The weapons used on the occasion were a couple of Dirkson's best rifles—the distance, 30 yards. They took one fire, without any damage being sustained by either party, except the ball of Thurston's gun passing through the crown of Hine's hat. Through the intercession of the Board of Honour the challenge was withdrawn, and the difference amicably adjusted.

While the aristocrats of the southern plantations dueled on the greensward, the frontiersmen of the lower classes, with less dignity but more effectiveness, gouged one another's eyes out.

The rough forebears of ours, the rip-tail roarers, have metatactically become playthings of children's literature—Davy Crockett and Mike Fink (and on the seas of the bathtub, pirates), but a century and a half ago they were not funny. The gang of John A. Murrell along the Natchez Trace was as ferocious a troupe of bad men as any society has produced. We have already met Bully Bill Sedley, the fellow who, while inebriated, killed a tiger, but we have not noted that Bully Bill was shortly thereafter killed in a fight with another bully.

The English visitors, seeing these people on their best behavior, were not terrified by them. Dickens tells of meeting one of the Kentucky horse-alligators, a fellow by the name of Porter,

> of the moderate height of seven feet eight inches in his stockings. There never was a race of people who so completely gave the lie to history as these giants, or whom the chroniclers have so cruelly libeled. Instead of roaring and ravaging about the world, constantly catering for their cannibal larders, and perpetually going to market in an unlawful manner, they are the meekest people in any man's acquaintance.

Our military men, too, were amusing to the visitors. In commenting on American dueling, Marryat said: "The majority of the editors of the newspapers in America are constantly practicing with the pistol, that they may be ready when called upon, and are most of them very good shots. In fact, they could not well refuse to fight, being all of them colonels, majors, or generals." Dickens complained about the disappearance of a servant: "I wonder what has become of the faithful secretary whom I brought along with me from Boston. He is supping with our late landlord—a Field Marshal, at least, no doubt." And poor, humorless, tobacco-spattered Mrs. Trollope:

> The total want of all the usual courtesies of the table, the voracious rapidity with which the viands were seized and devoured, the strange uncouth phrases and pronunciation; the loathsome spitting, from the contamination of which it was absolutely impossible to protect our dresses; the frightful manner of feeding with their knives, till the whole blade seemed to enter into the mouth; and the still more frightful manner of cleaning the teeth with a pocket knife, soon forced us to feel we were not surrounded by the generals, colonels, and majors of the old world.

Most northerners today would be shocked to know that there is at least one national cockfighting magazine circulating the country, advertising appalling devices to make the cocks more lethal and the illegal sport more bloody. Puritans, for all their sins, never galloped over the landscape after a fox (or, because of the scarcity of foxes nowadays, after a bag of fox dung, demonstrating in Oscar Wilde's phrase, "the unspeakable in pursuit of the uneatable").

In *The Theory of the Leisure Class* Thorstein Veblen gave a memorable name to a phenomenon that ethnologists found in many cultures besides our own—the transvaluation of animals used in transport and hunting to "honorific animals," serving the function of symbolizing Conspicuous Leisure, Conspicuous Consumption, and Conspicuous Waste. The chief honorific animals in our culture are dogs and horses, both exhibited in the competitive sports of the upper classes, and both justified by the remarkable rationalization on the part of their keepers that these animals possess the best qualities of human beings—intelligence (though few have learned to read or write), loyalty, affection, and the like. Dog-loving has evolved to the point that genuine enmity is shown by dog-keepers for cat-keepers. Veblen cuts to the heart of the matter:

> The cat is less reputable than the other two just named, because she is less wasteful; she may even serve a useful end. At the same time the cat's temperament does not fit her for the honorific purpose. She lives with man on terms of equality, knows nothing of that relation of status which is the ancient basis of all distinctions of worth, honor, and repute, and she does not lend herself with facility to an invidious comparison between her owner and his neighbors. The dog has advantages in the way of uselessness as well as in special gifts of temperament. He is often spoken of, in an eminent sense, as the friend of man, and his intelligence and fidelity are praised. The meaning of this is that the dog is man's servant and that he has the gift of an unquestioning subservience and a slave's quickness in guessing his master's

mood. Coupled with these traits, which fit him well for the
relation of status—and which for the present purpose may be
set down as serviceable traits—the dog has some characteristics which are of a more equivocal esthetic nature. He is the
filthiest of the domestic animals in his person and the nastiest
in his habits. For this he makes up in a servile, fawning attitude towards his master, and a readiness to inflict damage
and discomfort on all else. The dog, then, commends himself
to our favor by affording play to our propensity for mastery,
and as he is also an item of expense and commonly serves no
industrial purpose, he holds a well-assured place in men's
regard as a thing of good repute.

Caninophiles have devised many "games" in fulfilling the ulterior purpose Veblen identified. The more passive simply exhibit
them, often with excess jewelry and costuming their own bodies
are too overloaded to carry (Mrs. Potter Palmer in 1890 had a
collar made for her dog set with 2,268 pearls and eight large dia-
monds); the more energetic and ingenious breed them into fantastic and unnatural forms (the darling little dachshund is only an
achondroplastic dwarf, which defect in a human being has dis-
qualified him as a pet since the Middle Ages).

The sports of the leisure class, oriented around dogs and horses,
led to a double standard of morality that Veblen might have
pointed out. An aristocratic horse owner can get into *Who's Who*
on the basis of the racing successes of his stable, calculated in
money won, but a proletarian crap shooter can get only into jail.
Even in the province of legal and acceptable play, there is a wide
disparity in status—compare golf, for instance, with bowling, or
bridge with canasta.

There are survivals in sports as in other aspects of culture, especially in mental attitudes, since the essence of sport and play is
their basic impracticality and uselessness. The leisure class that
Veblen excoriated and its ideas are a survival of the medieval
aristocracy that still persists despite surtaxes and death duties,

devices that the lower classes invented to extinguish it. Aristocracy
was obsolescent in the fourteenth century, when Gaston de Foix
in his treatise on venery, *La Grande Chasse*, deplored the intrusion of the canaille into gentlemanly sports: "I should not teach
to take beasts unless it be by nobleness and gentleness, and to
have good disport, so that there be more beasts, and that they be
not killed falsely." "False" hunting was hunting for food, of which
Foix says: "I will speak no more of this chase, for it is one per-
taining to villains, to the common people, and to the peasants."
It is a tribute to the tolerance of the villains, the common people,
and the peasants, that this attitude has been allowed to continue
down to the present. Had Gaston de Foix survived along with his
ideas to the twentieth century, he would have got on famously
with Avery Brundage, who is their leading exponent today. Brundage cannot go so far in America as the English, who did not
permit Jack Kelly to row in the Henley regatta because he had
once worked with his hands, but it is not his heart that hinders
him. In a recent announcement, Brundage recommended to the
International Olympic Committee that winners of gold medals
be banned from subsequent competition in order to discourage
them from "making a career out of sports." Jack Kelly married
and had a son, who ironically won the Henley, and a daughter,
who became a genuine princess—ironically again, as the consort
of the hereditary owner of an amusement park.

Brundage and, to a lesser degree, the Amateur Athletic Union
and ancillary organizations are opposing an irresistible evolutionary
force which Lewis Henry Morgan a century ago located in time
on the dividing line between man the savage and man the barbarian, and which Veblen caustically adapted to our own society.
The phases of evolution about which Morgan and Veblen theorized are no longer defensible concepts, but the characteristics of
evolution are stronger than either imagined. One of the changes
that took place when man laid down his spear and picked up the
hoe was, said Veblen, that "gradually, as industrial activity further

displaces predatory activity in the community's everyday life and in man's habits of thought, accumulated property more and more replaces trophies of predatory exploit as the conventional exponent of prepotence and success . . . property now becomes the most easily recognized evidence of a reputable degree of success as distinguished from heroic or signal achievement. It therefore becomes the conventional basis of esteem." In less turgid language, college football players want wages instead of medals, and it is certain that they will get wages instead of medals, the N.C.A.A. notwithstanding. When such an inevitable change is opposed, the result is that an activity which should be legal becomes illegal, and sports are thereby delivered into the hands of the professional criminal, whose endeavor has always been to supply the demands of people which the law says must not be filled.

Boxing is an excellent example of a number of these cultural processes at work. As a blood sport, it is a survival of barbarism in a civilized society, certain to be eliminated, probably through the phase of becoming a contrived exhibition, like wrestling. Pugilists used to fight for belts and other trophies, but as they progressed from savagery to the level of barbarism, they were paid for their efforts in coin and cash. The more ancient blood sport, wrestling, has progressed further; its practitioners are not paid in purses, but in more or less regular wages, and the predatory, competitive aspects have entirely disappeared, except in the minds of ladies at ringside, for whom savagery is feigned by the wrestlers. The only hope for boxing to free itself from the grip of the underworld is for it to become so dishonest that, like wrestling, it is of no use to the gamblers. There is evidence that the manly art is very close to this point now.

A further social law illustrated by boxing is that the lowest elements in a class or caste society take up the lowest occupations. Except in the inextinguishable imagination of the *Lumpenproletariat*, boxing pays no rewards, and so its ranks have been filled chiefly from the race or nationality at the bottom of the social heap—first the Germans and the Irish, then the Italians, then the Negroes, and now the Puerto Ricans. The sociologist need go no further than the list of boxing licensees to identify the lowest class in our society at any given time. It is not entirely accidental that the heavyweight champion of the world is an illiterate.

Boxing (whose victims now come mainly from the South and from Manhattan) and the other violent physical sports cultivated by the Cavaliers and their descendants are losing popularity in America. Even such ameliorated physical competitions as baseball hang on mainly through the generosity of income-tax laws to over-rich oilmen and to sports writers who have nothing else to write about in the summer. The vital American sporting competitions are economic, and these are derived from those dour northern ancestors of ours, the Puritans.

Though the patterns of national character cannot be measured or numbered, they exist, and they have been used for a long time by people and nations who have not been so sociologically per-snickety about stereotypes. The Byzantines compiled summaries of the probable behavior of their enemies in war, just as modern Russians compile summaries of the probable behavior of their opponents in chess. Every nation that is truly a nation—that is, a fairly homogeneous ethnic group—exhibits a distinctive ethos; if this is a stereotype, it is a stereotype that has been fulfilling itself since history first recorded it. We have looked at the national character of the Mexicans and have seen it as insufficiency leading to morbidity, as in the sport of bullfighting, a brutal, brutalizing, and boring sport that perseveres in an otherwise civilized nation because as an adult toy it has been wrapped in a fantastic tissue of romanticism, trapped out with meaningless but impressive language ("moment of truth") and gay costumes and flamboyant posters. Even among Mexican children, the national morbidity affects their play. The English cow riddle:

Four stiff standers, four dilly danders, two lookers, two hookers, and a wig wag, becomes in Mexico:

> Cuatro pacapacas, dos miradores, dos matagente, y una
> matamosca (four stampers, two lookers, two mankillers, and
> one fly killer).

We have seen also the polar orientations of behavior proposed
by Ruth Benedict; these are evident in play also. The Apollonian
Hopi child engages in very little play competition; the Hopi girl
takes her amusement in playing house, while her brother indulges
in rivalry only as a member of a team. The Plains Indian boy,
growing up in a frenetic Dionysian atmosphere, imitates his con-
tentious and individualistic father, even to learning raiding and
theft by pilfering food from some other family in the band.

As for our own national character, we have probed our heritage
from the Puritans in several more important aspects of life, but
this heritage can be seen in sports as well. For the unproductive
competitions of their Royalist opponents the Puritans had as little
tolerance as they had for erroneous religious opinions. It was not
entirely true, as Macaulay said, that the Puritans outlawed bull
baiting not because it gave pain to the bull but because it gave
pleasure to the spectators; there was just no money in it. They
had come to catch fish.

Marryat understood this when to his horror the train in which
he was riding from New York to Providence ran through a churchyard with tombstones flashing by on both sides:

> In Rhode Island and Massachusetts, where the Pilgrim fathers
> first landed—the two states that take pride to themselves
> (and with justice) for superior morality and a strict sense of
> religious observances—they look down upon other states of the
> Union, especially New York, and cry out, "I thank thee,
> Lord, that I am not as that publican." Yet here, in Rhode
> Island, are the sleepers of the railway laid over the sleepers
> in death; here do they grind down the bones of their ancestors
> for the sake of gain, and consecrated earth is desecrated by

the iron wheels loaded with Mammon-seeking mortals. And
this in the puritanical state of Rhode Island! Would any
engineer have ventured to propose such a line in England?
I think not. After all, it is but human nature. I have run over
the world a long while, and have always observed that people
are very religious as long as religion does not interfere with
their pockets; but with gold in one hand and godliness in the
other, the tangible is a ways preferred to the immaterial. In
America, everything is sacrificed to time, for time is money.
The New Yorkers would have dashed right through the
church itself; but then they are publicans, and don't pretend
to be good.

The Puritans were too busy for unprofitable play. "You must
not think to goe to heaven on a feather-bed," warned one Puritan
clergyman. "If you will be Christes disciples, you must take up his
crosse, and it will make you sweat." But as long as one must sweat,
one might as well make a little money at it. There was some virtue
in the sweatless endeavor of gambling, since it made money at
times, but gambling was seen as a frivolous imposition upon the
Divine Will, and by no means a certain and predictable source of
revenue—and so we still do not permit any gambling to the working classes more serious than bingo; and it is significant that one
finds bingo more often in Catholic than in Protestant church halls.
As for the other sports, they were wholly unprofitable. The Puritans banned baseball long before baseball was invented. The
wolves of evening had indeed been loosed upon the world when
Assistant Governor Stephen Hopkins was arrested for "suffering
servants and others to sitt drinkeing in his house . . . and to play
at shovel board & like misdemeanors." In Salem Village they
hanged Brigit Bishop as much for providing a shuffleboard in her
tavern as for consorting with the Devil.
     The repression of the play impulse possibly did much to develop
in the American national character the tension that is evident in
everything from the high incidence of cardiac failures to Olympic

track performances. Americans are good at any endeavor that requires the sudden expenditure of built-up energy; they are, conversely, poor at anything that takes steady persistence. In war, our
reputation is good at taking difficult positions and bad at holding
them. In chess, we have never developed a "drawing master," one
who can steer the game between a win and a loss whenever he
chooses. American football is a series of short surges interrupted
by periods of energy-recharging. In Olympic track and field competition, we have won seventy-six first places in events up to 800
meters, and eighty-nine more gold medals in field events that
similarly require a short burst of tremendous effort, but in track
events from 1,500 meters up we have won only one gold medal in
the last half century.

Unluckily for us, the Olympics do not recognize economic
games, for that is what our Puritan heritage trained us to excell in.
In our contention with the Soviets, we have been told that the
approaches of these two great ideologies are symbolized by the
respective national games—the Russian by chess, the American
by poker. There is some validity in this epitome, but the American ethos would be better expressed in the game of PIT, the
perfect American game, a table model of the Chicago grain market where there are few rules but much fast and furious trading,
and in which a set of cards is worn out every few games—in line
with the seriocomic economic suggestion that what this country's
economy needs is a mandatory game whose equipment costs
$5,000 and must be replaced every year. Parker Brothers Inc.,
which sells the game under its patent says that the inventor is
unknown even to them, but that the game has been selling with
increasing popularity in this country since 1902, and that it has
had a longer life than any other proprietary game.

But the Russians refuse to play PIT with us; they are forcing
us to play games, from heavy missiles to chess, on their board.
Since 1957 they have been telling the rest of the world that we
are hopelessly lost in the missile race; now they are telling the

world that we cannot compete in intellectual enterprise either,
that the Soviet system has made them the best chess players in
the world. Let us look into the game of chess and see what meaning there is in it which might help us understand culture,
ourselves, and the Russians.

CHESS—A MICROCOSM

The anthropologist finds tongues in trees, books in the running
brooks, sermons in stones, and significance, if not good, in everything. He believes that if a principle of culture is valid, it should
be discernible in every aspect of that culture. A good teacher of
American civilization can teach a semester course out of *Huckle-
berry Finn*; a good teacher of anthropology can teach a semester
course out of a cigar, a watch, a case of incest, or a case of whiskey
—just as Huxley taught biology out of a piece of chalk. If the
approach of the cultural determinist is valid, the tyranny of culture should be seen as well in chess as in automobile accidents.

Gerald Abrahams, philosopher and chess master, denies that any
force controls chess play other than the human mind. If "there is
mental or volitional freedom to be found in human activity," he
says, "it is in Chess, and the Chess player comes as near as any
human being to demonstrating its reality. It follows, then, that
the Chess mind is of interest, not only to Chess players—many of
whom play very well without knowing anything about it—but to
any philosopher or psychologist who is interested in the intellectual background of the present age. For it so happens that this
impalpable mental freedom, which the Chess player manifests, is
one of those rock-like facts on which some of the most elaborate
constructions of modern deterministic materialism suffer ship-
wreck."

It is true that chess is among the least function-bound of all
human inventions. Clothing, whose purpose is almost entirely the
expression of various symbolic ideas, is highly bound to its culture;

a chair, whose purpose is to hold the human body in a sitting position, is almost free from the determination of culture; but chess, whose purpose is completely self-contained, is, like mathematics (with which it is so often compared), nearly function free. But no segment of culture is wholly independent of the laws of culture, not even mathematics. The mathematics of Newton was adequate for the eighteenth century but is inadequate for the twentieth, and there are, as we have seen, persuasive cultural reasons to account for the limitation of Greek mathematics to the conic section as well as for such polygenetic inventions as the calculus.

Every chess player in the Western world since the late fifteenth century has had the same equipment and the same purpose: a set of sixteen pieces being moved in an agreed and unchanging way upon a checkered board with the object of placing the opposing king into a position of imminent capture. This is the apparent extent of cultural interference; the rest is human, psychological, organic, as Abrahams implies. But through this small chink culture enters, for chess, while coldly mathematical in theory, is played by human beings, who are the instruments of culture. Therefore, a chess player is only as free as his culture permits him to be.

Everyone agrees that in any chess position there is but one efficient way to effect checkmate; so chess play should be, as Norbert Wiener said, "essentially no more difficult than the construction of a system of interlocking systems for a railway signal tower." Yet a person steeped in the history of the game in Europe and America can identify a typical master game of any period by the style of play. In the eighteenth century there is a cold unemotionality about the style, a striving to be mechanical; it is understandable that the most famous player of the century was Baron von Kempelen's Automaton Chess Player—quite in accordance with the dominant philosophical idea of the Age of Reason that the universe was a machine, created, wound up, and then abandoned by its Maker. In the early nineteenth century, chess play became infected with Romanticism, and games slowly took on the characteristic of emotional and artistic beauty, of brilliance, of apparently boundless imagination, and of shallowness. Compatibly and predictably within the principles of diffusion, Romanticism came to the United States several decades after it had been well established in England, and in chess it found expression in the play of Paul Morphy, whose "Game in the Opera Box" is perhaps the archetypical Romantic game (a minor form of diffusion can be seen in the elaboration of Morphy's brilliant coup in this game on the part of European masters in the following years).

Chess, like Western culture in general, became unemotional and mechanically stolid in the last years of the century, represented best in the deadly but unspectacular efficiency of Alexander Alekhine; the ideally representative game of this period was the "Evergreen Zugswang Game," in which the quietest and least aggressive move possible in the final position wins the game.

Romantics as human beings lasted on in chess as in poetry, but suffered the oblivion of any person who lives beyond his age. Time was out of joint for Frank Marshall, a player surely as brilliant as Morphy; Marshall won many beautiful games, but was humiliated in match play by the strongest players of the new school. As a final epitome of the effect of contemporary cultural ideas upon chess, there is the Russian chess composition created to honor Soviet space achievement; in it a queen revolving around the periphery of the board like a sputnik gives perpetual check to a king rotating in the center!

The principles of cultural invention and diffusion are strongly evident in the tangible aspects of the game—the pieces, the board, the rules. The game of chess was diffused to China from India at a time when the Moslem invaders were experimenting with boards of various sizes, so the Chinese board today is squared nine-by-nine, instead of eight-by-eight, which finally became the

Western standard. Chinese culture is an elaborating culture, and the game was almost grotesquely developed in the Orient, with such things as a dividing river added to the center of the board and a most devious piece (Oriental inscrutability!) which could exert power only through one of its own men, added to the forces.

More interesting to Western enthusiasts are the diffusionary changes that occurred as the game spread from India through Persia to the Dry World and into Europe. The piece known as the bishop in English-speaking countries was originally in Indian chess an elephant, but since the Koran prohibited the representation of living things in Islamic art, the realistic figure was represented in Arabian chess by a simple cylinder with a central wedge cut out of the top, supposedly representing the conventionalized ears of the elephant. In Europe, where the last elephants disappeared with Hannibal, this strange figure was misunderstood. In England it looked like a bishop's mitre, and so the piece became a bishop, incidentally affording moralists in that anti-clerical age with material for snide remarks about the sneaking sidewise movement of churchmen. In France the figure looked rather like a jester's cap, and with the compounding and abetting error of a mistranslation (Persian *pil*, "elephant" → Arabic *al fil* → Latin *alfilus*, meaningless → French *fou*, "fool"), it became a court jester. In Russian chess today, the piece is represented by a bishop's mitre but is called *slon*—"elephant."

Even more curious is the evolution of the queen. In India and Persia this was a very weak chessman that could move only one square diagonally. It was called a *farzi* (counselor); this name became the meaningless word *fercia* in Latin, and again was mistranslated by the French into *vierge*—"virgin," thus changing the sex of the piece. About this time in Europe Andreas Capellanus was writing his great treatise on Courtly Love, so the new chess pieced shared in the augmentation of women's privileges, and was promoted from the impotent *farzi* into the queen, and its power aggrandized beyond even that of the king.

A jocose side development out of Courtly Love was the French invention of a variant chess game in which another piece was placed on the queenless side of the king and called a "concubine." This abortive invention of an adulterous French game is only a single instance among uncounted hundreds of similar innovations that cultural drift, analagous to genetic drift, swamped out of existence. Every few weeks the assiduous newspaper reader can see, during lulls in more sensational news, an item about the invention of a three-dimensional chess game—usually by some juvenile player. There are several inconveniences and illogicalities in the rules of chess that nearly every player agrees should be changed, but they have not been changed, and they will not be changed, for it is obviously the intention of our culture that the game be kept as it is, and the nebulous "we" that we hear so much about cannot do much about it.

Polygenetic invention is as frequent in sport as it is in other areas of culture. Curious chess lore abounds with examples of similar positions from dissimilar places and ages. One striking instance is the following pair of problems submitted in a competition in 1898:

A. F. MACKENZIE
America

H. W. LANE
England

From Cherney and Reinfeld: *The Fireside Book of Chess*

Not only were the key move to the solution (Q-R2) and the subsequent lines of play identical, but both Mackenzie and Lane, the composers, were blind!

With regard to chess, the manifestation of cultural interference that is most difficult to explain concerns the way national prowess in the game parallels political position. In Europe, until the nineteenth century, France was the chess power of the world, but immediately after the Napoleonic era England rose to supremacy. She gradually lost out, in the latter part of the century, to the United States. And during the last several decades, we in turn have been struggling with Russia.

The development and perfection of competitive chess play in the Soviet Union since the Communist revolution is of more than mere recreational significance—one can see in it an epitome of the contention between the Communist and the capitalist cultures, and, even beyond that, to the contention of any two incompatible cultures. Though chess was always a favorite game of the Russians —three hundred years ago Burton in his *Anatomy of Melancholy* attributed their interest in chess to climate: "In Muscovy, where they live in stoves and hot houses all Winter long, come seldom or little abroad, it [chess] is again very necessary, and therefore in those parts (saith Herbastein) much used"—it did not become an instrument of national policy and prestige until the expansionist period following the revolution. One of the problems of the propagation of Communism was how to overcome the general Saxon idea that Slavs were as stupid as vegetables; since chess is taken by good chess players to be an infallible gauge of intelligence, the Soviets set about to become the best chess players in the world. They attained their goal beyond question of doubt in 1945, when they crushed the United States in a radio chess match. Those who like to draw mystical parallels may remember that this is the year we made our wrong historical decision—the often-fatal wrong response to a crisis that Toynbee gives as the triggering impulse to the downfall of a civilization—to put away the tools of war and get down once again to business as usual.

This is how the apparently impossible goal of the Russians was achieved. Through propaganda and education, chess was made into the national sport just as factitiously as baseball was made into the American national sport. One hundred thousand persons applied for admission as spectators to the Moscow tournament in 1935. Chess was taught in the grade schools and universities as a regular, and often as a required, subject. Among the working population, trade unionists channel off contentiousness into team chess play instead of strikes, so that a national championship will not attract two or three dozen contestants, as here, but a million, all trying to become Stakhanovites of the chessboard. Such a large number of competitors inevitably turns up a proportionately large number of potentially great players, who are then carefully nursed into mastery. When Botvinnik first became world champion, he was given two days a week off from his engineering work to perfect his play. The masters who represent the country internationally are trained physically like Olympic athletes and mentally like quiz contestants. But this is not enough.

The Soviets control the International Fédération des Echecs by applying the same political acumen they use to control more consequential international organizations; this control secures the best playing conditions for the Russian competitors in any tournament, including referees so sympathetic that the only comparable American parallel would be the home-town umpire who regularly knocked down the visiting first baseman every time a ball was hit. The conduct of pro-Russian referees is quite beyond belief. But this is not enough.

Russian players fill every legal place in a tournament, and when Russians in an international competition play Russians, Russians do not beat Russians unless a Russian winner of the tournament has already been assured. In the World Championship Challengers Tournament of 1953, the nine Soviet contestants treated one another to a total of 138 non-aggressive draws. At the

Saltsjobaden tournament of 1952, every game between a Russian and a Russian ended in a draw. This blatant collusion was so outrageous that the Soviets have been more subtle in recent competitions, but Communist morality will not change until we hear shrimp whistle. It continues perfectly consistent: a Russian must win—by fair means if necessary. But this is not enough.

A Russian team competing internationally is accompanied by several times its number in managers, physicians, cooks, bottle washers, and a second team of players scarcely inferior to the representative team in ability. These act as a two-platoon system. If a Russian is in a difficult position against a capitalist opponent, he will play temporizing moves until the game is adjourned, whereupon he retires for the night, turning over the uncompleted game to a second or a team of seconds, who spend the evening analyzing the game; the next morning they can give their competing master a prefabricated plan for winning. The non-Russian player, meanwhile, who comes to the tournament often alone and at his own expense, has to decide in this situation whether to lose sleep or the game, and generally winds up losing both.

What is the result of this strategy and these tactics? The result of the 1960 World Championship Challengers Tournament gives the answer:

1 Mikhail Tahl, U.S.S.R.
2 Paul Keres, U.S.S.R.
3 Tigran Petrosyan, U.S.S.R.
4 Vassily Smyslov, U.S.S.R.
5-6 Robert J. Fischer, United States, and
    Svetozar Gligorich, Yugoslavia
7 P. Olafsson, Iceland
8 Pal Benko, United States

Tahl then went on to win the world championship from his countryman Botvinnik with some of the weakest play ever seen in grandmaster competition on the part of Botvinnik—and in the rematch in 1961 Tahl promptly lost the championship back again with even weaker play. The credulous attributed the poor play to illness, poor training, age, youth, and the like; the cynical were sure that Botvinnik threw the championship to Tahl in order to add another Russian to the list of world champions—and their suspicions were affirmed when the Soviets after the 1961 event promptly made the brag that six of the twelve holders of the world chess championship were Russians. The 1963 championship saw Petrosyan winning the title from Botvinnik, making the Russian score seven out of thirteen.

If the Rusians can apply such deadly efficiency in so minor an activity as chess, what are they doing in missile development? The answer seems too frightening to contemplate; perhaps we should prepare ourselves for the burial Khrushchev has promised us. But take heart—all is not lost.

Late in 1960, the United States smashed out a stunning victory in the world junior chess championship against all the collusive teams from behind the Iron Curtain, and later, with a second-rate pickup team, finished a close second to the strongest Russian team ever to represent the Soviet Union in the senior world team championship.

The shock of these American successes fell upon the Russians like a kettle of hot water on an anthill—chess directors were scalded by official criticism; chess dialecticians were seen scurrying off, in all directions; and like the Americans after Sputnik, everyone underwent agonizing reappraisal. "They," however, are determined to do something about the situation. One of the first efforts was to adopt the American poker technique of "psyching" the eighteen-year-old American champion, Bobby Fischer, in the Bled Alekhine Memorial Tournament. Bobby scored four wins and a draw against the top five Russians; the fellow who got the draw came at the end, and had made the sobering decision to go back to the old Russian system.

In this difficult time, perhaps we should go back to the old

American system. We might train our chess players to emulate the old colonel who sat in the Mercantile Chess Club in Philadelphia from some time around 1850—by the look of him—to the late 1940's.

The colonel had a ploy. He chewed tobacco, whose juices ran like Aaron's hair oil freely down his otherwise white beard, yea, even to the hem of his garments; this disconcerted opponents who were at all fastidious about personal appearance. The colonel was wont also to set an old tin can by the side of the board, rather toward his opponent's side, in lieu of a spittoon.

When the colonel's aim was off, he won a remarkable number of games.

The Arts in America

In 1962 the Museum of Modern Art in New York hung a Matisse *gouache*. For forty-seven days some 116,000 art lovers filed by— before one of them realized it was hanging upside down. Shortly afterward Nikita Khrushchev visited an exhibition of modern art in Soviet Russia, and being more assertive in his expertise than the Americans, he declared that in his opinion the paintings had been smeared on the canvas by the tail of a deviationist donkey. The Russian artists agreed, yes, now that he mentioned it, gosh, it did look as if an ass had got loose in the studio, yes, it did indeed, yes, and scurried back to painting tractors. Not so the Americans. With typical Yankee ingenuity and disregard for the property rights of Russians, such as they are, one of them, Arthur Watson, director of the Baltimore zoo, dipped a donkey's tail in a bucket of black paint and backed the animal up to a canvas. The result, submitted without explanation to a Baltimore art authority, was pronounced to be a fine example of abstract expression, and was sold to a Texan for fifty dollars.

The Baltimore donkey was a late comer to primitive art, having been antedated by at least one chimpanzee, whose bank account is now probably larger than yours. But man forges ahead of his primate poor relations; there is the fellow who paints great murals by sloshing gallons of paint over a quarter acre of canvas laid on the floor of a loft and then stroking it out in bold lines with a pair of skis. Another, more advanced technologically, uses the same medium but delineates his imagery by running an automobile back and forth over it. Laymen in their ignorance think all this is aimless, but the artists know what they are doing, according to this paragraph excerpted by the New Yorker from a gallery catalog:

> Only the recourse to the hylemorphic principle of the individuation of a haecceity quanticly defined (*qua substantia fit haec*)—a universal formality may be applied univocally to all things—may still be possible as the last means of a volitive and actual achievement of the individual in deferring the ineluctible rarefaction of the critico-organic ontities and the corollary engulfing of all possibility of transumption of the epistomological reality into maximum intelection.

This is quite wrong. It is not true that the fundamental pseudo-duality of the substantiality of the I indicates its failure the moment the world plunges further into the myth of relative knowledge and anticipates the approaching decline of the privilege of the real demeanor—the intuitive realization of the vacuity of existence.

Not one artist in a hundred knows what he is doing. If they did, they would stop it. More than a century ago the greatest art critic of his time, John Ruskin, admitted that the function of the artist had passed away, and "the painter has no profession, no purpose. He is an idler on earth, chasing the shadows of his own fancies."

If Ruskin had had some knowledge of ethnology, he would

have had evidence to make a fact of what was only an opinion. Throughout the primitive world there is almost no art for art's sake, except when a culture begins its decline. Art is the perceptible expression of a philosophical concept, which means it is usually religious; but it also can be the support and essence of a social or political system, if such a system can take hold of men's minds like a religion. When Aurignacian man 30,000 years ago scratched the first pictures on a cave wall he was conjuring *mana*—plugging in to a spiritual electric outlet. Our troglodytic ancestors may have been fiddling around with the first prurient art in carving their hyperfeminine stone "Venuses," but, except for this insignificant genre of Paleolithic pin-ups, the art of the cave man was magical, as the recently-discovered La Colombière Pebble proved beyond all quibble. Living Paleolithic peoples make art for no other reason that a religious one—until the white man arrives with his irresistible materialism, which drives out the spiritual every time. As for the situation among ourselves, no further comment is needed beyond calling attention to Salvador Dali, as consummate a craftsman as ever set brush to canvas, whose function in modern culture is to be a clown.

Another circumstance operative in modern civilization makes it impossible for artistic genius to fulfill itself: what anthropologist Alfred Kroeber called the "exploitation and exhaustion of culture patterns." When an artifact is invented, it is developed through a series of improvements until its maximum efficiency is reached, after which begins decorative art; art in this sense is the master craftsman playing with his achievement. This is the phase of artistic exploitation, which evolves until the pattern is exhausted. Beyond this, there is nothing in either functional or artistic development except grotesquerie. The destiny of the Model T mudguard is to become the Cadillac tailfin, and of Rembrandt to become Picasso. The Second Law of Thermodynamics works as well in art as it does in physics: in the end, entropy overcomes order.

In the England of the first Elizabeth there were about five million people, only a small percentage of whom could read and write. Yet this population, half the size of that of metropolitan New York, turned out a half dozen or more playwrights of the same class if not rank as Shakespeare—Marlowe, Massinger, Ford, Beaumont, Webster, Jonson, Fletcher, Heywood, Dekker, Kyd, and the unknown author of *Edward III*, which would be among Shakespeare's greatest historical tragedies if he had written it. Marlowe's early dramas are easily superior to those of the young Shakespeare, but Marlowe had the bad luck to get fatally mixed up in a barroom brawl while still in his twenties. Now there are more than 300 million people in the English-speaking world, with incomparably better education than Elizabeth's subjects, incomparably more to write about, and three and a half centuries of dramatic experience to draw from, and whom do we have to put over against Shakespeare? Tennessee Williams.

Similarly with poetry. In Shakespeare's England everybody could write publishable verse, even Henry the Eighth, when he was not gourmandizing or wenching. Sir Walter Raleigh would be remembered in history if he had done nothing else than write his poetry. That was the age when a courtier could compose in verse recipes for almond tarts while fighting a duel, and a gutter rat such as Robert Greene could write lyrics as beautiful as *Sephestia's Song to her Child*:

> *Weep not, my wanton, smile upon my knee,*
> *When thou art old, there's grief enough for thee.*

Poetry lasted longer than drama—well into the nineteenth century before it sickened, and until 1963 before it died with Robert Frost. Poetic art and adventure died together; in this century the man who was Elizabeth's Walter Raleigh fulfills himself as Beverly Aadland's Errol Flynn.

At the time when a pattern is exhausted it is the part of genius to foresee the end of his art and to search for a new pattern. The magazine editors are just now realizing that prose fiction has run its course, but Joyce saw this two generations ago and and tried to fight his way out of the closed maze with two stupendous books that are now sadly revealing themselves for all their genius as grotesqueries. But his effort and that of Picasso in the medium of graphic art are the work of giants; lesser men like e. e. cummings bite at the cage in work that in every sense is lower case.

Of all modern civilizations, none has been affected more by the circumstances of cultural change than America, since none has moved faster. One of these circumstances is the exhaustion of patterns; therefore our art seems very poor. At first the process of function development—the settlement of a new and hostile environment—prevented the growth of art, and then the rapid change of the young agricultural nation into a mature industrial society bypassed the phase of artistic elaboration entirely. All along the way, foreign critics noticed and declaimed the barrenness of American art, few of them suspecting that forces beyond the ignorance and crudity of Americans were responsible for the situation. Alfred d'Alembert in his *Flânerie Parisienne* a century ago had a chapter on "Beaux Arts en Amérique"—followed by a blank page. Even de Tocqueville, who could be relied upon for a kind word, was no consolation here. And we have never been allowed to forget Sydney Smith's catechism of "In the four quarters of the globe, who reads an American book? or goes to an American play? or looks at an American picture or statue?" and the rest of it.

America had other handicaps in art—democracy, for instance. Democracies make fine machines, but they do not make fine art. Harry Lime, in *The Third Man*, observes that Italy under the Borgias was an oppressive tyranny of vice and corruption that produced the greatest art of Western civilization, whereas Switzerland, with five hundred years of democracy, produced—the cuckoo clock. Art and industry in a democracy are dependent upon popular acceptance, and the greatest good for the greatest number means absolute excellence for none. This is one of the consequences of having faith in the people, and it is a small enough concession for the benefits of democracy, even though at times the most liberal of us feel that some limit ought to be imposed on democratic freedom—for example, on the Natural Rights of the woman who complained to her local television station because Colonel Glenn's flight had pre-empted "The Price Is Right."

ART IN THE COLONIES

The failure of colonial religion to inspire art is a further indication of its basic irreligiousness. The Puritans flew in the face of their culture as well as of their God, but they were not alone. In Philadelphia the Quakers allowed neither music nor the theater, fine houses or good clothing, or expensive silverware or furniture. Philadelphia became a center of science and the crafts only after Franklin threw the peaceable Quakers out of the government during the Indian wars. Some of the other religions made respectable art in spite of themselves—like the sexless Shakers at Niskayuma, but they were the exceptions.

Early American art was industry. Cabinetmaking became one of the first indigenous American arts after the dependence on English imports ceased, but, predictably, this and the other artistic industries were nothern, Puritan. Of the first three dozen notable colonial cabinetmakers, only four were even marginally southern.

These northern artisans made several worthwhile inventions in furniture, among them the banjo clock, the butterfly table, and the rocking chair, all of which fell under the usual British ridicule of the unfamiliar. Dickens was the most prophetic of the lot when he said that "it would be impossible to get anywhere in America without a rocking chair." But before these inventions could begin artistic elaboration they were given over to the machine, which made them better and cheaper than the man with the chisel. Lambert Hitchcock's "Hitchcock Chair," made in Hitchcocksville, Connecticut, was the first of America's mass-produced furniture.

Materialistic America became a world center of craftsmanship in silver as soon as silver became common enough to be used as tableware, and spiritual Boston was the American center of materialistic silver working. Again, the South produced few artists of note in this medium, but in the northern colonies there were hundreds of silversmiths, many of them better at their work than Paul Revere.

Glassmaking was still another important consumer art in America from the time of the first settlement in Virginia, and the products of Henry William Stiegel of Manheim, Pennsylvania, and Caspar Wistar of Salem County, southern New Jersey, are highly valued today, even by Englishmen. Wistar established an industrial tradition in South Jersey that lasted almost to the present; nearly every man there over sixty used to be a glassblower.

Early colonial architecture is a good example of what the anthropologist calls environmental determination. The Puritans tried to build English houses on the rocky soil of New England, but the weather made them into something more appropriate. The storms tore the half-timbered daub apart; the low humidity, compared with that of the East Midlands, made thatch impractical, and the cold narrowed the windows and sloped the roofs. Log cabins would have been a better construction to begin with, but there were no log cabins in Puritan New England.

Philadelphia benefited architecturally from the Great Fire of London, which persuaded the British to let Wren have a go at designing their houses for awhile. Philadelphia, founded a few years after the fire, adopted the architectural style of Wren, and became for a little while the most beautiful city in the British world.

On the whole, architecture in America has been always too important to industrial function to be limited by artistic considerations, and it is therefore not an imposed art as it is elsewhere. American buildings are designed from the inside, to suit a particular use, and the outside has to shift pretty much for itself.

Invidious comparisons are often made between the flimsy glass-and-steel structures of contemporary America and the beautiful solidity of the Parthenon by those who understand the function of neither. Given the environment of Greece, the purpose for which the Parthenon was built, and the architectural precedents of Greek culture, even an American could build one. We have built several, as a matter of fact, including one in Nashville, Tennessee, more impressive than the original, but the American pattern of expansionism demands buildings that can be added to when a new child or a new car comes into the family or a new stock flotation into the company or a new product into the agency —and it is hard to put wings and upper stories on a Parthenon.

An art comparatively free from industrial function is painting, but it did not catch on in Puritan New England because the Puritans still had some qualms about that Second Commandment. Only the Quakers did anything of note with paint and canvas; more accurately, only the Quaker Edward Hicks did anything of note with painting in the religious colonies. Hicks put his life into painting "Peaceable Kingdoms" in which emaciated lions lie down with uneasy lambs. Other painting was mostly portraiture, and when an artist found a vain subject with money, he had a job for life. Gilbert Charles Stuart, we know, made a good thing of George Washington, but he was not the only one. Charles Willson Peale made fourteen portraits of Washington. A more stimulating drive than portraiture was lacking, so that the three greatest American painters—John Singleton Copley, Benjamin West, and James Whistler—all went to England.

Americans excelled in three of the arts—music, literature, and the theater—and Puritanism had nothing to do with two of them, music and the theater. Gilbert Chase, the important historian of American music, tries to make a case for the Puritans. He tells us that Robert Browne, the father of the Separatist Pilgrims, was known in his time as a "singular good lutenist," which is as may be, but he never came to America. He quotes also Edward

Winslow's statement that "many of our congregation [are] very expert in music," a claim that appears in a book significantly entitled *Hypocrasie Unmasked*. And he tells us further that while "specific references to musical instruments in New England before 1700 are rare, yet they *are* mentioned several times." He goes on to mention them—in sum, three viols, a guitar, and a virginal.

There are many more references in Puritan writing to music, but nearly all of them are in court records, being accounts of people fined for indulging in this vice. It should be kept in mind that one of the charges the Puritans of the Massachusetts colony tried to work up into a capital case against Thomas Morton was that he introduced music to accompany the revels on Merry Mount.

The Puritans did sing psalms, in a manner of speaking. In William Brewster's library of three hundred volumes there was one book on music—*The Palms of David in Metre*; but what we can glean from the commentaries tells us that Puritan psalm singing contributed infinitesimally to vocal art. In 1724 James Franklin's *New England Courant* describes it:

> . . . the same person who sets the Tune, and guides the Congregation in Singing, commonly reads the Psalm, which is a task so few are capable of performing well, that in Singing two or three staves the Congregation falls from a cheerful Pitch to downright *Grumbling*.

Thomas J. Wertenbaker says that in the Salem church there is this inscription carved into a pew:

> *Could poor David but for once*
> *To Salem church repair,*
> *And hear his Psalms thus warbled out,*
> *Good Lord, how he would swear.*

Before the close of the Puritan hegemony, things began to change in American music. Isaac Watts in England anticipated

the shift from intellectualism to emotion in religion and went to
the heart of the issue, questioning the propriety of the psalms
themselves and thereby giving himself the opportunity to write
songs more appropriate for both morality and the voice. In 1739
the first American edition of his enormously influential *Hymns
and Spiritual Songs* was published, a collection that at once became the chief fuel for the Great Awakening then blazing all
along the American frontier. About the same time Governor
Oglethorpe of Georgia invited the preacher John Wesley to come
to his colony. Wesley had been exposed to Moravian singing, and
decided to make lusty song his medium in spreading the gospel;
thus the singing and shouting Methodists.

John's effort was strengthened by his brother Charles, and the
two of them issued a number of popular hymn books. There was
nothing that could stop a Methodist from joyful singing; one of
their favorite hymns was "Over the Corpse of a Believer":

> *Ah, lovely appearance of Death,*
> *No sight upon Earth is so fair;*
> *Not all the gay Pageants that breathe,*
> *Can with a dead Body compare.*

Between the Methodists in the South and the latter-day Puritans in the North (whom Jonathan Edwards stirred up with his
terrifying sermons), there was an indescribable proliferation of
eccentric religious bands, some of them the shouting and singing
kind. A random example is the German Ephrata Cloister or
Community of the Solitary, led by Conrad Beissel and Peter
Miller. These Pennsylvania Dutchmen had several manuscript and
printed hymnals, the most impressive being the *Turtel-Taube*,
which contained 750 hymns.

Of secular singing we hear very little from the written accounts,
though Benjamin Franklin as a disgruntled shopkeeper gives us a
hint of how the popular interest was turning in the cities of
colonial America when he complains: "I have known a very

numerous impression of Robin Hood songs go off in this Province
at 2s per Book less than a Twelvemonth; when a small quantity
of David's Psalms have lain on my hands above twice the time."

While we have Franklin in mind, we should mention also his
invention, now wholly forgotten except by historians of music, of
the "Glassychord," a device he gave the more impressive name
of Armonica, later to be Cockneyized into "Harmonica" and
applied to a more plebian instrument. While in France Franklin
was exposed to a parlor game in which brief musical sounds were
produced by rubbing a wettened finger against the rim of a thin
tumbler; Franklin's Yankee mind extracted the essence of this
device, and he constructed an instrument on which were strung
glass bowls on an axle, like a shishkebab, and turned by a foot-
operated spindle. This is the most important American invention
in musical instruments until the autoharp; Mozart and Beethoven
composed serious pieces for it, and it was praised by Richter,
Schiller, and Goethe. Franz Anton Mesmer used it to hypnotize
his patients. Suddenly about the beginning of the nineteenth
century people admitted that the thing actually set their teeth
on edge, and it vanished from the musical scene.

Vernon Parrington said: "A world that accepted Michael Wigglesworth for its poet and accounted Cotton Mather its most distinguished man of letters had certainly backslidden in the ways of
culture." Both are poor candidates for the position Parrington
imputes to them, but the historical fact is that neither stood for
the position of poet or writer. Mather published 382 books, which,
on bulk alone, entitles him to some consideration as a man of
letters, but these writings were inspired by his vanity in wanting
his most inconsequential and bombastic talk preserved. We picture him running around a Boston street, picking up pages of
a sermon the wind blew out of his hand; he got them all, and
the Devil got nothing for his deviltry. Mather was a director of
Puritan society with the same relation to literature as President

Kennedy or Prime Minister Churchill, each of whom could be called a very successful writer if historians chose to ignore their other accomplishments.

Michael Wigglesworth got into poetry for the simple reason that he was too sick to preach.

> *Thou wonderest perhaps*
> *that I in Print appear,*
> *Who to the Pulpit dwell so nigh,*
> *yet come so seldome there.*
> *The God of Heaven knows*
> *what Grief to me it is,*
> *To be with-held from serving Christ:*
> *no Sorrow like to this.*

And no poet ever began his work with a more honest and accurate estimation of himself.[1]

Most critics of the vulnerable Puritan efforts at literature forget that Puritan expressive art was oratory, the most ephemeral of media and the hardest to convey in print. Jonathan Edwards's *Sinners in the Hands of an Angry God* is a fairly effective bit of fright to read, but no one who has not experienced while in the bonds of religious belief such a preacher delivering such a sermon can imagine how much is lost in the translation. There is still a masochistic pleasure in this kind of literature, and this perverse desire no doubt shot Wigglesworth's *The Day of Doom* into the position of one of America's all-time best sellers. Maugham was merely being arrogant in saying: "If I set down every action in my life and every thought that has crossed my mind, the world would consider me a monster of depravity," for everyone is like this to the best of his ability. As for Wigglesworth being a preacher, so was Mickey Spillane.

It is fashionable, too, to criticize the *Bay Psalm Book* for committing such literary atrocities as:

[1] "Reader, I am a Fool."

The Lorde to me a shepheard is
Want therefore shall not I

but this was put together by a committee, an agency that did no
better when it constructed the camel. Over against these easy-
to-find Horrible Examples in Puritan literature one could put
Edward Taylor, the metaphysical poet who ranks well with his
great English counterparts, but it is true that the greatness of
Puritan literature was only latent, kept from fruition by the religious delusion of the colonial church.

American literature stands so high today among the literatures
of the world that it does not even need to be surveyed here in
defense of American art. According to unimpeachable sources, it
has even been taught in some English universities. And it is all
Puritan, from Hawthorne to Hemingway, even when, from Hawthorne to Hemingway, it rebels against our inherited Puritanism.
When American literature is good, which is very often, it is dissentient, exercising the most important of the legacies from
Puritanism.

Southern literature suffers from the lack of the Puritan drive of
protest. In colonial times it was a vast literary Lubberland, weakly
imitative of obsolescent English writing, with readable material
found only in manuscripts not designed to be read publicly (like
the diary of the sotweed factor William Byrd, which contains such
eye-opening entries as his curious practice of rogering his wife on
the billiard table). Even after the Civil War, Southern literature
seldom rose out of its dullness to dissent. Anthologies are mislead-
ing in this respect; when they include such Southern writers as
William Gilmore Simms and John Pendleton Kennedy it is only
for the sake of geographical symmetry and the desirability of selling college texts to Southern colleges, and scholars who study them
for reasons other than regional patriotism are not so much literary
authorities as ethnographers. As one of the Southern lady poets
expressed it:

Poor South! Her books are fewer and fewer;
She was never much given to literature.

MUSIC—AMERICA'S UNRESPECTED ART

Americans abroad apologize for American music almost as eagerly as they apologize for American tourists; yet, of all things American, none is more avidly and universally wanted than our popular music. In India they still refuse to eat hot dogs; in China they eschew ice cream; in Australia they prefer chilblains to central heating; in England they spell tires "tyres" and drive on the wrong side of the road just to spite Americans; but our music has no opposition but the official, anywhere. All over the world American folk song and its derivatives—the blues, jazz, popular song, and hillbilly song—are driving out their aboriginal counterparts. On the island of Puka Puka in the remotest South Pacific, the only songs the last Polynesians sing are American hillbilly tunes. In Spain rock 'n' roll is displacing the *cante jondo*. In many parts of Africa Louis Armstrong is the only known American. In Australia the Stone Age natives often get guitars before they get trousers. And even in Russia, after two generations of ferocious anti-Americanism, Elvis Presley records are a prime item in smuggling.

One of the insights that anthropology provides is that there *is* an accounting for tastes. The Eskimo eats rotten fish, the Ubangi makes love to women with lips stretched over saucers, the Australian natives knock out their front teeth and mutilate their sexual organs, the Ona run around naked in the sleet—because their culture persuades them that these things are good, not because there is any intrinsic, universal good in the things themselves. We like to imagine that there are objective standards in music—whether the scales and modes are sophisticatedly complex, whether the intervals are in harmonious mathematical relationship, whether the lyrics are coherently structured and richly allusive in narrative songs and evocative of worthy emotions, whether the singing is polyphonous, whether the instruments are varied in type and unvaried in tuning, whether the musicians are long trained to their art—but to most peoples outside Western civilization these criteria are as irrelevant as judging automobiles by their taste. In the primitive world music seethes the savage breast. It is an adjunct to frenzy, a means of building up martial spirit, of bewitching a woman to love, of cursing an enemy, of ridiculing a fool, of frightening a ghost, of placating a god. Americans profess dislike of their most original and influential art because their culture tells them to do so. Across the centuries, Puritan intolerance forces a contempt for popular music because popular music owes nothing to Puritanism. Its rhythm came from the Dry World before the Negroes, its literature from England before the Normans.

Of the two primary elements of music, rhythm is the most vital. Rhythm comes early to the human animal; before he walks, he dances; before he talks, he sings. As soon as a child is old enough to stand, he will bob up and down in good time to strong rhythm, whether it comes from a mountain banjo, a Viennese piano, or an Australian *didgeridu.*

The best rhythm in the world, primitive or sophisticated, is beaten out by the ferocious nomads who surge across the 10,000-mile width of desert from Morocco to the Gobi. From Assyrian times these people—Mongols, Turks, Tatars, Moors, Bedouins, Kurds, Tuaregs, and other folk rather too close to ourselves to identify—have poured all of their psychic energy into the production of frenzy: war, pillage, murder, lust, greed, vengeance, religion, and music. In the few times in their history that the Dry World nomads settled into peaceful sedentariness, their energy created nearly everything we understand to be civilization. The ancient cultures of the Fertile Crescent from Egypt to Akkad did not drain away entirely when evaporation overtook precipitation in their climate. The substance, the seed—rhythm—washed along with the rest of the elevated Middle Eastern culture into India

and the Orient and there grew to an incredible degree, finally
turning away from its original purpose of feeding emotion and
becoming mathematical exercises. Running off to the south, the
rhythms of the desert nomads (together with many of the instruments of the ancient world) gave the African peoples a nucleus
around which their civilization built itself.

Before the African infant can walk, he absorbs rhythm, strapped
to his mother's back as she goes about her rhythmic chores. He is
taught to clap his hands in proper time before he is able to stand,
and when he walks, he begins his dancing. His games are designed,
as one authority on African music says, not only for amusement,
but to develop a strong feeling for compound rhythm. In line with
the ulterior purpose of children's games, the toys children play
with are musical instruments, which they are encouraged to make
themselves. As the African child grows older, he is put into competition with past standards and present performances of others
in dancing and its accompaniment, and ineptness is always ridiculed and often punished. By the time an African Negro reaches
adulthood, music has become indistiguishable from an instinctive
trait, as it once was thought to be; it has, in a manner of speaking,
become culturally instinctive, and he can no more escape it than
a lion can escape eating meat. African culture made the Negro a
slave—but it also made him a musician.

All American folk and popular music is run through with
African rhythm; jazz and its derived forms only show it more
plainly. Take for example the blues, which incorporates nearly
every technique developed in jazz. Specifically, the blues seems,
from internal evidence alluding to emancipation, the problems
faced by the Negroes during Reconstruction, and the like (as well
as from the fact that jazz instruments came into Negro culture
from surplus sales of military band instruments after the war),
to be a post-Civil War form, possibly an outgrowth of the "field
holler," the moaning song of the solitary worker. Technically, the
blues developed in three phases: first, the single line repeated over

and over, as in most primitive music, from two to four bars long; second, the eight-bar blues, two lines of four measures each; and third, the classic twelve-bar blues subdivided into three lines of four bars each.

Improvisation is a feature of all African singing, and in the classic blues the first line is repeated to give time to improvise the third. The blues singer does not take up all four bars (sixteen beats), but rather uses nine, ten, or eleven, letting the missing beats be supplied by the instrumental accompaniment which is an integral part of the blues, and which takes the place of the sung response in the typical African call-and-response antiphony. Purely African, too, is the "blue" element—the adaptation of the diatonic scale to the more characteristic African pentatonic by flatting the third and the seventh tones, the "blue notes." Of course, the genuine blues singer is not aware of these and other processes when he sings, for culture internalizes rather than intellectualizes its directives to its carriers.

Jazz is unquestionably the great contribution of America to world culture, though some of us would prefer to have our civilization represented by other things. It is a form that ranges from the infra-folk to the ultra-sophisticated, and, in the opinion of most liberal musicologists, it is the new pattern that must be developed when our calcifying serious music exhausts itself.

The bluegrass hillbilly is even less conscious of how his music was made than the blues singer, for his genre incorporates not only the African stream of influences, but also the lyric and metrical tradition of his Anglo-Saxon forebears. These oldest English were not anthropophagi whose heads grew beneath their shoulders, as the French would have us believe, but quite a civilized people, more advanced in many things than the 12,000 thieves who landed at Hastings.

One of these things was literature. The great epic of the Anglo-Saxons, *Beowulf*, is tedious and silly in the Frenchified language in which most of us must read it, but in the original Anglo-Saxon it is a poem of supreme mastery in theme, expression, and prosody. The language of the Anglo-Saxons was well fitted for literature, as the history of English culture since their time repeatedly shows; for every British or American or Australian sculptor, one can easily name a hundred writers, for the English genius lies in literary expression. And not only the genius for literature and the frame of mind necessary to make it last through the centuries, but the form and devices of literature as well. Many of the poets in English who had no knowledge at all of Anglo-Saxon language or prosody, from Marlowe on, nevertheless retained the essence of that ancient literature.

Whether English literature would have been richer, had King Harold Godwinsson not had to exhaust his army fighting off Earl Tostig and King Harold Hardraada at Yorkshire, we can never know, but English folklore would surely have been poorer, for it would have had to emanate from the Welsh and the Scots, who had little of that Celtic magic that enriches the literature of their Irish cousins. But Harold Godwinsson got an arrow in his eye at Hastings and the French swarmed in, driven by greed and helped by cunning (the two qualities of the Norman French mentioned as outstanding by their countryman Geoffrey Malaterra). There was no fraternization for the first century of conquest; the Normans put the Anglo-Saxons to work tending their swine, the Anglo-Saxon culture declined, and the Anglo-Saxon people became the English folk, sharing only meagerly in the new English civilization.

The Americans were folk from the beginning. Raleigh's unlucky settlers were drawn from the lowest and most ignorant classes in England. Francis Bacon was thinking of the Americans when he counseled his government that "it is a shameful and unblessed thing to take the scrum of people and wicked condemned men to be the people with whom you plant." Time went on, but the quality of the immigrants—so far as sophistication and social position determined quality—remained close to the folk level.

By one means or other, the Puritans drove the minority-group
later comers to the wilderness, to separate again a whole people
into a new division of civilized and folk enclaves. After 1745, the
collapse of the Scottish Jacobites and their Irish allies sent refugees streaming to America by the tens of thousands to settle in
the eastern mountains and become the hillbillies. Later, the Irish,
who came over in millions after the potatoes failed in the 1840's;
the Germans, driven out by reprisals after their mid-nineteenth
century rebellions; the Scandinavians and Central Europeans,
brought over in a culture capsule by the railroad entrepreneurs;
the Mormons, planting an Eden in the Utah desert after being
harried across the country by religious hate, their own and their
neighbors'—all these and countless others established the folk
groups that created American folk music.

The people who molded the influences of the Anglo-Saxons and
the Negroes into the folk music that produced sophisticated jazz
and popular song were the hymn singers who abandoned the
psalms almost a century before the nation's beginning, but hymns
spread sluggishly until the camp meeting was invented by the
Reverend James McGready, a Presbyterian minister, around 1800.
The great distances in America, which produced other momentous
inventions such as the telephone, made necessary the itinerant
preacher, the circuit rider. But even the most peripatetic of these—
for example, Francis Asbury, who traveled some 275,000 miles on
horseback—could not reach their parishioners often enough to
keep the frontier souls saved; hence, the camp meeting. Camp
meetings spread as fast as the circuit riders themselves, and in
many places each meeting developed into a new denomination.
They were beyond counting; there was even a sect called "The
Christians."

Of all these singing sinners, the most fascinating to the ethno-
musicologist were the shaped-note, "buckwheat note," fasola,
Sacred Harp (so-called after their first shaped-note hymnal) folk
who "jerked," as the saying went, from one end of the frontier to
the other, but who now have been compressed by encroaching

education into a thin line from east Texas to Georgia. Culturally, these are the real Tobacco Road folk, but their fugueing contrapuntal and modal harmonies, badly imitated by their Negro neighbors, engendered the spirituals.

Roy Harris, sometimes called America's outstanding living composer, recently visited the campus of the University of Colorado and spoke about the state of American music to fewer than two hundred and fifty people. A month earlier an undistinguished folk-singing trio drew an audience nearly ten times as large, though they had to pay to get in, whereas the Harris talk was free. Mr. Harris is a warm and genial man, but he is saddened by what he sees happening to his art. It is all downhill, he fears, with the symphony orchestra leading the funeral cortege into oblivion. Despite immense wealth, neither CBS nor NBC carries a symphony orchestra, though they could have one for much less than they would have to pay Paul Anka for his services. All over the country it is the same; where there is no patronage from the Conspicuous Consumers, there is no serious music. The few surviving orchestras play repertoires that include only four per cent of music composed by Americans. Mr. Harris knows what is at the heart of the trouble: Madison Avenue, materialism, football, the noise of civilization, materialism, the affluent society, materialism, juke-boxes, the Hidden Persuaders, Muzak, the Lonely Crowd, materialism, automation, and of course materialism. He asks that "we do something about it."

It is too bad, truly, but American musical genius, Mr. Harris, expresses itself in the deplored art of popular music, not in your "serious" music, which belongs to another time and another culture. Those in whose interest it is to praise American composers of respectable music cannot commend it, and those for whom the composers write will not listen to it. Warren Storey Smith, music editor of the *Boston Post*, said of Aaron Copland's *Piano Concerto* at its Boston presentation in 1927, "If there exists anywhere in the world a stranger concatenation of meaninglessly ugly sounds

and distorted rhythms . . . Boston has been spared it." Smith's
rival newspaper, the Boston *Evening Transcript*, concurred: "The
Copland Piano Concerto is a harrowing horror from beginning to
end. . . . The piano part of the composition is not played but
merely happened upon at random, as it might be if the performer
struck the keyboard with his elbows instead of his fingers."

Henry Cowell, another candidate for the position of America's
Most Distinguished Composer, inspired this remark in a German
critic: "It is said about Cowell that he has invented tonal groups
that can be played on the piano with the aid of fists and forearms!
Why so coy? With one's behind one can cover many more notes!"

American serious music could have had a quick death by drown-
ing in such calumny instead of perishing of disinterest if it were
not for the tradition that every great musical innovator must be
damned before he can be appreciated; no other art gives its practitioners such sublime comfort. Slonimsky has put together a
bookful of musical invective in which surprising things are said
by famous people about great musicians. John Ruskin, the bright
champion of Culture, wrote a friend that "Beethoven always
sounds to me like the upsetting of bags of nails, with here and
there an also dropped hammer." Nietzsche asked: "Is Wagner a
human being at all? Is he not rather a disease?" And Tchaikovsky
wrote in his diary on October 9, 1886: "I played over the music
of that scoundrel Brahms. What a giftless bastard!"

Invective is all that American composers seem to share with
their European predecessors, and as Roy Harris says, there is little
hope for the Americans. Ironically, the man who is unobtrusively
moving up to the historical lead in his profession is George
Gershwin, who was a Tin Pan Alley piano banger until Paul
Whiteman persuaded him to get into the high-status–low-pay
division of his trade. Gershwin applied for and received the necessary invective ("*An American in Paris* is nauseous claptrap, so
dull, patchy, thin, vulgar, long-winded and inane, that the average
movie audience would be bored by it"), picked up a St. John to

make straight his path (Oscar Levant), and gave himself respecta-
bility by changing the titles of early follies ("Rhapsody in Rivets"
became the *Second Rhapsody*).

An Englishman remarked in 1830 that Americans "have neither
made any music nor do they show the slightest appreciation of it.
Even their 'Yankee Doodle' and 'Hail Columbia' were not written
by Yankees." The name of Francis Hopkinson, "the first serious
American composer," the "greatest colonial musician," does not
appear in *Chambers's Biographical Dictionary*, which however
gives the biography of Jesse James. According to nearly everybody,
Edward MacDowell is "America's greatest composer," but it is
possible that some readers of this paragraph have never heard his
name. Certainly some have never heard his music. Not in our lifetime will Americans learn to appreciate the importance of their
only vital music, the music Roy Harris deplores; but they had
better learn to appreciate it, for they have no other.

A DEMOCRATIC GENRE: SOMATIC ART

Probably popular music would not come in for so much condemnation if it did not pretend, in the absence of any rival, to art.
Another democratic expression has made no such pretension, and
it therefore occupies even more of the attention of Americans,
with scarcely any criticism, even by British visitors. To give it the
pretension it deserves, let us call it somatic art—the beautification
of the body. God knows—or at least foreign commentators know—
that the ugly Americans need beautification, not only for the
reasons Burdick and Lederer made their fortunes by revealing, but
because in a democracy personal adornment must counterfeit
the inner beauty that in more noble countries comes through one's
genealogy. In neither case will zoological objectivity say much for
the natural attractiveness of the human animal. "A pair of pincers
set over a bellows and a stewpan and the whole fixed on stilts,"
was the way Samuel Butler described our poor species; "a forked

radish with a head fantastically carved," agreed Carlyle. Man became an upright animal at grievous cost to his health and his
looks. He cupped his pelvis and turned in the remnant of his tail
to keep his insides from falling out, subjecting himself thus to
hernias and hemorrhoids and all manner of internal weaknesses.
He is not to be compared with tigers for beauty or elephants for
grace of movement; in physical strength he is the puniest mammal
of his size as well as the slowest; and not even the most doting
father can honestly compare his infant with a kitten for either
looks or intelligence.

Man has used every conceivable means to make himself look
more presentable, even molding the body itself. Some Indians
flattened their heads, others elongated them, still others worked
them up into a point. Africans and Australians knock out teeth;
we put them in. We whiten our teeth, but Melanesians, despising
the dog-like natural whiteness, blacken them (and Americans, in
their limitless enterprise, have even made money by manufacturing
black false teeth for people who favor black teeth such as the
Melanesians). We cut off our fingernails; other peoples cut off
entire fingers.

Culture shows its sense of distorted humor in man's—or rather,
in woman's—notions of beauty: we are nearly the only species of
animal that has the strange notion that the female is handsomer
than the male. It is a curious and unnoticed fact that many
beautifying mutilations emphasize peculiar racial characteristics,
though in some cases the people involved have no knowledge of
other races and so could not know that they differ in any way
physically. The Australian natives exaggerate the long flat slope of
their very primitive skulls by plucking the hair away to the center
of their scalps. The extremely broad-headed Pueblo Indians six
centuries ago bound the heads of their babies; the fashion in adult
crania was to have them wider than they were long. The Nilotic
Negroes, the world's tallest people, further elongate themselves
by building their coiffures into a foot-long bun; some central

Africans extend their racially characteristic everted lip to incredible size (one Ubangi woman was photographed with the eight-inch can in which the motion picture film had come, in her lower lip; it is said that she was irresistible to Ubangi gentlemen). Negroid and Australoid skin has a tendency to form large keloid scars when cut, so these people often beautify themselves by slashing their bodies and rubbing ashes or some other irritant into the cuts. The glabrous Indians plucked out what little facial hair they had, whereas the hirsute Ainu of northern Hokkaido are so proud of their hairiness that women tattoo mustaches on their upper lips. Such examples are endless in the primitive world and not unknown in ours. Caucasoid hair has a tendency to waviness, which women exaggerate by mutilating their hair into curls.

Culture has its transitory fashions, just as human beings do. In times when food is hard to come by, the ideal woman is grossly fat—like the Paleolithic figurines that some scholars (bachelors with no direct knowledge of these things) think represent pregnancy and therefore "fertility goddesses." As our history of race prejudice demonstrates, we have no absolute admiration for dusky skin, but a tanned person exhibits to all observers that he can afford to withdraw from the industrial process long enough to acquire the color as a symbol of Conspicuous Leisure. Conversely, in Polynesia, the high-status woman was one who could sit indoors all day and develop the pallor that only leisured persons could afford to get. Long fingernails likewise proclaim exemption from manual labor, and have been used as symbols of exploit from Chinese mandarins to American private secretaries. In a strictly biological sense, one of the most amazing genetic adaptations in history is the speed with which women grew breasts when they became fashionable less than a generation ago. For a visual demonstration of this remarkable evolution, see any of Gina Lollobrigida's early movies on the late late show.

Some women are squeamish about pumping paraffin into their mammary glands or even poking holes through their ears, but all use cosmetics unless they propose to attract dissentient admiration. It is hard to believe that smearing one's face with grease, dirt, dust, or paint is beautifying, but people have done this ever since Neanderthal man, who, by the look of the skulls he left, doubtlessly needed to do something about his appearance. In a more direct line of diffusion, many of our cosmetic ideas, like so much else in our civilization, come from the ancient Near East. Since antiquity, in Mesopotamia and Egypt there was constant danger from eye infections; and so it seems that the earliest cosmetics other than the Neanderthal ochres were intended as medications at first, though they quickly lost this primary function. The Mesopotamian word for eye ointment was *guhlu*; this becomes *kohl* in ancient Egypt and *kuhl* in Arabia. The addition of the Arabic article *al* (which prefix, by the way, provides an easy reference to many elements of civilization that came to us through Arabia) takes us right to *alcohol*, which has a rather different function from the primitive *guhlu*. All the Semitic people (the Babylonians, Sumerians, Assyrians, Syrians, Phoenicians, and Jews) used cosmetics lavishly; even the Hebrew prophets did, despite their other-worldliness. When the Jews became Puritans, they tried to eradicate this heathenish custom; one of the charges made against Jezebel was that she "painted her face and tired her head" —but they had no more success than the latter-day Puritans. Even in the New Testament, Martha got nowhere criticizing Mary for anointing the feet of Jesus while she had to wash the dishes. And consider the gifts of the Magi.

The Egyptians had no such scruples, and so ancient Egypt is the real homeland of cosmetics. Though the texts are understandably scanty on this mundane subject, Egyptian records contain the names of thirty-five different cosmetics. The fashionable Egyptian girl prepared for a date by painting her upper eyelids black and her lower lids green,[2] rubbed red ochre into her cheeks to assure

---

[2] It is possible that the Copper Age discovered itself when a lady's cosmetic kit containing malachite eye paint burned, leaving a pure copper residue.

her boyfriend that she was not a yellowish Sumerian, brightened her hair with henna (in later Egyptian times she would have shaved her head and worn a blue wig), and reddened her lips with hematite, which, unhappily, was not kissproof. Gentlemen Egyptians were vain also, and so were ungentlemanly Egyptians. One of the first labor strikes we have a record of was called against the Pharaoh Rameses III by his workers at the Theban necropolis because he had cut the ration of ointments.

Though one of the first uses of butter among the German tribes was as a hair pomade, cosmetics did not get into Europe in any variety until the Crusades. Soldiers, as we know, always send home lots of odd junk, such as satin pillows with WELCOME FROM WEEHAWKEN on them; the Crusaders sent back the exotic cosmetics of the East in the forlorn hope of making their pale ladies as warmly attractive as the beauties of the harems, whose acquaintance, being soldiers, they undoubtedly made. Whatever the Western ladies might have thought of the implied criticism, they did take the hint. By Elizabeth's time they were taking milk and wine baths, and eventually the use of artificial beauty aids became so flagrant in England that a law was introduced into Parliament to curb the wicked wiles of women:

> . . . all women of whatever age, rank, profession, or degree, whether virgins, maids, or widows, that shall, from and after such Act, impose upon, seduce, and betray into matrimony, any of His Majesty's subjects by the scents, paints, cosmetic washes, artificial teeth, false hair, Spanish wool, iron stays, hoops, high-heeled shoes, bolstered hips, shall incur the penalty of the law in force against witchcraft and like misdemeanors and that the marriage, upon conviction, shall stand null and void.

This sounds like a Puritan legislation, for on these shores the Saints encouraged plain religion, plain singing, and plain women. And plain men—one political miscreant was given a suspended fine in Massachusetts on condition that he "cut off the long hair off his head into a civil frame." Women were treated more harshly. The godly elders of Salem Village—Samuel Sewall among them—hanged poor Brigit Bishop in 1692 for several infractions of Puritan etiquette, besides plain witchcraft; she hired a back-slidden Quaker to dye her clothes and otherwise made herself so attractive that the judges had spectral evidence of her witchcraft: her "familiar" appeared to Puritan men at night—some of them married, too—and tried to do you-know-what.

Today we are more realistic about these things: about two thousand brands of face powder are registered with the trademark bureau in Washington, and some of them have infiltrated, like other unrespected elements of American culture, into the most remote parts of the world. When Heinrich Harrer visited Tibet, that intensely religious country was so isolated from the rest of mankind that it seemed to be on another planet; yet he saw Elizabeth Arden cosmetics on sale in Lhasa.

THE DRAMATIC ARTS

The musical and somatic arts owe nothing to the Puritan heritage dominant in so much of American life; drama owes even less. Even in Europe, drama was the youngest of the arts and a purely indigenous invention. To trace English theater back to the Greeks is nice, but erroneous. The Church, as part of the effort to keep knowledge alive in the Middle Ages, cut out the theater, root and branch, and for five hundred years drama wholly disappeared in Europe. It is ironic that when drama re-invented itself, it did so in the Church.

The revival started with the last "a" of an "alleluia"—the end of the Epistle of the Mass, lengthened into a sung sequence and finally into a drama. Specifically, at the end of the ninth century the phrase in the Introit of the Easter Mass *Resurrexi et adhuc tecum suum* was extended into an antiphonal colloquy between two halves of the choir, representing on one side the angels and on the other the faithful who came to watch at the tomb of Christ after the crucifixion. The Mass itself, with a thousand years of conservative establishment behind it, did not permit much elaboration, but the idea was transferred two centuries later into the less sacred morning office, the Matins. We even have manuscript evidence of stage directions before the eleventh century.

The first play, the *Visitatio Sepulchri*, was presented in three acts: the Grave Scene, in which the Marys are invited to inspect the shroud; the Race Scene, in which medieval realism showed Peter beaten up the aisle by John; and the Gardener Scene, in which Mary Magdalene confuses Christ with the gardener. The *Visitatio Sepulchri* was thrown out of the church into the adjoining graveyard when it threatened to displace the Matins, and was thrown out of the churchyard when the audience trampled down the headstones. Driven thus into the secular world, drama for several centuries retained its religious orientation in the Mystery and Miracle Plays, though more and more the religious *raison d'être* settled into a feeble excuse for earthly entertainment. Manuscript accounts—the first reviews—tell us that when the Flight into Egypt was presented, the liturgical ass stole the show every time. Herod and the Slaughter of the Innocents was enormously popular, though it may be suspected that some people complained about violence in the theater. And virgins were sure-fire then as now, though, except for the imminent possibility of their losing that status (perhaps right on stage, as in *Dark of the Moon*), virgins are the dullest of characters in or out of literature. Long before drama re-established itself, the plight of besieged virgins was a popular theme—there are innumerable legends of martyrs to virginity, and the erotic element in the Lives of the Saints is often the strongest. Critics of television who View with Alarm the education of young criminals might just as well settle down into acceptance of this use of drama, for throughout history villains are ahead in ninety-eight per cent of the action, regardless of what the audience is asked to believe about their final reward.

The "natural lout behind the cassock," as E. K. Chambers maligned the clerical actor, was worldly enough in these first dramas, but when the theater was driven out of the church into the innyard, the personnel did not improve in morality. The history of vice in the theater is almost as old as the theater itself; by Shakespeare's time actors were officially condemned as vagabonds and were liable to severe punishment. Shakespeare and his fellows got around the law by the patently dishonest device of hiring on as some nobleman's servants.

Mrs. Trollope ridiculed an American who told her, in Cincinnati: "Shakespeare, Madam, is obscene, and thank God, WE are sufficiently advanced to have found it out." Mrs. Trollope's informant was quite right; Shakespeare is obscene, though the rapid linguistic change in words and phrases referring to sexual intercourse has purged him of what he was conveying to the groundlings. It is doubtful that Mrs. Trollope or the local PTA would be such champions of Shakespeare if they knew what lines like "Pillicock sat on Pillicock hill" really meant.

Obscenity and the titillation of vulgar taste seem to be organic functions of the drama, rather than organic functions of television and the movies, as self-critical Americans like to think. In ancient Rome serious and respectable drama starved while the coarse and vulgar *mimes* prospered. Until the end of the nineteenth century, Japan was completely isolated from the West; yet the history of the kabuki theater is so like the history of the British stage as to suggest a mystical rapport. Kabuki developed from an elaboration of Buddhist ritual dances, just as English drama developed from an elaboration of Christian ceremony. As time went on, kabuki was driven out into the market place, and by the seventeenth century it had become primarily a showcase for prostitutes. In 1629 the Shogunate banned kabuki for flagrant immorality, just thirteen years before the Puritans in England banned the theater for the same reason. Women thereafter were not permitted to appear on the Japanese stage; in England the first woman did not set foot on a public stage until the end of the Puritan interregnum. In Japan the *yo jo* kabuki—the "prostitutes' play"—was replaced by the *wakashu,* or "young men's kabuki," which differed from the *yo jo* kabuki in that the sex of the prostitutes was different. This was banned in 1652, and replaced by the *yaro* kabuki, the "men's kabuki," but provisions were made to guard against immorality; for instance, bangs were thought lascivious, so the actors shaved the front of their heads, as they still pretend to do in kabuki. Skill instead of physical attraction became characteristic of the kabuki players, and lavish production, high salaries, luxuries for the actors, and other things commonly thought to be unique and diabolical inventions of Hollywood flourished for half a century—just about the age span of the Hollywood era—and then settled into a long decline.

The first American theater was built in Williamsburg at the beginning of the eighteenth century. Puritan New England obviously did not permit this plumbing of damnation to infect its new Jerusalem. Plays were presented in early colonial times in New York, since it was under Dutch rather than Puritan influence, but the Dutch were rather dull so far as the mimetic arts were concerned, and did not take advantage of their opportunity. In early Philadelphia the Quakers were just as firmly opposed to play acting as their persecutors in the north. When they were ejected from the government during the French and Indian War, the theater followed in close behind them, but cautiously—the first Philadelphia theaters, like the first theaters in Shakespeare's London, were built outside the city limits.

Mrs. Trollope, whose incisive criticisms of the American theater actually did clean things up a bit, has been ashes for exactly a century, so we are bereft of her perceptive opinion about American movies and American television. Probably she would have approved of neither, but in her absence we have adequate substitute critics. Anybody, in fact. A cartoon in the University of Colorado student newspaper showed two beatniks sitting side by side at an avant-garde foreign motion picture; one of them whispers a furtive confession out of the corner of his mouth: "I saw an American movie last night." Many of the faculty at the University of Colorado categorically refuse to have a television set in their homes, which is understandable in people who each June promenade into the football stadium for Commencement Exercises in medieval caps and gowns.

The stage—or legitimate drama, as it is invidiously called by many devotees who do not know that this adjective refers not to the elevation of live acting but to the legal status of two London theaters—is quite respectable now. It has become a Fine Art—an Art becoming Fine when it is on its deathbed. For half a century the movies pushed the live theater up off the floor of American culture; now, suddenly, criticism of the movies shows signs of abatement, as television inherits the obloquy that at one time in our history was the monopoly of Shakespeare's theater.

Culture evolves in much the same way as living organisms. Primitive forms develop, compete, die or survive, and mutate into better organisms. The stage was fine for Shakespeare; for us it is an obsolete survival, an anachronism kept alive by people whose own way of life is passing and who support the doomed and dying theater largely because it is a symbol of the past. At this writing, theater critics are agonizingly reappraising Broadway, and finding blame for its decline in utter innocents such as the ladies who hold stage parties. The critics must know that the Broadway theater lasted as long as it did only because of the visiting firemen to whom play acting was Hot Stuff, O You Kid. Now even the yokels have become sophisticated enough to understand that if they come to New York to see girls, they ought to go to see musicals, not turgid dramas of male sex deviates, problems of minority races, and Biblical allegories.

The small praise Hollywood gets from the intelligentsia comes grudgingly when a serious play is translated to the screen. Such fare is easily detected, because motion-picture directors seem somehow unable to overcome the restrictions of the stage. Perhaps the directors are not sufficiently encouraged to do so since they know reviewers will commend immobile movies as "tight dramas." Left to its own boundless resources, the motion picture is the greatest medium for making reality out of illusion—and television gives us this and immediacy besides. Shakespeare would have written for the movies had he lived in the twentieth instead of the seventeenth century, and he would have had television in his home, for he explicitly recognized the limitations of his theater. After all, he asked his audience to piece out these imperfections with their thoughts.

Television must play to the groundlings most of the time, but so did Shakespeare, for it is the groundlings who make it financially possible for the less profitable drama to be seen at all—and to be seen by more people now than was ever dreamt of by Shakespeare in his philosophy. When *Hamlet* was last telecast in the United States, it was seen by thirty million people—an audience six times the entire population of England in the early seventeenth century, a single audience larger than all the audiences who saw *Hamlet* on the stage since the day it was written. Television is no worse than the people who watch it, and no true believer in democracy can say there is very much wrong with the people.

☆ X ☆

In Praise of a Materialistic Culture

Three years after World War II, when the United States had poured more than 25 billion dollars into the economies of the combatant nations to get them started competing with us once more in the markets of the world, the Common Council for American Unity got the idea that this might be the best time in history to record a little gratitude and admiration, however grudging, for the Americans. At least the Europeans would confess that we were not just selfish money grubbers, and it might just possibly be that they would find some small love in their hearts for us, despite our faults. Accordingly, the Council conducted a survey among the Marshall Plan countries, which was published in 1949 as *European Beliefs Regarding the United States*.

But its disclosures were disillusioning. The Europeans turned out to be like the farmhand who complained that he did not like the farm ner the work ner the pay ner the food ner the farmer ner his wife ner *none* of his children. They were grateful enough for the handout, certainly they were, but even that went to show the soulless materialism of Americans. We had provided food and tractors and that sort of thing, but we had sent over no composers or piano players and damned few preachers. The typical attitude was expressed by a German:

We in Germany make a difference between civilization and culture. America is considered to be the country of civilization. This refers to material goods, but culturally all Europeans consider themselves above America. This refers to spiritual goods.

This, just three years after Adolf Hitler, with the ovens of Dachau still smelling of ashes.

This German respondent had never been to the United States, but that little matter has never handicapped our foreign critics. When Karel Čapek, the great critic of mechanical civilization, wrote his estimate of the United States in *The New York Times Magazine* of May 16, 1926, he had never visited America, but he knew all about our lack of spirituality:

It is possible that an American tailor makes three coats while our tailor makes one; it is possible that an American tailor earns three times as much as ours, but I ask whether he consumes a three-times larger portion of life, whether he is three times as much in love as our tailor, whether he whistles three times as many songs at his work, and whether he has three times as many children?

. . .

European morale . . . has assured us since time immemorial of different values of life than those of success. If I am not mistaken, it talks here and there of the futility of all success, inspiring us to look for values higher and more permanent.

Čapek did not live to criticize the Marshall Plan, for he died in 1938 just a few months before his country died, as a wave of

Kultur poured over Czechoslovakia with Hitler's Germans, who knew all about the higher values.

Possibly the Europeans are right; we should not be so smug in our material prosperity. We might be better people if our appreciation of Art were strong enough to make us see the inherent beauty of lampshades made out of Jewish skin. We might care less about tailfins and television, had our education been received in religious schools amid an atmosphere of such elevated piety that, like Adolf Hitler and Joseph Stalin, we entered adult life with the intention of serving God as ordained priests. Our lives might be fuller of the higher values if we aspired to be connoisseurs of art like Hermann Goering. Surely we should give up comic books and movie magazines and learn a little philosophy, like Alfred Rosenberg. Speaking of books, why can't we patronize letters as Reinhard Heydrich, Benito Mussolini, and Julius Streicher did? Certainly we should be ashamed of the low standard of our education when we think of Paul Joseph Goebbels, who attended eight universities. Unhappily, we are not like these paragons of Old World spirituality; we are just Americans, unfortunate prisoners of our culture, who must go on doing the best we can, producing Coca-Cola instead of Calvinism or Communism. It is regrettable that we cannot at least keep our crassness to ourselves, but now that nearly 200 million Europeans are regularly watching Hollywood movies, the elevated *Kultur* of the spiritual nations will be abraded. It is a sad thing.

Criticism of materialism is not based on reason, so there is no use arguing with people about it. If the subject is brought up at a cocktail party, as it inevitably is, by someone whose wife has been nattering at him since he came home from the office, where his bright idea for the day had been run up the flagpole without anyone saluting it, whose stomach is upset and whose baseball team lost, and who is just feeling spiritually insufficient, you can safely go on with the conversation so long as you realize that you are enterting what semanticists know as a non-sense area—that is, a linguistic situation in which no sense data are being communicated. There is, rather, an exchange of snarl sounds or purr sounds, as when a member of the John Birch society talks about Earl Warren or a Liberal talks about Adlai Stevenson. Your unhappy friend will complain that our country is becoming too damned materialistic, that no one gives a damn about the other things in life, that we should get the hell out of Laos, that we should give television back to the Indians, and Christ isn't this damned drink flat. In this situation, assuming you are complacent about our materialistic culture, you can make the appropriate soothing noises, or you can be brutal and ask him what *he* did this day to increase the nation's spiritual treasury. Or ask him what he is talking about.

Alfred Korzybski in one of the saner passsages in his *Science and Sanity* presented the concept of the Abstraction Ladder, which Hayakawa in *Language in Thought and Action* illustrated by the way most people define red.

What is red?
A color.
What is color?
A quality.
What is quality?
Say, what are you trying to do?

Critics of materialism are not only unable to define the opposite of materialism; they are unable even to name it. There is no substantive noun for what they advocate in the place of materialism, except as they borrow from materialism to make a definition, such as "the meaningful *things* in life," or "the *things* of the spirit." Roget's *Thesaurus* gives as antonyms "immaterialism," "not of the earth," "beauty of holiness," "unsubstantiality," and other ideas in the Cloud Cuckoo Land above the top of the Abstraction Ladder. *Webster's New International Dictionary* has no antonym at all for materialism.

Very probably your cheerless friend cannot even define materialism. If he is a philosopher and has not had too much to drink, he may run up the Abstraction Ladder and talk about the different kinds of materialism, like hylozoism and monism. If so, it would be best to leave him floating in the semantic clouds, criticizing materialism as the *Encyclopaedia Britannica* does, "because it has not been elaborated into a consistent metaphysic."

Let there be no ambiguity about what we mean here by materialism. We do not mean a philosophy, since the approach of cultural determinism, described in the first chapter, denies that there is any philosophy of culture. We have studied logic and have found it to be a lot of nonsense, as the lady said when she bought a pair of shoes two sizes too small for her. We will accept the definition of materialism in Webster's: "a tendency to give undue importance to material interests; devotion to the material nature and its wants." Your friend will agree that this is exactly what he is opposed to; indeed it is.

For most people, opposition to materialism is not the philosophy they imagine, but a vague feeling of guilt growing out of the realization that we have too much material wealth while the rest of the world has so little. They are like the rich man who has quite convinced himself that the only thing his money is good for is to pay his psychiatrist; they are like the melancholy gas-station attendant in *The Grapes of Wrath* who continually whined: "What's it comin' to?" And they can be answered as Tom Joad answered the attendant.

"You ain't askin' nothin'; you're jus' singin' a kinda song. 'What we comin' to?' you don' wanta know. Country's movin' aroun', goin' places. They's folks dyin' all aroun'. I see too many fellas like you. You don' want to know nothin'. Just sing yourself to sleep with a song—'What we comin' to?'"

Or you can ask him what spiritual nation in particular he would recommend that we imitate. There is Pakistan, for a starter, which is devoutly Moslem. And India, which for the most part is devoutly Hindu. Of course, these two spiritual nations are having a little disagreement just now about how to save all those souls over in Kashmir, and therefore, as Bertrand Russell cynically remarks in *The Impact of Science on Society*, "one of them must support Russia and the other the United States. It will be obvious to anyone who is an interested party in one of these disputes that the issue is far more important that the continuance of life on our planet."

Since we have mentioned India, it would be instructive to look more closely at this wellspring of many of the forms of immaterialism that dissatisfied Americans find consolation in, whether they contort themselves in yoga or follow the old-time religion that was good enough for father. Spirituality has always been important in the civilization of this part of the world. As long ago as five centuries before Christ, when the Greeks were still wary of spirits in trees and the inhabitants of the British Isles were still eating one another, the Buddhists had combined theology and social morality into a sophisticated philosophy. But Indic religion was only incidental to a sturdy materialism that drew our barbaric forefathers on journeys as difficult for them as space travel is for us. It was not just pepper that Columbus was looking for; travelers two thousand years before his time and nearly half a thousand afterwards went to India to bring back to Europe the inimitable riches of the Indus. You can turn back to the paragraphs in Chapter One about that 100 per cent American to see some of the fundamental possessions of our civilization that came ultimately from India.

Just what turned Indian energy away from worldly prosperity is not clear. Certainly the repeated invasions through the northern mountain passes, east and west, crashing one upon the other over the continent, had something to do with it, for the caste system and its attendant religious sanctions tried to force some order upon the chaos of racial and cultural clash. It has been suggested also that the destructiveness of nature—the cataclysmic storms, floods, and earthquakes, plagues of locusts and rats, epidemics and famines—convinced the Indians that reality was unbearable. We conquered our environment, the Australian aborigines adapted themselves to it, but the Indians withdrew from it. Since Hinduism offered the best method of ignoring the world, it eventually overwhelmed the other religions; as nearly as we can count the churchgoers in India today, there are 100 million Mohammedans, 26 million pagans, 6.5 million Christians, 6 million Sikhs, 1.6 million Jainists, 250,000 Buddhists, 120,000 Parsees, and 25,000 Jews—but there are 275 million Hindus. In Hinduism the sophistication of Buddhism deteriorated into an animistic view of nature, full of spirits to be propitiated, from cows to constellations; the material world became a transitory vale of sorrow and pain, from which one retreats toward *dharma* by mortifying the flesh and ignoring emotions emanating from the animal nature of man, both painful and pleasurable. The spiritual enthusiasm of Hinduism would shame an Oklahoma Campbellite: in 1954 four and a half million people gathered for the feast of *Kumbh-Mela*; some three hundred and fifty were trampled to death and another two hundred disappeared in one way or another, but the spiritual enrichment of the survivors was incalculable. And to think that some Americans, wallowing in materialism, have never even heard of *Kumbh-Mela!* If it is any consolation, devout Hindus do not think much about the United States or its civilization, and if they do, it is to regard both with ineffable contempt. Some advanced Hindus are concerned about America; the expression "We show the way to America" in regard to racial tolerance is common among Indian intellectuals who call in Untouchables to sweep the streets with their hands—but we do not understand that the caste system is only an economic device to reduce competition for such jobs as sweeping the streets with one's bare hands. Americans have a lot to learn.

Such spirituality is a great comfort to the people of India and, we are assured, makes them impervious to things we should not like at all. As one observer put it, India is a vast slum, its streets swarming with lepers and cows that one dare not kill for fear of offending the Cow Goddess. If a man cannot beg, he must work— for an average income of two cents a day. Less than a quarter of the population have adequate food; half live perpetually in a state of near-starvation. In the next ten years, 50 million children will die of starvation's diseases in India. Some others will be killed, especially if they are girl babies with no prospects of marriage. Part of India's economy is based upon its people's death; a Calcutta agency will sell fresh Indian skulls to physical anthropologists five for a dollar. Any kind you want, first to third grade (second grade is pretty good—only a few teeth missing), any sex, any age. Catalog sent on request.

Materialistic America is interfering with the ancient ways of the Indian people. Under Public Law 480 ("Food for Peace") the United States has shipped more than two billion dollars worth of surplus corn, wheat, cotton, and other commodities to India. This officiousness has not pleased Thailand, another spiritual country, because it has cut into the Thai wheat trade. And the suppliers of skeletal material to medical students and physical anthropologists are upset because of the American switch from real to plastic skulls. It is no wonder that Indian holy men, sitting in their filth and philosophy, have bad thoughts when American jet planes, carrying fat American tourists, disturb their meditation these days.

But it is not necessary to study the wisdom of the East to learn the benefits of spirituality. We have a long history of looking upward in our own culture—nearly fifteen hundred years of it, in fact. Everyone knows that before the Industrial Revolution life was hard in Europe, so there is no need to describe how the flesh was mortified by a hostile environment in those dark days. Everyone knows this, but everyone knows too that the spirit soared and knowledge was nurtured like a flickering candle by the men of the Church. This is interesting and would bear looking into. Let us see how things were before, as Emerson put it, Things got in the saddle and rode mankind.

THE INTELLECTUAL LIFE IN AN AGE OF SPIRITUALITY

In the twilight beginning of the Dark Ages, the thought occurred
to some irreverent people that perhaps Christianity had a little to
do with the lights going out all over Europe. The Christians naturally blamed the barbarian conquerors (though there were no barbarian conquests of Eastern Christendom, where the intellectual
sky was just as murky as in the West), and to counteract such
irresponsible talk, the Christians set the scholars among them—
those who could write—to preparing themes *adversum paganos*.
Orosius's *Historia* was the first important tract on the subject,
having been commissioned by St. Augustine himself; King Alfred
of England, who was greatly concerned because his priests were
saying Mass in a language they did not understand, translated the
Historia, and so did others. Spengler may have taken more from it
than he admitted for his *Decline of the West*. But after thirteen
hundred years of such dissertations, some people still persist in
slandering the Age of Faith. In the spirit of Orosius, the *Encyclopaedia Britannica* nails the slander; beginning with the fourteenth
edition (1929), we are told in the article "Dark Ages" that the
term is no longer used by historians (a strange remark, since this
was the first time the phrase was discussed in the *Britannica*)
because we understand now that these spiritual centuries were
"dark through the insufficiency of historical evidence," and that
"it is necessary to remember that intellectual work of the highest
quality was done by exceptional individuals." This is right, in a
way; there is in truth not much historical evidence, since there
are no books. There was the great library at Alexandria, estimated
by Aulus Gellius to have 700,000 volumes, but that did not last
very long after the coming of spirituality; not even the Christians
maintain any more that the Arabs burned the books. Joseph
McCabe says the pious Emperor Theodosius burned them, just
before Saints Philip and John appeared to him and turned back
the arrows of the army led against him by the grammarian
Eugenius—but McCabe was a notorious apostate and atheist.

Whatever happened to the books, they were not saved for us by the monks who were going about preserving knowledge in the Middle Ages.

The pagan Romans, everybody admits, had good facilities for learning. Throughout the empire there were free schools, none of which remained at the end of the first century of Christianization. Rome itself had twenty-eight libraries, and as in other aspects of Roman culture, there were branches in the suburbs and provinces. These are gone too; James Westfall Thompson laments in *The Medieval Library* that not even the memory of Roman libraries survived to the Middle Ages. Thompson goes through several centuries of spiritual enlightenment in so many sentences, saying that there was no evidence of a papal library until Pope Damasus I (366–384), from whose time until the sixth century there again emerges no information about a papal library. For the next thousand years libraries steadily grew, as the monks diligently preserved knowledge. By the twelfth century the great Benedictine Abbey at Peterborough, the last repository of Anglo-Saxon historiography and a center for the "new learning," had seventy books. Malmesbury, another locus of education, where the eminent scholars Aldhelm and William worked, contained in Leland's time twenty-four books—but others were certainly destroyed when the Defender of the Faith, Henry VIII, got to them. The largest of the cathedral libraries in medieval England was at Canterbury, where longen folk to goon on pilgrimages; it had 698 volumes. It does not need to be said that nearly all these works were theological, and not many readers of this book, unless they are professional medievalists, have ever read any volume written during the seven centuries that followed the triumph of spirituality over materialism in Europe. The famous library at York Minster, praised by the scholarly Alcuin, had only Bibles. In the rest of spiritual Europe during the Dark Ages, the largest libraries could boast of no more than two thousand books.

Meanwhile the pagans—the Arab agnostics who built up a high

civilization in Syria and Spain before the religious fanatics of Mohammed went on a spiritual rampage—had many colleges and large libraries; those at Baghdad, Cordova, Cairo, and Tripoli were the most famous. Their lance of learning penetrated the thick European skull in Andalusia, where there were seventy different libraries. In the caliph's palace at Cordova one could choose among 400,000 books—eight hundred times as many as in the largest library in all Christendom—and this library flourished until our spiritual forebears destroyed it. An inventory of some of the knowledge that filtered into Europe from these Arabs can be made, as we have noted, by checking words beginning with *al*—the Arabic definite article. For example, the Arabs had algebra when our ancestors were counting on their fingers (eleven: Anglo-Saxon *endleofan*—"one left after counting ten"). For further example on the subject of counting, Christian Europe had to get along on Roman numerals and the abacus until a materialistic merchant, one Fibonacci of Pisa, brought back the Arabic system of numeration (which we still use) from his commercial partners in north Africa at the end of the twelfth century. But the Arab civilization had its Dark Ages, too, when spirituality descended on it, first from the sword-wielders of Islam and later from the last barbarian invasion from the West—the Crusades.

As for books, we remember that Emerson said that a person can be a scholar without reading books. There were some such Emersonian scholars in spiritual Europe who, to recall the phrase in the *Britannica,* did "work of the highest quality." There was Pope Silvester II (999–1003), recognized as the most accomplished scholar of his time. He was so learned, in fact, that it was thought (even by the scholars William of Malmesbury and Cardinal Bruno) that he had sold his soul to the Devil for knowledge, and he gets into our folklore by contributing to the beginning of the Faust legend. It is a pity to have to say that Silvester received his education from Arabs at Cordova.

The Arabs were not entirely unreceptive to infidels who came to them for knowledge, for these students could then be shown the backwardness of their spiritual homeland. The Arab Usāmah tells an illustrative story to this point regarding a physician among the spiritual Crusaders in the twelfth century; to appreciate it fully, one should know that European medicine until the middle of the seventeenth century was based on a very bad translation of the *Canon of Medicine*, written by the great Arab physician Avicenna six centuries earlier.

The Lord of al-Munaytirah wrote to my uncle asking him to dispatch a physician to treat certain sick persons among his people. My uncle sent him a Christian physician named Thabit. Thabit was absent but ten days when he returned. So we said to him, "How quickly hast thou healed thy patients!" He said:

"They brought before me a knight in whose leg an abscess had grown; and a woman inflicted with imbecility. To the knight I applied a small poultice until the abscess opened and became well; and the woman I put on diet and made her humour wet. Then a Frankish physican came to them and said, 'This man knows nothing about treating them.' He then said to the knight, 'Which wouldst thou prefer, living with one leg or dying with two?' The latter replied, 'Living with one leg.' The physician said, 'Bring me a strong knight and a sharp axe.' A knight came with the axe. And I was standing by. Then the physician laid the leg of the patient on a block of wood and bade the knight strike his leg with the axe and chop it off at one blow. Accordingly he struck it—while I was looking on—one blow, upon which the marrow of the leg flowed out and the patient died on the spot. He then examined the woman and said, 'This is a woman in whose head there is a devil which has possessed her. Shave off her hair.' Accordingly they shaved it off and the woman began once more to eat their ordinary diet—garlic and mustard. Her imbecility took a turn for the worse. The physician then said, 'The devil has penetrated through her head.' He therefore

took a razor, made a deep cruciform incision on it, peeled
off the skin at the middle of the incision until the bone
of the skull was exposed and rubbed it with salt. The woman
also expired instantly. Thereupon I asked them whether my
services were needed any longer, and when they replied in the
negative I returned home, having learned of their medicine
what I knew not before."

The labors of such dear and glorious physicians as the Frankish
Crusaders were so frightful that one is not quite so surprised by
the casual view taken of physical torture in these centuries. There
was torture in other cultures, as one would expect of barbarism
anywhere, but nothing was done in the age of the spirit in Europe
to ameliorate the common practice of torture in law, medicine,
and religion, despite the kindly example of Jesus Christ, except to
outlaw crucifixion as a penalty for capital crime—and some suspect
that there was another motive than humanitarianism for this reform. The subject of torture, incidentally, has not had the attention of scholarship, so that when we read passages such as that
quoted earlier from Curtis Bok's *Star Wormwood*, we are hesitant
to credit them. Nevertheless, one comes upon such things constantly in reading in medieval texts, and it is a consolation to
know that after all this was an age of the spirit, when the trials of
the flesh were generally unnoticed by the praying population, so
that persons who for their crimes, irreverence, or stubbornness
had noses, ears, tongues, fingers, hands, feet, and other appendages
cut off did not really feel much pain.

While on the subject of amputating appendages, it would be
unkind but not irrelevant to mention here the *castrati*, male choir
singers permanently fixed as sopranos by a bit of clerical surgery,
who raised the "shrill celestial whine of eunuchs" in the Sistine
Chapel until *1878*, to the horror of American heathens who wrote
of this abomination as relentlessly as Englishmen wrote about
tobacco spitting.

But this sort of thing got the kids off the street corners and kept them out of the kind of mischief the age of spirituality was most concerned about. You couldn't trust them otherwise; boys were known even to seduce the celibate clergy, and well along in the Middle Ages priests nominated for promotion had to swear that no bad boy had succeeded with them. We remember Fra Lippo Lippi, caught out after curfew by the watchmen charged to prevent young religious men from running after women:

> . . . *but a monk!*
> *Come, what am I a beast for? tell us, now!*
> *I was a baby when my mother died*
> *And father died and left me in the street.*
> *I starved there, God knows how, a year or two*
> *On fig-skins, melon-parings, rinds and shucks,*
> *Refuse and rubbish. One fine frosty day,*
> *My stomach being empty as your hat,*
> *The wind doubled me up, and down I went.*
> *Old Aunt Lapaccia trussed me with one hand,*
> *(Its fellow was a stinger as I knew)*
> *And so along the wall, over the bridge,*
> *By the straight cut to the convent. Six words there,*
> *While I stood munching my first bread that month;*
> *"So, boy, you're minded," quoth the good fat father,*
> *Wiping his own mouth, 'twas refection-time—*
> *"To quit this very miserable world?*
> *Will you renounce" . . . "the mouthful of bread?" thought I;*
> *By no means! Brief, they made a monk of me;*
> *I did renounce the world, its pride and greed,*
> *Palace, farm, villa, shop, and banking-house,*
> *Trash, such as these poor devils of Medici*
> *Have given their hearts to—all at eight years old.*

Young Lippo was not so badly off, as he admitted. Today a minister of the gospel is rewarded with neither high salary nor status by our materialistic culture. In the age of faith it was differ-

ent; spirituality was appreciated. A man could receive praise in
this life and a nimbus to assure heaven in the next by such an
effortless act as having himself walled up standing in a shallow
niche, where he would be fed regularly through a hole left by a
missing brick, living in indolent meditation—until he drowned in
his own excrement. Or, if he preferred a more active path to salvation, he could assure himself of eternal bliss by killing Jews and
Saracens. Even a woman, though her sex had been degraded ever
since Hebraic times, could attain some prominence in spiritual
work. Catherine de Medici conducted the Massacre of St. Bar-
tholomew's Day with only a little advisory assistance from Church
authorities; 50,000 Huguenots were slain, and Pope Gregory XIII
had a special medal struck for her. And that hotbed of Courtly
Love, Provence, was cleared of its sinners in the early thirteenth
century by wholesale massacres; a hard remedy, to be sure, but it
achieved, in the words of the *Encyclopaedia Britannica*, "a state
of peace and political and religious unity."

The spiritual reader will be interrupting this catechism about
this time with the protest: "But that was the CATHOLIC
CHURCH! It was the CATHOLIC CHURCH that did those
things!" He will be right, but only in a narrowly technical and
immaterial sense. This is where the professional atheists of recent
times went wrong, pathetic men such as Robert G. Ingersoll,
Clarence Darrow, and Joseph McCabe, who squandered their
great intellects in quixotic charges against Christianity.

These things were not perpetrated by the Catholic Church, or
even by Christianity; they were perpetrated by the universal destructive nature of man, which, as we have argued, religion was
designed to control—to control, ameliorate, channel destructive
urges away from man's own social group—not to eliminate, for
elimination of these drives does not seem to be biologically possible. Massacres of infidels and heretics are common occurrences
in the history of any philosophy that intrudes into this area of
man's nature. Lincoln Steffens tracked down the origin of the

acquisitive stimulus when he blamed it, not on Adam and Eve or the Serpent, but on the apple. There was in the Garden of Eden another force which he did not perceive, far more destructive than acquisitiveness. This was the *belief* of Adam and Eve in what was told them by both sides in the celestial controversy.

The apple causes much less unhappiness in this world than the belief. Believing is the denial of reason; it is the willing abandonment of man's unique intelligence to his animal gullibility. There is no human utterance so frightening as the sentence that begins, "I believe," no matter what the predicate is, for it is an announcement that the speaker is about to give himself up to irrationality—and for human beings, there is no good irrationality. Through the whole history of Christendom man's lot was deprivation, oppression, indignity, and restriction, but now that we have given up spirituality our behavior toward one another has become truly human. One might go so far as to say that we became good only when we gave up morality. The virtues that Americans cherish most—freedom, democracy, equality, tolerance, and dignity of the individual—are not spiritual virtues; they are absolutely incompatible with dogmatic belief, and no dominant religious philosophy in our history has ever tolerated them. The medieval Church ordered nature in a rigid hierarchy from God to the lower animals and forcibly prevented men from moving out of their ordained station. The Protestant reformers were of the same opinion; Luther, the gentlest of them, advocated violent suppression of the peasants' revolts in Germany. "No one need think that the world can be ruled without blood," he said; "the civil sword shall and must be red and bloody." When during the Industrial Revolution some of the denominations went down to stand by the side of the oppressed lower classes, they were trying to save themselves as much as the downtrodden.

Progress and improvement in the world began when people said "I want" instead of "I believe." This is a fact established by the overwhelming evidence of our entire culture, but those who want us to turn back toward believing have so intimidated us that even in the face of the plainest evidence such a statement seems outrageous if not blasphemous. We have seen some of the things that happened when "I believe" dominated thought and behavior; let us look briefly at some of the changes that followed when "I want" displaced "I believe."

LIFE IN AN AGE OF MATERIALISM

Henry Adams had no formal training in anthropology, but his close studies of the Middle Ages led him independently to the understanding that "man's function as a force of nature was to assimilate other forces as he assimilated food." "To the highest attractive energy, man gave the name divine, for its control he invented the science called Religion, a word which meant, and still means, cultivation of occult Force whether in detail or mass. Unable to define Force as a unity, man symbolized it and pursued it. . . ." And so long as man believed in the omnipotence of unreason, he would not invest his little money in "complicated machines when he could hire an occult force at trifling expense."

The difficulty, though it took us more than a thousand years to admit it, was that the occult force was not getting the work done. I remember driving through the San Joaquin Valley with an old settler of the area who had been driven close to atheism by his dislike for the Okies who swarmed into the region with their children, wives, chickens, dogs, and Bibles. On one side of the road, the land was in its pristine state; on the other, irrigation had turned the desert into the kind of garden the Okies read about in Genesis. The old farmer spoke proudly of the lush fields and then pointed to the other side of the road, where lizards shot across the sand from one tuft of salt grass to another. "That's the way it was," he said, "when God was running it."

The professional atheists tell us that no Father of the Church ever spoke out against slavery, and that slavery was so common a state during the Age of the Spirit that few thought even to mention it. It was the lot of man. They tell us too that not until the materialistic Deists agitated for abolition was there any moral indignation against slavery. This is true, but we need not give so much humanitarian credit to the Deists. Their culture was the first to take the machine seriously as a source of energy; in earlier times, as Henry Adams said, occult power was the prime mover, and the "world was incredibly poor. It knew but one productive energy resembling the modern machine—the slave."

The cobwebs of cultural inertia are thick in the mind, and we have yet to clear our thinking of the notion that man's duty on earth is to work, a notion that Christianity has some responsibility for. The Greeks saw work as a curse, and so named it *ponos*, from which the Romans took *poena*, sorrow. According to Cicero, the Romans felt as the Greeks did about it, and he would allow only two kinds of occupation to be worthy of a citizen: big agriculture and big business. The Christians took instead the Hebraic idea: that labor was the payment for the apple. The Talmud says: "If man does not find his food like animals and birds but must earn it, that is due to sin." Christ thought work no more worthy of man's attention than its gains, but Paul, a more practical man, quickly corrected this idea: "We commanded you, that if any would not work, neither should he eat." Medieval Christianity made use of the ideas of both these founders of the Church: man must work, as the avenging angel commanded his ultimate ancestors, but he should not enjoy the fruits thereof. Developing this philosophy, the ascetics, among whom must be counted even St. Francis of Assisi, made a positive virtue of profitless labor, all the better if it was "painful, humiliating, a scourge for the pride of the flesh," in the phrase of Adriano Tilgher in his *Work: What It Has Meant to Men through the Ages*. "With Calvinism," Tilgher went on,

> comes a new attitude toward labor. All men, even the rich, must work, because to work is the will of God. But they must not lust after the fruits of their labor—wealth, possessions, soft living. Their sweat and toil have value only as they help

to establish the Kingdom of God on earth. And from this paradox—the command to ceaseless effort—must needs follow a new economic practice. The miser's sterile hoarding, the money-lender's usury, are both swept away. A new use—the only worthy one—has been found for profit. As soon as earned it is used to finance fresh ventures, to breed new profit, again to be reinvested . . . and so on to the end of time.

All this sounds like the beginning of modern business. And so it is.

Now, as we approach the time when we can transfer Adam's curse to the machine (which has no philosophy about labor), and have in sight, after thirty millennia of spirituality, the human use of human beings, the spiritualists show their bitter resentment at losing the basis of their philosophies. For the religious believer, automation will mean that we can finally wipe away the sweat beaded on our brows since Adam's time. For the Communists, automation means the end of their beloved working class and its ancillary institutions, such as labor unions and the small business-men—and what will become of their theology then?

These moribund strata left over from the age of spirituality will not disappear immediately, and we ease their passing by romanti-cizing and even idealizing them, the way we did with the Indians after enough of them had been killed off to permit us to make pets of the remainder. At the moment the small businessmen are our national economic heroes, and we delay the inevitability of their passing by letting them become a temporary proletariat. General Electric, for instance, hires some 40,000 small business-men, whose true position as employees is disguised under the pleasing name of "subcontractors." For a while also, the cultural lag that occurs in such changes in technology and society will mean hardship and deprivation among the displaced workers, but means are being instituted to distribute more equitably the profits of the machines' toil. One such device is the graduated income tax, which, if only because it forces a distribution of wealth to the classes that in other times and other civilizations were the dangerous, grumbling dispossessed, deserves to be called the greatest act of leveling social legislation in the history of mankind. It has other claims to this primacy; it forces, for instance, excess value, or wealth, back into industry instead of allowing it to remain in what Veblen contemptuously called exploit. This means full employment of technology to increase efficiency of production, thus accelerating the whole movement away from using man as a beast of labor.

It would be easy to make an imposing inventory of what materialism has given us, things that spirituality was not even able to promise: 70 million telephones; 99 per cent of our homes supplied with electric power; 90 per cent of the population with at least one television set; money in our purse. But everyone knows our material wealth, even if few appreciate it as it should be appreciated. Moreover, statistics such as this are what drive the anti-materialists mad. Probably a good fraction of that ten per cent who do not have television reject it out of anger, since television sets are so perfect a symbol of materialism. They are not so angry, when they are ill, about the materialism of medicine. During the Black Death, four of five Englishmen died, though it may be supposed that four of five Englishmen sought a spiritual cure. Believing was just as bad in medicine as it was in morality; medicine progressed only when it gave up philosophy. Today a child who intends to die eventually in bed will have to tax his ingenuity. Spirituality promised eternal life, and never convinced people firmly enough for them to hurry toward that conclusion; materialism is now seriously working at achieving eternal life, and everybody who has heard about it is wondering where he can make his down payment. In the meantime, American bodies are developing in size, strength, and health to the point where vital statistics and even skeletal measurements of the average man and woman have to be revised every ten years. We have two doctors for every 1,500 people, one dentist for every 1,750 people, and three nurses for every 1,100 people. And in the hospitals, one bed for every hundred Americans. These figures would be better if the force of conservative opinion would allow national responsibility for the health of all to be exercised, and if they did not include the spiritual states, whose citizens rely on evangelists for curing their ailments and who do not need good teeth for eating corn-meal mush. Materialism makes penicillin; spirituality says we must not use it. So long as medical practice included believing in occult power, people died.

The spiritualists can be driven back easily on every front of argument, but on art they make their firmest stand, for the reason that most people know so little about art. Let us assault them there as well, and say that art, too, is a product of materialism. The cave paintings of Paleolithic Europe were a means of producing, by homeopathic magic, the things necessary to life at the end of the Ice Age. Of course this practice worked badly, but its failure does not affect the principle. Magic among all primitive peoples is made for the purpose of overcoming the environment and thus producing material wealth. Later on, Bertrand Russell says in *The Impact of Science on Society*:

> When Leonardo wanted to get a job from the Duke of Milan, he wrote the Duke a long letter about his improvements in the art of fortification and in the last sentence mentioned briefly that he would also paint a bit.
>
> . . .
>
> When Galileo wanted employment under the Grand Duke of Tuscany, it was on his calculations of the trajectories of cannon-balls that he relied.

Gottfried Semper in 1879 propounded a theory that art derives from industry, a theory that subsequent investigation by archaeologists and anthropologists has tended rather to corroborate than to refute. Semper as an architect traced the elaborate wall designs in classical and Mesopotamian structures to the beginning of their evolution in mats hung on mud walls. Gene Weltfish has further shown that such mat patterns invent themselves through the processes of weaving—the way a knot invents itself. All that the human being contributes to the process is the recognition of the design as something that can be abstracted from the fabric and transferred to other media—pottery, for instance. Weltfish's analysis of designs on the masterful pottery of the American Indians—the ware of the Mimbres people of the Southwest—is an irrefutable proof of how this self-invention of art works.

Scholars in disciplines other than anthropology have independently come to the same discovery by analysis of our own arts and crafts. The Swiss art authority Sigfried Giedion told the Harvard University community in 1939 that utilitarian artifacts, including architecture, were often better expressions of American artistic culture than the conscious productions of professional artists. John Kouwenhoven shows that some artistic inventions in furniture were belated discoveries of previous inventions of what he calls "vernacular" artists. The cantilever chair, designed by the Austrian Marcel Breuer, was an adaptation of the cantilever seat put on farm tractors by American mechanics, who died without knowing they were artists. They might have received the credit they deserved, if it were not part of modern American folklore to believe that art and industry are quite incompatible.

If art cannot get along with industry, so much the worse for art. It can sulk in Greenwich Village until urban renewal cleans it out. The wise man will go uptown and see what good things Madison Avenue has. Some men who as children read in comic strips about Buck Rogers and his flying belt have invented what is now a reality—a Fiberglas, twin-jet, hydrogen-peroxide flying belt for soldiers. This is not yet art, but in the nature of things, the war product comes first, then mass utility, and finally art.

Fortune in April, 1959, published the results of a two-year survey made by Jay Doblin, director of the Institute of Design at the Illinois Institute of Technology, to determine the hundred "best designed mass-produced products of modern times." The awkward redundance in Professor Doblin's title may not appeal to literary taste, but his list is a catalog of the latest Fine Art, the things that man and his machines have fashioned into a union of beauty and utility. Significantly, most of the nominations, distilled by two votes of the hundred-man jury of professional designers from all over the world, are American. In order of number of votes received by each artifact, this is Professor Doblin's list, with American products (appropriately) printed in small capitals.

1. Olivetti Lettera 22 portable typewriter, 1950
2. EAMES SIDE CHAIR, 1947
3. Barcelona chair, 1929
4. STUDEBAKER HARD-TOP COUPE, 1953
5. PARKER 51 FOUNTAIN PEN, 1939
6. LINCOLN CONTINENTAL, 1940
7. EDISON VOICEWRITER, VP DICTATING MODEL, 1952
8. FRIGIDAIRE SHEER LOOK APPLIANCES, 1957
9. HALLICRAFTERS COMMUNICATIONS-RECEIVER, MODEL SX-42, 1946
10. BELL "500" TELEPHONE, 1951
11. GEODESIC DOME, 1954
12. Necchi "Mirella" sewing machine, 1956
13. SAARINEN "WOMB" CHAIR, 1948
14. CORD 810, 1936
15. Vespa 125 cc motor scooter, 1956
16. BORG "FLIGHT" BATHROOM SCALE, 1954
17. VW-Karmann-Ghia coupe, 1955
18. SINGER VACUUM CLEANER, 1948
19. G.E. WALL REFRIGERATOR, 1954
20. Leica IIIc camera, 1940
21. "AMERICAN MODERN" DINNERWARE, 1937
22. REVERE WARE COOKING UTENSILS, 1939
23. FLINT STAINLESS STEEL KITCHEN TOOLS, 1946
24. Breuer chair, 1928
25. Raleigh bicycle, sports model no. 22, 1925
26. BISSELL SWEEPMASTER CARPET SWEEPER, 1954
27. IBM 305 RAMAC COMPUTER, 1955

28. Cisitalia "Gran Sport," 1946
29. TOASTMASTER AUTOMATIC TOASTER, MODEL 1B2, 1930
30. PLANNER GROUP FURNITURE, 1947
31. STUDEBAKER STARLIGHT COUPE, 1947
32. EAMES FIBERGLAS CHAIR, 1951
33. Aalto chair, 1934
34. Bell & Howell 16 mm movie camera, Model 240 EE, 1957
35. WILLYS JEEP, 1941
36. CHEMEX COFFEEMAKER, 1941
37. SCHICK "20" ELECTRIC RAZOR, 1950
38. CRANE "CRITERION" LAVATORY, 1951
39. "Hardoy" chair, 1938
40. Porsche 1500 Super, 1952
41. FORD THUNDERBIRD, 1955
42. DOUGLAS DC-3, 1935
43. THERMADOR "BILT-IN" RANGE AND OVEN COMPONENTS, 1946
44. IBM ELECTRIC TYPEWRITER, 1948
45. Olivetti printing calculator, 1948
46. DIRECTOR'S CHAIR, TRADITIONAL DESIGN
47. Wagner chair, 1949
48. Arzberg White china, 1931
49. BRUNSWICK CLASSROOM FURNITURE, 1953
50. G.E. KITCHEN CENTER, 1956
51. G.E. PORTABLE TELEVISION RECEIVER, 1955
52. ZIPPO LIGHTER, 1932
53. MUSEUM WHITE DINNERWARE, 1946
54. NELSON STORAGE WALL (MODULAR GROUP FURNITURE), 1949
55. WINCHESTER MODEL 73 LEVER ACTION RIFLE, 1873
56. NOGUCHI LAMP, 1947
57. "Vienna" café chair, 1876
58. NUTONE BUILT-IN MIXER, 1955
59. AMERICAN TOURISTER "TRI-TAPER" LUGGAGE, 1953
60. Gense "Focus" stainless steel flatware, 1955
61. STEINWAY GRAND PIANO, MODEL B, 1910
62. Finn Juhl chair, 1949
63. PYREX CHEMICAL FLASK, before 1934
64. Hasselblad 500c camera, 1947
65. Ponti toilet, 1954

66. Citroën DS-19, 1955
67. EAMES LOUNGE CHAIR AND OTTOMAN, 1957
68. "LINEAR" ROOM DIVIDER, 1956
69. NELSON WALL CLOCK, 1948
70. BELL & HOWELL HIGH-FIDELITY RADIO AND TELEVISION CONSOLE, 1955
71. BEECHCRAFT BONANZA, 1945
72. EASTMAN BROWNIE CAMERA, 1900
73. COLDSPOT REFRIGERATOR, 1937
74. Luxo drafting lamp, 1937
75. SAARINEN PEDESTAL CHAIR, 1957
76. BSE motorcycle, Super Rocket Model, 1955
77. MOEN ONE-HANDLE MIXING FAUCET, 1946
78. VERSEN CEILING LAMP, 1933
79. Rolls-Royce Phantom II Millinen Continental Tourer, 1930
80. FRIGIDAIRE FOLD-BACK SURFACE COOKING UNIT, 1955
81. Hermes Rocket portable typewriter, 1932
82. FORD MODEL T, 1923
83. HAMILTON "TURNIP" POCKET WATCH, 1892–1925
84. Aalto stacking stools, 1954
85. Luger Standard Army 9 mm pistol, 1908
86. IBM TIME-DATA PUNCH, 1957
87. TALON ZIPPER, 1913
88. LA SALLE, 1935
89. MG Model TC, 1948
90. FRANKLIN STOVE, *ca.* 1750
91. AMPEX PORTABLE TAPE RECORDER, MODEL 601, 1954
92. BUDD PIONEER ZEPHYR, 1934
93. Borletti sewing machine, 1956
94. NELSON BUBBLE LAMP, 1952
95. HOUGH "PAYLOADER" MODEL HH, 1955
96. SCENICRUISER BUS, 1954
97. VICTOR TALKING MACHINE WITH MORNING GLORY HORN, 1901–1906
98. TAPPAN "400" WALL-HUNG ELECTRIC RANGE, 1951
99. Futura type face, 1927
100. GILBERT ERECTOR SET, 1909

No one, least of all the voting designers, would accept this list unquestioningly. There are indefensible inclusions and inexplicable omissions; why, to mention the first omission that comes to mind, was the Coca-Cola bottle excluded? One finds it hard to disagree with its creator, Raymond Loewy, who said flatly that, except for the egg, this is the best designed functional object on earth. But any other list unhampered by cobwebbed ideas of the past would return the same proportion of American-made artifacts. Of the thirty foreign designs, eight (not counting number 65) are chairs, which might suggest some unkind remarks about the disposition to inactivity in foreign character. This kind of art is all materialistic—there is not a crucifix in a carload of industrial products—but this is a boast, not an apology.

Art can be defined as the master craftsman playing with his work. Most of us have confidence in the idea that the machine has achieved master craftsmanship but cannot yet play at its craft—this is the exclusive province of human beings; a poor thing, but our own. Still, human beings had better look to their leisure as well as to their work, for the machines are creeping into that endeavor, too. Raymond Auger has invented a painting machine that can be programmed to make paintings, abstract patterns, or semi-abstract figures. However, Auger consoles us with the knowledge that it still takes a human being to make the decision as to when the painting is finished.

If this does not please those who long for more spirituality in American life, we can look into the matter of books and reading, a form of diversion most of them approve of, though there is little precedent for it in their history. Although Americans spend all their time bug-eyed before the television set, library circulation somehow has increased nearly thirty per cent in the last five years, and paperback books are selling at the rate of nearly a million a day. To state that fact another way, materialism is producing more books in a few hours than the Age of Spirituality produced in a thousand years, and that does not include comic books. Bringing up the subject of libraries once more, the largest library in the world is the Library of Congress, which in 1957 had 36,100,000 volumes. This is a worthwhile fact to remember if you have to do any research in the libraries of the spiritual nations in any area other than medieval theology.

If nothing else suffices, the spiritualists can sulk by the window, which, it will have to be conceded, is less interesting a pastime now than it was a couple of centuries ago in London. It was all more spiritual then, in the good old days, when one could watch during a city shower:

Sweepings from Butchers Stalls, Dung, Guts, and Blood,
Drown'd Puppies, stinking Sprats, all drench'd in Mud,
Dead Cats, and Turnip-Tops come tumbling down the Flood.

While we have in mind both books and the second item in Swift's poetic inventory of the flotsam in a London rain, let us not forget idyllic Stratford-upon-Avon when Shakespeare was a boy and London was stalked by adherents of one spiritual philosophy or other, seeking whom they might devour. The first time a Shakespeare got the famous name into public record was when John Shakespeare, the poet's father, was fined for leaving a pile of human excrement in front of his house without proper authorization. It must have been a whopping big pile, for it was a whopping big fine. As Robert Benchley once said, the "thing which makes me distrust spiritualism [is] the quality of the material offered from the spirit world."

IN SUMMING UP

And so ends our catechism. We have looked surreptitiously into a few corners of American civilization and we have seen some things that are bad, more that are silly, and very many that are good. A longer and deeper view would turn up the same proportion of good, evil, and frivolity, but these value judgments are ir-

relevant in the anthropological approach of this book. As Preacher
Casy concluded after a lifetime of observing human behavior:

> There ain't no sin and there ain't no virtue. There's just stuff
> people do. It's all part of the same thing. And some of the
> things folks do is nice, and some ain't nice, but that's as far
> as any man got a right to say.

Cultural determinism sees man as a constant and culture as the
variable in the equation that makes behavior. It is just as futile to
criticize American acquisitiveness as it is to criticize the ignorance
and inhumanity of medieval churchmen. The churchmen were
the very best men in their society, and if what they did does not
seem nice to us, the fault was in their culture. American behavior
seems good to us, but whether it is good or bad is quite beside the
point, which is that it is inevitable, the end point in our time of
forces that began working when man was still chipping his tools
out of stone. Both medieval spirituality and American materialism
are phases in the evolution of culture. The materialism grew out
of the spirituality and therefore, according to the rule of irreversi-
bility of evolution, seems the better of the two approaches to life.
What will grow out of the materialism we cannot say, but that
too should be better. Doubtlessly, the next phase will see American civilization superseded as all civilizations must be, but it is a
worthy accomplishment to have set the direction of world culture
for a century or more, and it will be an honor to become the Old
World of the Age of Technology. We know that for some time
to come other cultures will not advance unless they develop along
the path we have set to them; they will progress only as they
borrow from our pattern.

As they borrow, they will criticize our petty weaknesses and silly
idiosyncrasies, as the British visitors of the last century criticized,
and for the same reason—for their own peace of mind. And we
will be glad to have the criticism and to participate in it—for our
peace of mind, since it relieves us of the guilt of being too pros-

perous. We will assuage our conscience further by giving away
much of our prosperity, like the boy who stole the cookies easing
his mind by giving some to his little brother. Since 1945 we have
given away some $85 billion dollars in major assistance programs,
including nearly a billion dollars to the U.S.S.R. Under Public
Law 480, we have in eight years sent more than 100 million tons
of surplus food to 114 foreign countries. Our cynics and those
abroad say we do these things not out of altruism but for military
expediency. If this were so, the money could have been spent
more effectively on weapons, instilling fear into foreign hearts
instead of love, for charity engenders resentment, whereas terror
engenders respect.

Not only will our character be impugned in the future as in
the past, but our method of perpetuating our culture also. Here
again, we will see the paradox of followers criticizing their leaders.
The British, native and colonial, will maintain their absurd standards of education; the Australians will continue to send their best
young men to England; and the best young Englishmen will
continue to emigrate to the United States.

Our behavior—that is, our social responsibility—will become
ever better, and it will harm no one very much if it is believed
that our better conduct is a result of more and more Americans
going back to church. Only professional students of man read
sociology books, so the generality of Americans will never know
that people go to church now to satisfy the animal drive of gregariousness. As the old social organizations such as the Elks, the
Odd Fellows, the Masons, the Knights of Columbus, and even
the family weaken in numbers and cohesiveness, the churches
grow stronger in everything but piety. Advisors to the lovelorn—
Ann Landers, Abby van Buren, and Helen Gurley Brown—will go
on telling incipient old maids to go to church to find a husband,
but rarely will they send anyone there for faith.

Our legacy from Courtly Love will go on running like a warm
current through our culture, making us more than ever beholden

to our women folk and easing still more their slight labors. Look again at those hundred best designed products of the machine age and notice how many were made to emancipate women from the chores that were her natural inheritance in the spiritual ages. Notice too that the only sewing machines—those obsolescent vestiges of home weaving—are foreign-made.

Every nation has areas of unreality to cherish; our are harmless enough. We shall go on making factitious heroes to symbolize our ideals, such as Abraham Lincoln—but we shall not make any Adolf Hitlers. We shall persist in cultivating and tolerating our dissenters, the nuts among the berries. Dissenters are the mutations in the cultural organism; ninety-nine per cent of them are harmful but are swamped out by natural selection. Still, every healthy culture, like every healthy organism, welcomes mutations, for only in these is there possibility for evolution to something better.

And through everything in our culture, from play to politics, the tendrils of materialism will grow, for materialism is just as inevitable as Americans. It is even working its way into things of the spirit. The May 2, 1960, issue of *Newsweek* showed Lee Davidson, Grand Dragon of the Georgia Ku Klux Klan, exhibiting a portable, electric-powered fiery cross. Not far in spirit from Georgia, the Reverend Billy Graham has a staff of eight secretaries slitting open thousands of letters every week and underlining in coding colors the key words in the plaints—"unsaved husband," "serviceman," "liquor," and so forth—and feeding the letters into robot typewriters which are thus activated to type personal letters in reply to the soul-troubled, together with pertinent verses from Scripture. Our spiritual heritage has always been concerned about the sins of the flesh, as some of us know. In the seventeenth century one spiritual inventor decided to do something about sexual intercourse, since the exhortations of the Church had gone unheeded for so long. With the mechanical knowledge that materialism was then making available, he invented a device for artificial parthenogenesis, and made supplication to the Crown to prohibit coition for one year to test his invention. It is not known how he made out. The spiritualists have always been resourceful, though; this is nothing new. Hypatia, the Alexandrian Neo-platonic philosopher and the most revered woman of her time (370–415), was chopped to pieces by a Christian mob. Later she was refabricated into the otherwise non-existent St. Catherine of Alexandria.

Materialism is more powerful than spirituality, and since cultural evolution proceeds in proportion to the amount of energy available to humanity, it will get more things done even in the areas traditionally in the province of spirituality. There is, for example, more racial integration in lunchrooms than in churches. We have in history overrated the power of spirituality. The dedication of the masses to their otherworlds has always been questionable; of the millions of members the Church claimed as communicants in the bad years when it was fighting for its life against the other proletarian religions, it has been able to recover only a few hundred genuine martyrs. In fact, the Church made an incomparably greater number of martyrs to other religions than it inspired in its own, by repressing with fire and the sword any deviationism that arose while it had the power to deal forcibly with heretics and heathens. Fear was the spur, as it always has been in getting human beings to behave themselves, and in our heritage it is an emotion that was nurtured well during the Age of Spirituality. We retain much of it still, and it is a culture trait that is not likely to pass out in the form of metataxis.

The old fear is none the less real for having become secularized, for its being based now on nothing more substantial than words. Next to "materialism," the word that liberal American intellectuals seem to fear most is "capitalism," and as with the Devil, it will take a long time for them to be convinced that there is no such thing. The stock-market crash of 1962—quite as severe for a short time as that of 1929—had no noticeable effect on the economy (except as it gave automated companies an excuse for getting rid of another batch of obsolete employees) because risk capital is no longer an important source of industrial finance. Buckingham in his study of *Automation: Its Impact on Business and People* sums up the change this way:

> The capital market itself has been losing influence over industry. Over three fourths of private corporate investment is financed from internal funds, meaning depreciation allowance and plowed in profits. Most of the rest comes from bonds and bank loans. Less than one twelfth of new private industrial capital comes from stock sales today and nearly half of this is from notvoting preferred stock. This leaves no more than five per cent of all new capital investment being financed from risk capital which is supposed to be the mainspring of capitalist enterprise. Some studies estimate this percentage to be as low as three per cent. So there may be plenty of private capital in industry but it is getting harder to find any capitalists.

What Buckingham should have said is: "It is getting harder to find any *big* capitalists"—the capitalists of the old political cartoons. The Bell Telephone System has 1,736,681 shareholders and 729,035 employees (1959)—or more capitalists than proletarians. The national debt is making even more capitalists than the Bell System. But as long as the Communists believe in the old bugaboo, we will believe in it, and they have a remarkable capacity for believing in things, as the examples in the first page of this book show. After their successful orbital flights, the Russian cosmonauts announced gleefully that while they were up there they looked all around for God, but they saw nobody. Only the Russians would have thought to look for Him. Still and all, we must remember that the Russians are new at being materialists and, as Khrushchev cannily observed, "Moscow was not built in a day."

We are even afraid of being healthy, because national health is infected with a bad word, "Socialized Medicine." Culture will get around our fear and opposition in the area of medical welfare by letting charity appeals for sufferers from psoriasis and bubonic plague proliferate until we beg the government to give us relief by taking over the entire job. At the moment, though, Americans prefer every sort of inconvenience and expense to parting with money for taxes, which their folklore tells them are somehow different from prices, or for the welfare state, which their folklore tells them is somehow different from insurance. In the anonymity of public-opinion polls the real feeling behind the fear is apparent; a recent Gallup Poll gives these figures on public welfare:

75 per cent in favor of old-age pensions for everyone over 65
74 per cent in favor of medical care for everyone who needs it
68 per cent in favor of public works for the unemployed
87 per cent in favor of public relief

Culture is a resourceful administrator and it can use our fears as well as our desires to effect the inevitable future. Our greatest fear now is the Bomb, which culture is playing upon very cleverly. We fear the Bomb even more than we fear taxes, so that expenditures for defense are the only kind we will make without protest. Already so much money is being spent on defense that a cessation of the Cold War would destroy our economy; in a few years this rate of expenditure by the government will become permanent, and peace will mean, without the least doubt, a transferral of tax money from armament to urban renewal, public health, education, welfare, conservation, and similar things that our present fear of words will not permit us to support.

As we are not far away from our legacy of fear, so we are not far from other heritages of spirituality. Rejection of materialism on a philosophical plane gives a perverse satisfaction that man has enjoyed through most of his history; since humiliation is so very easy to achieve in this competitive life, it has been made a virtue by the spiritual philosophies, and this, like other sustaining emotions, cannot be opposed by reason. So it is useless to argue with the anti-materialists, just as it is useless to argue with anti-Americans. Like the Quakers who went up to Boston from free Rhode Island to have their ears cut off, such people are happy only when they are unhappy, and it is best to leave them to their pleasures in the face of the inevitable—with possibly now and then (just for the fun of it) a turning off of their electricity for twenty-four hours so that they can better meditate the worthlessness of materialism and the crass Americans who put such stuff into ninety-nine per cent of American homes. For the rest of us, all that either our country or our materialism needs is a little appreciation.

A Note on Sources

*Parenthetical numbers preceding paragraphs
refer to pages in the text.*

Every teacher dreams of someday escaping from the narrow
syllabus of his course and wandering off like my uncle *Toby* into
the delightful byways of digression. Anthropology more than most
academic disciplines allows its teachers to deviate from knowledge
into wisdom, but even anthropologists are usually bound by a
course title to stay on the announced subject. After all, if you are
teaching Anthropology 497, the Material Culture of the Hodmadods of Monomatapa, you are more or less required to begin
a lecture by saying something like: "Students, today we will consider the footgear of the Hodmadods of Monomatapa. The footgear of the Hodmadods of Monomatapa (take this down; you
will be examined on it) falls generally into three categories: (1)
sneakers, (2) saddle Oxfords, (3) patent-leather slippers. Sneakers
among the Hodmadods of Monomatapa are woven in a coiled

pattern with the use of stone axes and *atlatls* from the fibrous stem of the Coreopsis plant (*Carduaceae drummondii*), which must be gathered on the night of the first full moon after the Hodmadod Feast of the Sneaker-Plant. . . ."

I do not mean to imply that this sort of information is not valuable; we have record of some students remembering it as long as a week after the final examination. But it is not much fun for the teacher, however much his students enjoy it.

When I first came to the University of Colorado I was given an opportunity beyond my dreams to exercise the mania which I share with my uncle *Toby*; I was assigned to teach a two-term course called Foundations of the Social Order. Since this was an inter-disciplinary course and its several instructors were drawn from economics, political science, history, sociology, and anthropology, and since the director believed in the Jeffersonian principle of government by noninterference, each teacher was given no more co-ordinating directive than the course title. Thus freed from all supervision, I organized my section in the following way. In the first term I took my freshmen on a guided tour of the primitive cultures of the world, drawing, from a heterogeneous mass of unique and universal behavior traits, anthropological principles and regular phenomena which in the second term I applied to American civilization. I like to think that at the end of the course my students knew a little something about why they did the things they did. Some were resentful that I had led them out of the Egypt of their ethnocentricity into the wilderness of objectivity, but some were grateful, for even after the final grades were in, a few came to ask me to autograph copies of my phonograph records.

This book is an outline of the second term of my course in Foundations of the Social Order, with a few references to material covered in the first term, for the benefit of those who joined the class late. As an outline, it is not nearly so digressive as the original course, nor does it provide for argumentative communication from the reader, who will be upset by having his comfortable beliefs, biases, and prejudices battered by my contentions. If he were a student in class, he would be able to ask questions, but, as a reader, all he can do is scribble violent objections in the margins. I am content that the reader should express his objections in this way (though he should be warned that second-hand dealers do not buy marked-up books), for most student questions are intended not to clarify the teacher's startling statements but to change the teacher's mind. The reader interested in going further into the issues I raise will consult the sources mentioned in the following paragraphs. He will not find in these references documentation for everything in the book, for I give only those sources from which I have consciously drawn material, and some of the ideas are my own, I think.

A WORD TO BEGIN

(3) I much regret to say that the one-hundred-and-forty-six-year-old fellow I mention in this brief list of Soviet accomplishments will not be able to read this book, for he died while it was in the making, in September, 1963, at the age of one hundred and forty seven. In reporting the untimely demise, the *Moscow Medical Journal* gives us the intelligence that he fathered a child at the age of one hundred and twelve, which is about the most unlikely story on this subject since Old King Pharaoh's daughter brought home that tale of finding Moses in the bulrushes. He is survived by a daughter, aged ninety, who would bear watching. We must lament the passing of old Ashkanger Bzania, but there are others to hold the red banner high. Norris and Ross McWhirter's *Guinness Book of World Records* (New York: Sterling Publishing Company; 1962) passes on the claim that two Soviet citizens reached the age of one hundred and eighty.

(3) The newspaperman is Robert Ruark, but since I am annoyed by his continual criticism of Americans at home and abroad, I am reluctant to put his name in the beginning of my book.

(4) For the same reason I do not identify the army officer on the following page. He is Lieutenant Colonel William E. Mayer, against whose 100,000 circulating tape recordings I have two or three of my own being broadcast by radio stations of little coverage and no influence. I urge those who have been exposed to Colonel Mayer to read my evaluation of his speeches and those of his supporters in "The Colonel's Korean 'Turncoats,'" which appeared in *The Nation*, November 10, 1962.

ONE: THE TYRANNY OF CULTURE

(7) The rhyming lines about tobacco are paraphrased from Graham Lee Hemminger's charming poem, "This Smoking World," which may be read in its entirety in Franklin P. Adams's anthology of light verse, *Innocent Merriment* (Garden City, New York: Garden City Publishing Co.; 1945).

(9) Readers who are really keen on documentation can look up the Hopi attitude toward time in several writings by Benjamin Lee Whorf, e.g., "The Punctual and Segmentative Aspects of Verbs in Hopi," *Language*, XII (1936), pp. 127–31, and "An American Indian Model of the Universe," *International Journal of American Linguistics*, XVI (1950), pp. 67–72.

(11) For the application of Darwinism to coinage, see John Evans, "On the Coinage of the Ancient Britons and Natural Selection," *Journal of the Royal Anthropological Institute of Great Britain and Ireland*, VII (1875), pp. 476 ff.

(12) Alfred L. Kroeber has developed his thesis of the pendulum swing of the dress styles of women in several writings, but I should like the reader to make Kroeber's acquaintance with his most stimulating book, *Anthropology* (New York: Harcourt, Brace and Company; 1948), the book that made me decide to go into anthropology professionally. So much has been learned about physical anthropology since 1948 that the first part of his book, which deals with questions in that area, is out of date, but his

discussion of culture is timeless. Harcourt, Brace, and World has thoughtfully re-issued *Anthropology* in two volumes, so that you do not have to buy the first part; get the second, entitled *Anthropology: Culture Patterns and Processes* (Harbinger Books Edition, 1963). Kroeber's great work is the best introduction to the approach of cultural determinism, the "superorganic," "supra-biological," "extrasomatic" view of culture which is the principal argument of *The Inevitable Americans*. Kroeber does not push the thesis to the point of mysticism; those who wish to go that far can read the leading proponent of the approach, Leslie A. White, in *The Science of Culture* (New York: Farrar, Straus and Cudahy; 1949), not to be confused with *The Evolution of Culture*, which contains some indefensible notions. I have on several occasions called Leslie's attention to his errors, but since he has recently repeated them in my presence, I must judge that he intends to be stubborn about this. His thesis that there are no great men who invent new ideas allows me, without danger of offending him further, to say that the main point of *The Science of Culture* is not original with him. Among earlier writers on this subject, the most outstanding was Émile Durkheim, whose *The Rules of Sociological Method* (eighth edition, translated by Sarah A. Solovay and John H. Mueller and edited by George E. G. Catlin; Chicago: the University of Chicago Press; 1938) shows how far ahead of his time he was. I am constrained to warn the reader that cultural determinism is not generally popular with anthropologists, any more than it is with theologians.

(13) Kroeber's book will also serve as a primer for understanding the concept of culture in the event that I have not made it clear. Although the concept was first isolated by Sir Edward Burnett Tylor in the book that established anthropology as a serious academic discipline, *Primitive Culture* (London: J. Murray; 1871), Kroeber was one of the earliest scholars to make use of it. Kroeber has kept his eye sharply on others who have considered the concept; the few definitions I have quoted here can be supple-

mented by the enthusiastic reader from Kroeber and Kluckhohn's *Culture: A Critical Review of Concepts and Definitions* (Cambridge, Massachusetts: Peabody Museum of American Archaeology and Ethnology, XLVII; 1952), which contains more than two hundred pages of definitions.

(13) I have used, in these preliminary pages, some biological suggestions from Garrett Hardin (whose book *Nature and Man's Fate*, New York: Holt, Rinehart and Winston; 1959, you had better read if you wish to know what radiation mutations are going to make of us eventually), and from Theodosius Dobzhansky. Hardin and Dobzhansky also informed me personally that in having only one child I am not reproducing myself; for very good reasons, I am ignoring their suggestion.

(17) You will find Kenneth Oakley's fascinating bit about the bottle-opening birds in his survey, "Skill as a Human Possession," in the first volume of *A History of Technology* (edited by Charles Singer, E. J. Holmyard, and A. R. Hall; New York and London: Oxford University Press; 1954-8), which, if you are at all interested in the making of this technological world, you already have on your bookshelves. The entire set of five volumes is a magnificent accomplishment, the best-edited cyclopedia I know.

(17) Isaac Goldberg's *The Wonder of Words* (New York: D. Appleton Century Co.; 1938) provided me with most of the summary on what is known about animal speech. In books on language written by linguists, the subject is ignored.

(18) The signal reaction, the symbolic process, and other fascinating aspects of semantics are most sanely discussed in S. I. Hayakawa's *Language in Thought and Action* (New York: Harcourt, Brace and Company; 1949). Avoid other, more promethean, books on semantics unless you are dissatisfied with your present religion.

(20) L. S. B. Leakey is holding out for an age of one and three quarters million years for his *Zinjanthropus*. I examined a cast of this skull when Leakey was in Boulder, and it didn't look anywhere

near that old to me—as I told Leakey, without his being much impressed, so far as I could tell. Some of Leakey's supporters are willing to grant Zinjy an age of four million years, which even Leakey is hesitant to accept. On this business of fossil man, the most recent and, without any near rivals, the most complete compendium of information is Carleton S. Coon's *The Origin of Races* (New York: Alfred A. Knopf; 1962). This is a most stimulating book; it has nearly all the conventional physical anthropologists brachiating from the ceiling.

(21) So far as I know, the idea that the bow was conceived of as a musical instrument before it was made into a weapon is one of my own original notions.

(23) Anacleto Apodaca's story about the Spanish-American farmers and the hybrid corn is in Edward M. Spicer's book *Human Problems in Technological Change* (New York: Russell Sage Foundation; 1952). Anyone who has ideas on how to handle primitive and folk groups ought to read this book.

(24) My information on the packaging of eggs came from Dean M. Wakefield, public-relations manager of the Dobeckmun Division of Dow Chemical Company.

(25) The figures on the number of building-code restrictions in California came from the California State Building Standards Commission.

(26) The concept of cultural lag was first described by William Fielding Ogburn in *Social Change* (New York: Huebsch; 1923).

(28) Ralph Linton's *The Study of Man*, from which the paragraphs on the hundred-per cent American were taken, is the best introduction to anthropology for the layman (Kroeber's *Anthropology* assumes more preparatory knowledge than the average reader possesses). It was published in New York by Appleton-Century-Crofts; 1936.

(31) The material about penicillin came largely from *Eleven Blue Men and other Narratives of Medical Detection*, by Berton Roueché (Boston: Little, Brown & Company; 1953).

(33) I first heard about the Great Vowel Shift from Albert C. Baugh, who suffered me as a student at the University of Pennsylvania. He describes it in his fine textbook, A History of the English Language (New York: Appleton-Century-Crofts; 1935), though he does not recognize it as a continuing phenomenon.

(36) The first series of "We musts" were extracted from John K. Jessup et al.: The National Purpose (New York: Holt, Rinehart and Winston; 1960).

(37) The Travelers Insurance Companies' booklets containing accident data can be had from that organization, in Hartford, Connecticut.

TWO: TO SEE OURSELVES

(41) This is the most opportune place to list those visitors to early America who have supplied me with so many pertinent quotations. Since the books of most of these have been published in many editions by several printers, some of whom are long out of business, I will give here only the authors, titles, and dates of publication:

Lord James Bryce, The American Commonwealth, 1888

Alexis, Comte de Tocqueville, Democracy in America, 1835 (first American edition, 1838)

Charles Dickens, American Notes for General Circulation, 1842

Henry Bradshaw Fearon, Sketches of America, 1818

T. C. Grattan, Civilized America, 1859

David Mackay, The Western World, 1846

Frederick Marryat, Diary in America, with Remarks on Its Institutions, 1839

James Fullarton Muirhead, The Land of Contrasts, 1898

Michael Scott, "Tom Cringle's Log," Blackwood's Magazine, 1829

Frances Trollope, Domestic Manners of the Americans, 1832

(42) Jonathan Swift's derogatory remark about the American cannibal is of course in his outrageous *Modest Proposal* (1729).

(43) George F. Kennan's derogatory remarks were printed in the *Rocky Mountain News* (Denver), October 28, 1959.

(44) Very few anthropologists will express themselves publicly on the subject of national character, for fear of being thought ethnocentric and pejorative. However, Margaret Mead, who will express herself on anything, has a survey of scholarship on the question in A. L. Kroeber's *Anthropology Today: an Encyclopedic Inventory* (Chicago: The University of Chicago Press; 1953), pp. 642–67.

(45) David M. Potter's *People of Plenty* (Chicago: The University of Chicago Press; 1954) has more to it than snide allusions to behavioral scientists preoccupied with toilet training.

(46) Ambrose Bierce's snide allusion to the probity of ethnologists is in *The Devil's Dictionary* (New York: The World Publishing Company; 1944; sixth printing).

(47) Stanley Milgram's experiments were reported in "Nationality and Conformity," *Scientific American*, CCV (December 1961), pp. 45–51.

(48) Ruth Benedict's *The Chrysanthemum and the Sword* (Boston: Houghton Mifflin Co.; 1946) was criticized most effectively by Jean Stoetzel in *Without the Chrysanthemum and the Sword: A Study of Youth in Post-War Japan* (New York: Columbia University Press; 1955). (49) The poll of Japanese college students regarding the retention of the Emperor was reported in the press on May 9, 1959. (50) Douglas C. Haring's study of Amami Oshima is titled "Japanese National Character: Cultural Anthropology, Psychoanalysis, and History," and was published in the *Yale Review*, XLII (1953), pp. 375–92.

(50) The studies of the national character of Mexicans are summarized in a well-documented article by Gordon W. Hewes, "Mexicans in Search of the 'Mexican,'" in *The American Journal of Economics and Sociology*, XIII (January 1954), pp. 209–23.

(52) Ruth Benedict's classic tract on differences among people, *Patterns of Culture*, was first published by Houghton Mifflin in 1934 but is most often purchased in the paperback edition (New York: Penguin Books; 1946). In spite of the invalidity of the thesis she developed from Nietzsche, it is a beautiful book, and is deservedly recommended in many other college courses besides those in anthropology.

(53) Another beautiful book is Alfred L. Kroeber's *Style and Civilizations* (Ithaca, New York: Cornell University Press; 1957) —short, but stimulating and, like most of Kroeber's work, well written.

(54) Ralph Linton's perceptive remark about the Semitic preoccupation with sin and sex is in his posthumous book, *The Tree of Culture* (New York: Alfred A. Knopf; 1957). This is a good book on the diversity of culture, but not so good as his *The Study of Man*, which should be a warning to all writers against letting wives finish their books. I do not subscribe to Linton's statement, I hasten to say. Some of my best friends are Jews, and they are all well behaved. Well, most of them, anyhow.

(54) The test of a great book is its ability to withstand clear refutation of its thesis—like Ruth Benedict's *Patterns of Culture* and James Frazer's *The Golden Bough*. In this category also is Frederick Jackson Turner's *The Frontier in American History* (New York: Henry Holt and Co.; 1920).

(55) Lawrence Housman's biography, *My Brother, A. E. Housman* (New York: Charles Schribner's Sons; 1938), has many memorable ephemera in it besides the definition of chastity, but the reader must be embarrassed by Lawrence's abasement before his more talented brother.

(55) I have taken several things from *The Portable Medieval Reader*, edited by James Bruce Ross and Mary Martin McLaughlin (New York: The Viking Press; 1949), beginning here with the merchant career of Godric of Finchale.

(56) Charles A. Beard's list of Puritan vices and virtues is in

his article, "On Puritans," *New Republic*, XXV (1929), p. 13.

(58) Governor Winthrop's reasons for not shooting birds out of season are given by Samuel E. Morison, the great authority on the early Puritans, in his *Builders of the Bay Colony* (Boston: Houghton Mifflin Co.; 1930). I suspect I have unconsciously used Morison's work more than I have acknowledged.

(58) Arthur M. Schlesinger, Sr., epitomized the American character in *Contemporary Psychology*, May 1961.

(59) Davy Crockett's boast is in *Davy Crockett's Almanac* (1837), but I quote it from Benjamin A. Botkin's *A Treasury of American Folklore* (New York: Crown Publishers; 1944) in order to recommend the latter anthology of customs and sayings from all of America, folk and sophisticated.

(60) Another book of informal American history, possibly the liveliest study of American history in print, is Herbert Asbury's *The French Quarter* (New York: Alfred A. Knopf; 1936), from which I had the story of Bully Bill Sedley.

(67) The cute verses on Freud were written by me, and can be heard, together with other satiric and acidulous stanzas on the Freudian psychology, on *The Cat Came Back and Other Fun Songs Sung by John Greenway* (Bergenfield, New Jersey: Prestige Records; 1961). The songs are good but the singing is frightful.

(69) Much more entertaining than the latter item is Felix Grendon's survey, "The Anglo-Saxon Charms," in the *Journal of American Folklore*, XXII (1909), pp. 105–237.

(69) The patron saints of illnesses are gathered together from William Rose Benét's *The Reader's Encyclopedia* (New York: Thomas Y. Crowell Company; 1948)—another book which you must have on your shelves—and from my own childhood memories of invoking them with rather poor results.

(71) Samuel Sewall's onerous charge to God, and other delightful things, can be savored in *Samuel Sewall's Diary*, edited by Mark van Doren (n.p.: Macy-Masius; 1937).

THREE: BRINGING UP AMERICANS

(7) The reader fervently interested in more source material on the Australian aborigines can peruse some 11,000 items in the first part of my *Bibliography of the Australian Aborigines* (Sydney, Australia: Angus and Robertson; 1963). Those whose interest is more casual can read about initiation surgery and ritual in the classic work on the central Australians, *The Arunta: A Study of a Stone Age People* (London: Macmillan & Co.; 1927), by Sir Baldwin Spencer and Frank J. Gillen. I have a motion-picture film, taken by Norman B. Tindale, of these horrendous operations, but I do not show it to strangers.

(74) The man with the queer idea that women are naturally superior to men is Ashley Montagu, and he has written a book on the subject which I will not further identify, lest it get into the hands of more women and spread the mischievous notion.

(77) Curtis Bok's *Star Wormwood* was published in New York by Alfred A. Knopf, in 1959. It is a morbidly fascinating study of a cannibalistic murderer, interspersed with Bok's comments on the legal ramifications of the case.

(77) Margaret Mead has described Samoan education in several famous books, principally in *Coming of Age in Samoa* (New York: William Morrow & Company; 1928), from which the quoted observations were taken.

(78) Northwest of Samoa, on the edge of the great Polynesian triangle, is Tikopia, the special province of Raymond Firth. The most important of his several works about these isolated Polynesians is *We the Tikopia* (New York: American Book Company; 1936).

(78) At the southern apex of the Polynesian triangle is New Zealand, home of the Maori, whose chief ethnologist was Peter H. Buck (Te Rangi Hiroa). The most complete study Buck made of his people is *The Coming of the Maori* (Wellington, New

Zealand: Whitcombe and Tombs; 1940). The layman will find his *Vikings of the Sunrise* (Christchurch, New Zealand: Whitcombe and Tombs; 1954) more readable.

(79) There is very little in print about primitive education, since anthropological fashion has not yet swung into this area. Though limited to one group, George Pettitt's *Primitive Education in North America* (Berkeley: University of California Publications in American Archaeology and Ethnology, XLIII; 1956) presents some universal principles.

(80) William Grayden's *Adam and Atoms* (Perth, Western Australia: Frank Daniels Pty. Ltd.; 1957) is a *cause celèbre* in Australia. Grayden is short on anthropology but long on compassion for the aborigines still dodging missiles in the western deserts.

(82) Weld's description of Princeton in the old days was taken from Henry Adams's *The Formative Years: A History of the United States During the Administrations of Jefferson and Madison* (originally published in nine volumes, 1889–91; condensed by Herbert Agar and issued by Houghton Mifflin in 1947). Adams took it from Isaac Weld's *Travels through the States of North America, and the Provinces of Upper and Lower Canada, During the Years 1795, 1796, and 1797* (London: J. Stockdale; 1799).

(82) My critical description of education in England was drawn from several sources, but my conscious debt is to that excellent study of lower-class life in England, *The British People 1746–1946* by G. D. H. Cole and Raymond Postgate (New York: Alfred A. Knopf; 1947). The most recent condemnation of the English university system is in Anthony Sampson's *Anatomy of Britain* (New York: Harper & Row; 1962).

(86) My analysis of higher education in Australia is primary work done while I was attached to the University of Sydney as a Fulbright research scholar in 1956–7. I intended originally to write and publish this analysis in Australia, but I lost my nerve.

(87) In July of 1963 the London County Council announced its

decision to abandon the prole-making eleven-plus examination in the 911 primary schools under its jurisdiction. The Labour Party is jubilant that this means the beginning of the end for the terrifying written examination that eleven-year old schoolboys take to determine their future life. I, however, have more faith in the British Empire. Some Oxford don will pontificate—in Latin—that the London County Council's move is another step toward Americanization of British education, and that will be the end of that. For the present, we should know that only about a dozen of the 146 British education councils have dropped the eleven-plus examination.

(95) The reference to what happens to editors of *Honi Soit* is borne out by Murray Sayle in his scathing novel, *A Crooked Sixpence* (New York: Doubleday and Company; 1961). Sayle denies that his *Sunday Sun* is based on any existing journal, and equally observant of the laws of libel, I shall not venture any identification. But apropos of nothing, I must mention that I was interviewed by a reporter for *Weekend* and had my photograph published therein. The editor evidently did not like my looks, for he drew in a mustache. Again apropos of nothing, Sayle's book is brought to a climax by the doctoring of a photograph by the editor of the *Sunday Sun*.

(97) Arther S. Trace's *What Ivan Knows that Johnny Doesn't*, which gave me most of my material about contemporary education in the U.S.S.R., was published in 1961 by Random House.

(99) Conway Zirkle's *The Death of a Science in Russia* (Philadelphia: The University of Pennsylvania Press; 1949) is the basic source, to the time of its publication, of the Lysenko scandal. I have borrowed some additional material from Garrett Hardin's *Nature and Man's Fate*. Carroll Atkinson and Eugene Maleska's *The Story of Education* (Philadelphia: Chilton Co. Book Division; 1962) gave me some further information about Russian education, as did Charles W. Thayer *et al.*: *Russia* (New York: Time, Inc.; 1960).

(105) Those intrigued by the hint that Shakespeare is rather more obscene than they had suspected while plowing through him in high school can see what they missed in Eric Partridge's *Shakespeare's Bawdy: A Literary & Psychological Essay* (London: Routledge Paul; 1955; revised edition) and then go back to Shakespeare with new understanding and appreciation. Or perhaps they would rather go on to other books of this nature by Eric Partridge. Or if they would prefer to hear rather than to read, I have had the privilege of writing notes to a startling series of phonograph records published by Prestige under the general title of *Lyrica Erotica*, though I know nothing at all about this sort of thing.

(105) Robert Jungk's *Brighter Than a Thousand Suns* (New York: Harcourt, Brace & World; 1958) has many passages of insight equal to the one quoted.

FOUR: BEHAVING OURSELVES

(107) The ancient Hebrews' appropriation of the religious ideas of the Mesopotamians is described most completely in Sir James George Frazer's *Folklore in the Old Testament* (London: Macmillan & Co.; 1923). Less systematic but more recent is *Studies in Biblical and Jewish Folklore*, edited by Raphael Patai, Francis Lee Utley, and Dov Noy (Bloomington: Indiana University Press; 1960).

(111) The Kurnai "nation" (actually a group of loosely associated tribes, the Krauatungulung, Brabralung, Braiakaulung, Bratauolung, and Tatungalung—all, together with their neighbors, now extinct) was studied chiefly by Alfred W. Howitt and Lorimer Fison in some seventy books and articles, of which the most important is *Kamilaroi and Kurnai*, published in Melbourne in 1880.

(113) Many books have told the story of the *Bounty* mutineers, though the original accounts are contradictory and unreliable. Of these, the most popular is Charles Nordhoff and James Norman Hall, *Mutiny on the Bounty* (Boston: Little, Brown & Company;

1932). Nordhoff and Hall continued the story in *Pitcairn's Island* (Boston: Little, Brown & Company; 1934). Excerpts from the journals and testimony of the participants make up Irvin Anthony's *The Saga of the Bounty* (New York: G. P. Putnam's Sons; 1935). Anthropologically, the most valuable book about the Pitcairn Islanders is Harry L. Shapiro's *The Heritage of the Bounty: Six Generations* (New York: Simon & Schuster; 1936). For my description, I made use of all of these books, together with some material I had by correspondence from Fred Christian, great-great-great-grandson of Fletcher Christian, who lives on Pitcairn Island.

(114) Freud's *Totem and Taboo*, whose thesis I have irreverently summarized, was originally published as four essays in *Imago*, a Viennese journal, in 1912, and as a book in 1913. The English translation by A. A. Brill was published in New York by Moffat, Yard, in 1919. Incidentally, 1912 saw the publication of several other highly original and influential books in psychology, but true to the principle of the simplification and personalization of great events, Freud gets all the credit, if what came out of it is creditable.

(118) The song illustrating confused marital relations along Tobacco Road is called "I'm My Own Grandpaw," and was written by Dwight Latham and Moe Jaffe (copyright assigned to General Music Publishing Company, Inc., New York, 1944), who are probably not aware that I or anyone else knows they took the idea from a letter allegedly published in a Pittsburgh newspaper by an intended suicide and quoted by John Graham Brooks in *As Others See Us* (New York: The Macmillan Company; 1910).

(120) W. Lloyd Warner did first-class scholarly work in several areas of sociology and anthropology, and is now making money in motivational research. *A Black Civilization*, dealing with a group of people not called the Murngin, who are not black, and who do not have a civilization, is nevertheless one of the best general studies of an Australian tribe (New York: Harper and Brothers; 1958; revised edition).

(121) The "Fry Framework" is inaccessible to most Americans, including anthropologists. It was published in *The Transactions of the Royal Society of South Australia* in two articles: "Aboriginal Social Systems," LXXIII (1950), pp. 282–94, and "Concerning Aboriginal Marriage and Kinship," LXXX (1957), pp. 1–16. The schema with the arrows was devised by me to make the whole thing look harder. Works on social organization are generally written by scholars who want to make it all look hard, so only one book can be recommended to the layman who might like to see it made easy: Elman R. Service's *Primitive Social Organization: An Evolutionary Perspective* (New York: Random House; 1962).

(125) Courtly Love has been treated excellently in C. S. Lewis's *Allegory of Love* (Oxford: Oxford University Press; 1936) and in W. P. Ker's *Epic and Romance* (London: Macmillan & Co.; 1908). John Jay Parry translated *The Art of Courtly Love, by Andreas Capellanus* (New York: F. Ungar Publishing Co.; 1941, 1959). The term "Courtly Love" was coined by Gaston Paris in an article, "L'Amour courtois," in *Romania*, XII (1883).

(134) The classic treatise on primitive law is Sir Henry Maine's *Ancient Law, Its Connection with the Early History of Society and Its Relation to Modern Ideas* (London and Toronto: J. M. Dent & Sons; New York: E. P. Dutton & Co.; 1917).

FIVE: THE UNREAL AMERICANS

(138) Theories on the origin and function of religion are too numerous even to sample fairly. Max Müller, for example, the leader of the "Solarists" (who found the origin of myth to be in celestial phenomena), wrote great volumes of stuff which you will not want to read. Just one of these works, *The Sacred Books of the East,* ran to fifty-one volumes. For a survey of these theories, see the chapter on "The Scholars" in my *Literature among the Primitives* (Hatboro, Pennsylvania: The Folklore Associates; 1964). A delightfully readable and authoritative book, for all its

wit and irreverence, is William Howells's *The Heathens: Primitive Man and His Religions* (New York: Doubleday and Company; 1948); this I can highly recommend as a first reader in the scholarship of comparative religion. Durkheim's great work was translated by Joseph Ward Swain as *The Elementary Forms of the Religious Life* (Glencoe, Illinois: The Free Press; 1954). Again I caution the reader that many anthropologists have not yet come to see the truth of Durkheim's explanation, but that is their misfortune and none of our own.

(141) Alfred L. Kroeber's *Anthropology* deals with the nativistic endeavor in Section 180 under "Culture Change." (143) Peter Worsley's account of messianic movements in the southwestern Pacific, "Cargo Cults," is in *The Scientific American*, CC (1959), pp. 117–28. (145) Nativistic endeavors among the American Indians (and a fine descriptive summary of the phenomenon in general) are best analyzed in James Mooney's magnificent work, *The Ghost Dance Religion and the Sioux Outbreak of 1890* (Washington: Bureau of American Ethnology Annual Report Number 14, Volume II; 1895). Short Bull's prophecy has been quoted from Mooney.

(146) *Funk & Wagnalls Standard Dictionary of Folklore Mythology and Legend*, edited by Maria Leach (New York: Funk & Wagnalls Company; 1949, two volumes), is the only adequate and reliable compendium of its kind. There are several other dictionaries of folklore; avoid them.

(148) Gladys Reichard's description of the Coeur d'Alêne Trickster is in her monograph, *An Analysis of Coeur d'Alêne Indian Myths* (Philadelphia: American Folklore Society Memoir 41; 1947). My *Literature among the Primitives* has a full description of the Trickster, the Culture Hero, and other characters in folklore. Most anthropologists writing this paragraph would recommend Paul Radin's study, *The Trickster*. I do not.

(150) The quotation of Joseph Ritson on Robin Hood's genealogy is taken from his *Robin Hood: A Collection of All the*

Ancient Poems, Songs, and Ballads, Now Extant, Relative to that Celebrated English Outlaw, to Which Are Prefixed Historical Anecdotes of His Life (London: T. Egerton and J. Johnson; 1795, two volumes). I wish I could recommend this book, but I cannot, for it is written in the style of the eighteenth century, with *s*'s that look like *f*'s; an hour's reading will leave you speaking with a lisp. A convenient summary of Robin Hood scholarship, prepared by William Simeone, is "The Historic Robin Hood," *Journal of American Folklore*, LXVI (1953), pp. 303–8.

(151) Lord Fitzroy Raglan's *The Hero: A Study in Tradition, Myth, and Drama* (London: Watts; 1949; reprinted in a Vintage paperback by Alfred A. Knopf) should be read, if only for its mordant writing; the ritual theory at the end is best ignored. Raglan's iconoclasm is the most delectable since H. L. Mencken carried his criticism to higher regions.

(153) The ballad "Pretty Boy Floyd" I had from Woody Guthrie himself, together with about two hundred other songs of social protest composed by him. It has been sung on record by several folksingers. Woody Guthrie, by the way, will one day be acknowledged as the greatest figure in all American folksong, and that includes scholars, informants, singers, and composers. You can hear his songs on a number of records by his admirers, e.g., "Jack Elliott Sings the Songs of Woody Guthrie" (Prestige 13016) and "Cisco Houston Sings the Songs of Woody Guthrie" (Vanguard VRS 9089), and by himself on various records now in the catalog of Folkways Records, 117 West 46th Street, New York, New York. Guthrie's autobiography, *Bound for Glory* (New York: E. P. Dutton & Co.; 1943), will some day be recognized by literary critics as one of the great American autobiographies.

(155) Marshall Fishwick's article, "Uncle Remus *vs.* John Henry: Folk Tension," is in the journal *Western Folklore*, XX (1961), pp. 77–85. Fishwick's *American Heroes: Myth and Reality* (Washington: Public Affairs Press; 1954) deserved a publisher with greater distribution resources. Richard M. Dorson's *American*

Folklore (Chicago: The University of Chicago Press; 1959) will lead the reader to primary studies in the construction of "folk" heroes. Dorson's apt term for this kind of thing is "fakelore."

(159) The folklore of Henry Ford has been compiled from several books: Fishwick's *American Heroes*; William C. Richards's *The Last Billionaire* (New York: Charles Scribner's Sons; 1948); Ralph H. Graves's *The Triumph of an Idea: the Story of Henry Ford* (Garden City, New York: Doubleday, Doran & Company; 1934); Allen L. Benson's *The New Henry Ford* (New York: Funk & Wagnalls Company; 1923); Allan Nevins and Frank Ernst Hill's *Ford: The Times, the Man, the Company* (New York: Charles Scribner's Sons; 1954); and especially from Keith Sward's thoroughly documented *The Legend of Henry Ford* (New York: Rinehart & Company; 1948). The serious reader interested in learning more about Ford, apart from the folklore, will confine himself to Sward.

(164) The "scholarship" of wolf children has been dissected in Bergen Evans's *The Natural History of Nonsense* (New York: Alfred A. Knopf; 1946), which is no less delectable for its inclusion of several small items of Professor Evans's own nonsense. Speaking of wolf children, J. P. V. D. Balston in *Roman Women: Their History and Habits* (New York: John Day; 1963) reminds us, regarding the rearing of Romulus and Remus, that in Latin, *lupa* meant not only "female wolf" but "prostitute."

(165) The "Kallikak" (both names are fictitious) story is even less credible, if possible, than the "Jukes" story, yet the often-serious journal *Science*, carried a defense of it as late as 1942. Henry H. Goddard was the creator of the Kallikak lore, and his *Feeble-Mindedness: Its Causes and Consequences* (New York: Macmillan; 1914) is a valuable study indeed of feeble-mindedness, but not the Kallikaks'.

(167) Theodore Roosevelt is in a period of debunking. The quotation here is from Thomas C. Cochran and William Miller's *The Age of Enterprise: A Social History of Industrial America*

(New York: The Macmillan Company; 1942), a very useful book, packed with information, but still quite readable.

(168) The Lincoln quotations were conveniently assembled for my use in Ralph Korngold's *Thaddeus Stevens: A Being Darkly Wise and Rudely Great* (New York: Harcourt, Brace and Company; 1955), *passim*. It is instructive to look, in the several collections of Lincoln quotations now in print, for these views on slavery —they will not be found. Korngold's book is the best corrective to the romantic legend.

SIX: THE ACQUISITIVE AMERICANS

(173) We begin with *The Autobiography of Lincoln Steffens* (New York: Harcourt, Brace & World; 1931). Few books contain a more profound analysis of the motivating forces in American politics and economics. But Steffens is still regarded, by most people who know him at all, by the petty and petulant name given him by Theodore Roosevelt—muckraker. Just how good a book this is, is indicated by the fact that, although Steffens was close to Communism, he is occasionally quoted by the *Reader's Digest*.

(175) The classic study of territoriality among the lesser primates is Clarence Ray Carpenter's *A Field Study of the Behavior and Social Relations of Howling Monkeys* (Baltimore: The Johns Hopkins Press; 1934). Robert Ardrey's *African Genesis* (New York: Atheneum; 1961) is an emotional indictment of the savagery of man. The reader should pay no attention to his screed on the failure of anthropologists to consider the things he as a playwright discovered about the origin of man in South Africa. The anthropologists discussed and largely rejected the wilder Africanist contentions nearly forty years ago.

(178) Some of the paleolithic trade routes mentioned are illustrated in Stuart Piggott's *Approach to Archaeology* (Cambridge, Massachusetts: Harvard University Press; 1959). *The Inevitable Americans* has had little to say about archaeology, for, no matter

what else the Americans may be, they are not fossilized; but archaeology strikes most laymen as the most fascinating field in anthropology. If you have not succumbed yet to its charms, or if you have come to it through the best-selling popular works on the subject, you really should get a copy of Piggott's book; it is the best introduction to the science.

(180, 185) The scholarly proprietor of the Yir Yoront tribe of northern Cape York Peninsula is Lauriston Sharp, whose article "Steel Axes for Stone Age Australians," which appeared first in Edward H. Spicer's *Human Problems in Technological Change* (already recommended), should be required reading for anyone who writes letters to the editor on how to deal with people unfortunate enough not to be Americans. Sharp's material on this subject has often been reprinted.

(180) Often reprinted, too, is the description of the Dobu, originally given by Reo Fortune in his *Sorcerers of Dobu* (London: Routledge; 1932). The principal borrower from him was Ruth Benedict, in her *Patterns of Culture*, which contrasted the wabu-wabuers of the world with those who get wabuwabued.

(184) For additional charming proverbs of the Ashanti gold merchants, see R. S. Rattray's classic ethnography, *Ashanti* (Oxford: The Clarendon Press; 1923), from which this sample was taken.

(184) To see how hard life is among the Eskimo, read the fine ethnographic novel by Hans Reusch, *Top of the World* (New York: Harper and Brothers; 1950). The plot is weak, but the incidents are harrowing.

(191) The best elementary source book of the economics of feudalism, from which the duties of the peasants are quoted, is Charles Seignobos's *The Feudal Regime* (New York: Henry Holt and Co.; 1902; translated by E. W. Dove).

(192) A more general, but equally convenient, source of information about life in medieval times is Ross and McLaughlin's *The Portable Medieval Reader*. My debt to this work has already been

acknowledged. (192) Like most secondary and tertiary writers about the economics of the Reformation, I have relied heavily on Richard Henry Tawney's great book, *Religion and the Rise of Capitalism* (New York: Harcourt, Brace and Company; 1926), but, more than most, I have been aware of his political orientation and the effect it had on his interpretations. I can say the same for *The Age of Jackson*, by Arthur M. Schlesinger, Jr. (New York: Little, Brown & Company; 1945), which I have also used here and there in this book.

(193) Having taught courses on American civilization on the college and graduate level for some years, I am not able to document all my information about the Puritans, but I know I have drawn in this section from James Truslow Adams's *The Founding of New England* (Boston: The Atlantic Monthly Press; 1921); Thomas J. Wertenbaker's *The Puritan Oligarchy* (New York: Charles Scribner's Sons; 1947) and *The Golden Age of Colonial Culture* (New York: New York University Press; 1942); William Bradford's *Of Plymouth Plantation*, edited by Samuel Eliot Morison (New York: Alfred A. Knopf; 1952); *Winthrop's Journal, History of New England*, edited by James Kendall Hosmer (New York: Charles Scribner's Sons; 1908); George M. Waller's *Puritanism in Early America* (Boston: D. C. Heath & Co.; 1950); and the other books dealing with this period of American history referred to elsewhere in this bibliographic summary.

(200) The quotations of Alexander Hamilton were appropriated from Nathan Schachner's biography, *Alexander Hamilton* (New York: D. Appleton Century Co.; 1946).

(204) A lively book about the antics of the nineteenth-century American capitalists whom I had space only to name is Stewart H. Holbrook's *The Age of the Moguls* (New York: Doubleday and Company; 1953). Matthew Josephson, in *The Robber Barons: the Great American Capitalists* (New York: Harcourt, Brace and Company; 1934), does not think these rascals were so funny.

(205) Andrew Carnegie expressed his philosophy in "Wealth,"

first published in the *North American Review*, CXLVIII (1889), pp. 653-4, and reprinted, with other material of the sort, in *Democracy and the Gospel of Wealth*, edited by Gail Kennedy (Boston: D. C. Heath & Co.; 1949).

SEVEN: THE DISSIDENT AMERICANS

(207) I have been unable to locate a copy of Timothy Root's dirty book, but for the history of the incident, see Perry Miller's *Jonathan Edwards* (New York: William Sloane Associates; 1949). Edwards's *Sinners in the Hands of an Angry God* can be found in any number of college readers in American literature.

(210, 232) A good biography of Roger Williams, upon which I have drawn, is Samuel Hugh Brockunier's *Roger Williams: the Irrepressible Democrat* (New York: Ronald Press Co.; 1940).

(211) Joe Hill, "The Man Who Never Died," is quite dead, as he should be. Those who have accepted the folklore about him can read some evidence to the contrary in my *American Folksongs of Protest* (Philadelphia: University of Pennsylvania Press; 1953. The Sacco-Vanzetti folklore is impossible to overcome now; this pair of rogues is inextricably established in our liberal history. But read, anyhow, Robert H. Montgomery's *Sacco-Vanzetti: the Murder and the Myth* (New York: Ronald Press Co.; 1960), or Francis Russell's *Tragedy in Dedham: the Story of the Sacco-Vanzetti Case* (New York: McGraw-Hill Book Co.; 1962), though the latter is a bit too ambivalent for my satisfaction. It is instructive, too, to look up the reviews of these books—especially Montgomery's—and see what gratuitous calumny a person receives for trying to look at Sacco and Vanzetti objectively.

(212) Social deviancy of the criminal sort in the United States is outlined in an elementary fashion by Reece McGee in *Social Disorganization in America* (San Francisco: Chandler Publishing Company; 1962). For the crimes of our big businessmen, the classic study is Edwin H. Sutherland's *White Collar Crime* (New York: The Dryden Press; 1949).

(214) For opium addiction in Chicago, see *Opium Addiction in Chicago*, by Bingham Dai (Shanghai: The Commercial Press; 1937). To learn how you must go about appreciating marihuana, read Howard S. Becker's "Becoming a Marihuana User," *American Journal of Sociology*, LIX (1953).

(214) Anything by Emile Durkheim is recommended for meaningful anthropological explanations of human behavior; for *anomie* and suicide, his *Suicide*, translated by John Spalding and George Simpson (Glencoe, Illinois: The Free Press; 1951), is the chief source.

(215) More specialized, but still readable by the layman, Homer G. Barnett's *Being a Palauan* (New York: Henry Holt and Co.; 1960) is good ethnographic reporting, as are the other paperbacks in Holt's Case Studies in Anthropology.

(215) My undergraduate curriculum was very catholic (or aimless), and so I had among my varied teachers Thorsten Sellin, one of the greatest criminologists of all time. My references to his theory are drawn from my lecture notes.

(216) One hesitates to recommend paperbacks if one is a writer who prefers the prestige of hardback publication, but since, in the section *A Sample Assortment of American Nuts*, I have taken so many leads from Ronald M. Deutsch's *The Nuts Among the Berries* (New York: Ballantine Books; 1961), it must be recommended. It should have been published in an edition that could withstand the hard reading the book will get.

(220) The sly dig at Aristotle and his notions about teeth refers to his belief that women biologically had fewer teeth than men, a fancy that shows he did not look into Mrs. Aristotle's mouth. He had other weird ideas about women that probably caused Mrs. Aristotle some consternation; for instance, he believed that the direction of the wind on the night of a child's conception directed its future. But it has always been hard on a woman to live with a genius.

(220) I have taken the results of The National Economic League's poll on "Paramount Problems of the United States for

1937" from Thurman W. Arnold's *The Folklore of Capitalism* (Garden City, New York: Blue Ribbon Books; 1941), a book which, I am told, some people have not given themselves the pleasure of reading, though this is hard to believe.

(221) I am currently proprietor of Aunt Molly Jackson, though other folklorists have braved her wrath to study her songs. For more about this most remarkable woman, see my *American Folk-songs of Protest* (which, if you must buy it, can be had in paperback edition: New York: A. S. Barnes and Company; 1960). To hear her stories told by herself and her songs sung by me (Aunt Molly was too old at the time of this recording to sing), my record, *The Songs and Stories of Aunt Molly Jackson* (New York: Folkways Records, FH 5457; 1961), is worth getting, even if you have to buy it, which is more than I can say for most of my efforts as an entertainer. The *Kentucky Folklore Record*, VII (October–December, 1961), is a special Aunt Molly Jackson Memorial Issue; it contains some frank and fascinating accounts of the old girl by several folklorists who knew her.

(223) In *American Folksongs of Protest* I have gone rather deeply into the history of the I. W. W. as a singing movement. The Manifesto which I quote can be read in any of the multi-edition *Little Red Song Books* ("To Fan the Flames of Discontent") of this organization. The primary source for the I. W. W. and its history is Ralph Chaplin's reminiscent *Wobbly* (Chicago: The University of Chicago Press; 1948.

(225) Because of Herbert Aptheker's political affiliations, I suppose I cannot recommend his books, but I can mention his *Negro Slave Revolts in the United States, 1526–1860* (New York: International Publishers; 1939) and *American Negro Slave Revolts* (New York: Columbia University Press; 1945).

(226) Any ethnographical survey of Africa will confirm my remarks about slavery in tribal Africa, though Simon and Phoebe Ottenberg's *Cultures and Societies of Africa,* (New York: Random House; 1960) manages skillfully to go on for six hundred pages

without discussing it. Less considerate of contemporary African ideas about African culture is George P. Murdock's *Africa: Its People and Their Culture* (New York: McGraw-Hill Book Co.; 1959).

(227) My statement regarding Negro drummers in white jazz bands has met with some opposition, which I am unable to appreciate. Any book on the history of jazz will bear me out, though most do so negatively—that is, by omission of any discussion of Negro jazz drummers. Joachim E. Berendt's *The New Jazz Book* (New York: Hill and Wang; 1959; translated by Dan Morgenstern) is nearly unique in that it devotes a long section to jazz drumming. In it, the scarcity of Negro drummers is discussed.

(228) Claude Bowers's *The Tragic Era: the Revolution After Lincoln* (New York: Blue Ribbon Books; 1929) contains several amazing things besides the account I have used about the origin of the Ku Klux Klan. For a quite different point of view, see James S. Allen's *Reconstruction: the Battle for Democracy, 1865–1876* (New York: International Publishers; 1937) and W. E. B. DuBois's *Black Reconstruction* (Philadelphia: A. Saifer; 1935). DuBois, who wrote some wildly lyrical things about the Negro, constructed some folklore for Ghana before his recent death. The political orientation of all three of these authors should be kept constantly in mind by the reader.

(229) J. C. Furnas's anecdote about Haitians and Negroes is on page 378 of his *Goodbye to Uncle Tom* (New York: William Sloane Associates; 1956). Furnas has never pretended to be anything else than a journalist, but his reading in anthropology has been extensive and his use of what he has read has been judicious. An excellent example of his best work is his *Anatomy of Paradise*, about the South Pacific. *Goodbye to Uncle Tom*, however, suffers from Furnas's inability to make up his mind on some aspects of the racial question.

(230) Wigglesworth's *The Day of Doom* can be found much too easily in anthologies of literature. It belongs rather in histories

of mania, but there are not many of these—which is a great lack.

(230) Thomas Morton gets less fair treatment than he deserves in American histories (Stephen Vincent Benét put him on the jury of the American damned, in his story "The Devil and Daniel Webster"). George F. Willison in *Saints and Strangers* (New York: Reynal & Hitchcock; 1945) gives Morton a better shake. There is also a chapter devoted to him in Morison's *Builders of the Bay Colony.*

(233) The story of Salem witchcraft is told in readable fashion by Marion L. Starkey in *The Devil in Massachusetts: a Modern Inquiry into the Salem Witch Trials* (New York: Alfred A. Knopf; 1949). The standard American treatise on witchcraft is George Lyman Kittredge's *Witchcraft in Old and New England* (New York: Russell & Russell; 1929). Margaret A. Murray, who is celebrating her hundredth birthday as this is written (and who is publishing two more books this year), wrote one of the great studies of witchcraft: *The Witch-Cult in Western Europe* (London: The Oxford University Press; 1921). Dr. Murray draws a good bit of her evidence from the Salem witch confessions, but she differs from most other modern authors in that she believes the Salem suspects were really witches.

(234) If your library does not contain the deistic works of Ethan Allen, Elihu Palmer, and Thomas Paine on its open shelves, you can read about deism generally in Herbert M. Morais's *Deism in Eighteenth Century America* (New York: Columbia University Press; 1934), though it is not nearly so much fun as the originals.

(237) It would be best not to read any of the Transcendentalists if you are past the mental age of a college sophomore. If you must know more about Emerson and his strange companions, get the information painlessly by reading Octavius Brooks Frothingham's *Transcendentalism in New England* (New York: G. P. Putnam's Sons; 1886), which, despite its date, the name of its author, and its title, is quite lively stuff, or George F. Whicher's *The Transcendentalist Revolt against Materialism* (Boston: D. C. Heath & Co.; 1949).

EIGHT: THE PLAYFUL AMERICANS

(239) The fascinating story of the diffusion of tobacco around the world is told best, to my knowledge, in Robert V. Sayce's *Primitive Arts and Crafts* (Cambridge: Cambridge University Press; 1933), though what it is doing in that book I cannot tell.

(243) Alfred Cort Haddon's far-seeing prediction about kites and explosives is in his anthropology text, *The Study of Man* (New York: G. P. Putnam's Sons; 1908).

(247) The stanza from "The California Stage Line" was written by John A. Stone and published in his *Put's Golden Songster* (San Francisco: D. E. Appleton & Co; 1858). We have few genuine folksongs from the California gold rush because "Old Put" saved the miners the trouble of writing them. Curiously, the same thing happened in Australia during its gold rush of 1851; there Charles Thatcher wrote all the funny and satirical songs the miners needed.

(250) Gordon W. Hewes's experiments on primate bipedalism were first reported in *Southwestern Lore*, XXVII (1962), p. 69, under the title "Observations on Stumptail Macaques," and more extensively later in "Food Transport and the Origin of Hominid Bipedalism," in *American Anthropologist*, LXIII (1961), pp. 687–710. His work continues, despite the sad demise of his most adept bipedal monkey. The poor animal ironically died in a fall —which should teach others of his ilk not to presume upon their intellects.

(256) On boxing prowess as an indicator of low position in the social strata I can cite my maternal grandfather, Joe Rafferty, who was heavyweight champion of the British Isles (and a friend of Skin-the-Goat, who appears in James Joyce's *Ulysses*). Grandfather Rafferty lived in the same slum that Sean O'Casey and Brendan Behan later inhabited. Rather more taken to the vice of drinking than even Brendan Behan, he died literally in the

gutter. His genes were inherited by myself, who achieved a B in boxing at college.

(261) Gerald Abrahams's *The Chess Mind* (Hammondsworth, Middlesex: Penguin Books; 1960), is one of the curiosities of chess literature, of which there are too many for my comfort. The literature of chess is ancient and enormous; the first book printed in the English language may have been Caxton's *The Game and Play of the Chess*. The irreplaceable history of the game is Harold James Ruthven Murray's *A History of Chess* (Oxford: Clarendon Press; 1931), which runs nine hundred pages. My sources for this section are difficult to acknowledge, since I have been studying the game for more than twenty years. For most of that time I have been a regular reader of *Chess Review*, and a lot of my knowledge comes from the news printed in that journal. I am constrained to say that I owe nothing of my analysis of how the Russians win chess tournaments to Robert Fischer's article in *Sports Illustrated* last year. A good while before Fischer wrote this piece, I submitted to the editors of that magazine an article that I have expanded upon here. The editors generally liked the piece, but while I was revising it slowly with little enthusiasm, they bought Fischer's account, which is much the same as mine, for the silly reason that Fischer happens to be the United States chess champion. They entirely disregarded the fact that I was playing chess before Fischer was born.

(265) The remarkable example of polygenesis in chess problems was taken from Irving Chernev and Fred Reinfeld, *The Fireside Book of Chess* (New York: Simon & Schuster; 1949), p. 90.

NINE: THE ARTS IN AMERICA

(271) My opinions on modern art are firmly based on assertion and intuition. I have had quite enough argument from students in my class in Primitive Arts and Crafts, and want no

disputatious letters from Greenwich Village about this.

(273) Kroeber's ideas about pattern exhaustion are discussed in his *Anthropology* and *Style and Civilizations,* both mentioned earlier.

(281) I have inserted the short quotation from Vernon Parrington's *Main Currents in American Thought* (New York: Harcourt, Brace and Company; 1927, 1930) in order to recommend that classic interpretation of American literature to a generation that may have overlooked it.

(282) Mickey Spillane as a communicant of the Church of Jesus Christ of Latter-Day Saints was required to put in some time as a preacher and missionary to the heathens.

(283) If the allusion to William Byrd's activity on the billiard table excites the curiosity of any readers, they can go read as much as editors Louis B. Wright and Marion Twining dared print of *The Secret Diary of William Byrd* (Richmond, Virginia: Dietz Press; 1941). (283) The couplet about Southern literature was printed in Wyndham Lewis's collection of bad verse, *The Stuffed Owl* (New York: Coward-McCann; 1930). This, incidentally, is Dominic Wyndham Lewis, not Percy Wyndham Lewis.

(290) The origin given here of Negro spirituals is well known to folklorists through the work of George Pullen Jackson (e.g., *White and Negro Spirituals,* New York: J. J. Augustin; 1943).

(291) Nicholas Slonimsky's book, which provided me with the criticisms of composers referred to here, is titled *Lexicon of Musical Invective: Critical Assaults on Composers Since Beethoven's Time* (New York: Coleman-Ross; 1953).

(292) For cosmetics, see Volume I of *A History of Technology,* already recommended in another connection, and the article therein (pp. 238–98) by J. Forbes, "Chemical, Culinary, and Cosmetic Arts." The history of changing ideas in beauty is excellently given in text and photographs in Madge Garland's *The Changing Face of Beauty: Four Thousand Years of Beautiful Women* (London: Weidenfeld and Nicholson; 1937).

(297) Heinrich Harrer's experiences with American cosmetics in Lhasa are described in his *Seven Years in Tibet* (New York: E. P. Dutton & Co.; 1954).

(297) The story of English drama I had first as a student of Albert C. Baugh, whose knowledge of medieval English was encyclopedic. For those less fortunate than I, some of this information is available in Sir Edmund Kerchever Chambers's *The Medieval Stage* (Oxford: The Clarendon Press; 1903; two volumes). Baugh has released some of his knowledge in his textbook *A Literary History of England* (New York: Appleton-Century-Crofts; 1948).

TEN: IN PRAISE OF A MATERIALISTIC CULTURE

(306) I shall not give publication details of Alfred Korzybski's *Science and Sanity* because I have already told you not to read any books in semantics except Hayakawa's. Especially avoid Korzybski.

(308) Bertrand Russell's *The Impact of Science on Society* (New York: Simon & Schuster; 1953) is a good book, and shows only hints of the eccentricity that he is presently devoting all his time to.

(308) A few recommended books about India are Frederick G. Bailey: *Caste and the Economic Frontier; a Village in Highland Orissa* (Manchester: Manchester University Press; 1957); Arthur L. Basham: *The Wonder That Was India* (London: Sidgwick & Jackson; 1954); John Henry Hutton: *Caste in India: Its Nature, Function, and Origins* (Bombay and New York: Oxford University Press; 1951); and Sir Herbert Risley: *The People of India* (London: W. Thacker & Co.; 1915). A secondary work, but useful for its up-to-date statistics, is *Culture Worlds* by Richard J. Russell and Fred B. Kniffen, abridged by Evelyn L. Pruitt (New York: The Macmillan Company; 1961).

(311) Joseph McCabe in his time, which was only a dozen years ago, was referred to as "the world's greatest scholar," but it does

no good to be famous if no one has ever heard about you. The sharp work of this professional atheist can be read in any of seventy pamphlets he wrote for Haldeman-Julius's series of *Little Blue Books*, published in Girard, Kansas. At the suggestion of McCabe, I compared the eleventh edition of the *Encyclopaedia Britannica* with the fourteenth (the twelfth and thirteenth editions were only reprints) in items referring to Church history. You should do the same; you will find the comparison very instructive indeed. In speaking of the Church, by the way, I mean the Christian church of Western Europe, not the Catholic Church, except as the Catholic Church traces a direct line back to Saint Peter. Tracing this line is not as easy, incidentally, as we were told it was back in parochial school; try it in James A. Corbett's *The Papacy* (Princeton, New Jersey: D. van Nostrand Company; 1956).

(312) I had the onerous job, while in a university graduate course, of tracking down a catalogue of a medieval library and commenting on the entire holdings. It is not a job I care to recall. The figures on libraries in the Age of Spirituality come largely from James Westfall Thompson's *The Medieval Library* (Chicago: The University of Chicago Press; 1939).

(314) The Arab Usāmah described other interesting Christians among the Crusaders besides the physician with the axe; see P. K. Hitti's translation of the *Memoirs of Usāmah* (New York: Columbia University Press; 1929).

(316) The poem on Fra Lippo Lippi is of course by Robert Browning.

(319) Anyone who is himself educated has read *The Education of Henry Adams* (Worcester, Massachusetts: Massachusetts Historical Society; 1918), so there is no need to mention it.

(320) A semi-classic study is Adriano Tilgher's *Work: What It Has Meant to Men through the Ages* (translated by Dorothy Canfield Fisher; New York: Harcourt, Brace and Company; 1930).

(321) Norbert Wiener rewrote his *Cybernetics* (1948), for the

understanding and edification of the layman, as *The Human Use of Human Beings: Cybernetics and Society* (New York: Houghton Mifflin Co.; 1950). Men who have the time to read it now because they are technologically unemployed will find some satisfaction in doing so.

(322) The figures on American materialism were drawn from *Statistical Abstract of the United States: 1961* (Washington, D.C.: Bureau of the Census; 1961; 82nd edition) and *Historical Statistics of the United States, Colonial Times to 1957* (Washington, D.C.: U.S. Bureau of the Census; 1960). Mentioning these volumes gives me an excuse to say that anyone interested at all in the United States should own a copy of *A Guide to the Study of the United States: Representative Books Reflecting the Development of American Life and Thought* (Washington, D.C.: Library of Congress; 1960), a huge compendium of 6,487 books, each with a review of more than a hundred words. The whole thing goes to 1,193 pages, and costs only seven dollars.

(323) The stimulating theory that art derives from industry is well presented and illustrated in Gene Weltfish's *The Origins of Art* (Indianapolis, Indiana: The Bobbs-Merrill Company, Inc.; 1953). Sigfried Giedion's addresses to Harvard have been published as *Space, Time, and Architecture: The Growth of a New Tradition* (Cambridge: Harvard University Press, 1954). John Kouwenhoven's idea about "vernacular art" is discussed in his badly titled work, *The Beer Can by the Highway* (Garden City, New York: Doubleday and Company; 1961).

(329) The winsome verses about London in the rain are from Jonathan Swift's poem *A Description of a City Shower* (1710), which, since it is not everywhere accessible, you can find in a book by another of my college teachers, John C. Mendenhall: *English Literature 1650–1800* (Chicago: J. B. Lippincott; 1940). For the Shakespearean dung and other solid facts about Shakespeare, the only work without airy inferences is Edmund K. Chambers's *William Shakespeare, a Study of Facts and Problems* (Oxford: Clarendon Press; 1930; two volumes).

(332) The note on Sir John Hill rears up the subject of sex, which one aspect of my national character forbids me to discuss. For those who want information about our sexual inheritance, Albert Ellis and Albert Abarbanel's *The Encyclopedia of Sexual Behavior* (New York: Hawthorn Books; 1961; two volumes) is the frankest thing our presses will publish (its foreign counterparts are less reticent). Among other things, it contains Robert M. Frumkin's "Early English and American Sex Customs" (Volume I, pp. 350–65). No browsing, now.

(334) Though it will be out of date by the time you read this, the latest thing at this moment on automation is Walter Buckingham's *Automation: Its Impact on Business and People* (New York: Harper and Brothers; 1961). I have drawn two or three facts from this work, including the quotation about capitalism and its disappearance.

(336) On this last page I must acknowledge a most pervasive debt, evident in almost everything I have said: to E. H. Crussell's *Jobbing Work for the Carpenter* (New York: U. P. C. Book Co., Inc.; *ca.* 1916), which taught me to stand in awe of no task, however difficult; and to Edward E. Winner, my first employer as a carpenter, who taught me to stand in awe of no man, however eminent.

INDEX

A NOTE ABOUT THE AUTHOR

JOHN GREENWAY was born in England in 1919 and came to the United States in 1922. After leaving high school, he worked for seven years as a carpenter and builder before entering the University of Pennsylvania in 1945. He graduated Phi Beta Kappa two years later, and now has four university degrees in anthropology and English, together with a bewildering variety of academic honors, prizes, and awards, including a Fulbright Research Scholarship to Australia (1956–7) and a Nuffield Foundation Award (1957). Though his main field of activity has been folklore, he has had experience in all the areas discussed in this book; for example, he was a ranking track athlete in college, a chess champion, and is well known as a folksinger—he has nine phonograph record albums to his credit. He has taught at several institutions in this country and abroad, giving courses in chess, American civilization, all periods of English and American literature, ethnomusicology, and many areas of anthropology. He is presently editor of the *Journal of American Folklore* and of *Southwestern Lore*, the latter an archaeological journal. Among his publications are three pioneering works: *American Folksongs of Protest* (1953, 1960), *Bibliography of the Australian Aborigines* (1963), and the forthcoming *Literature Among the Primitives*; four college textbooks: *Principles of Anthropology* (1959), *Peoples and Cultures of Australia* (1962), *Primitive Music* (1962), and *Peoples and Cultures of the Pacific* (1963)—besides a plethora of articles and book reviews. Dr. Greenway lives with his wife and small son in Boulder, Colorado, where he is an Associate Professor of Anthropology at the University of Colorado.

A NOTE ON THE TYPE

THIS BOOK is set in *Electra*, a Linotype face designed by W. A. DWIGGINS. This face cannot be classified as either modern or old-style. It is not based on any historical model, nor does it echo any particular period or style. It avoids the extreme contrasts between thick and thin elements that mark most modern faces, and attempts to give a feeling of fluidity, power, and speed.

Composed, printed, and bound by
The Haddon Craftsmen, Inc., Scranton, Pa.